# RIVER ROAD RECIPES II

## A Second Helping

PUBLISHED

BY

# THE JUNIOR LEAGUE

OF

## BATON ROUGE, INC.

### BATON ROUGE, LOUISIANA

The purpose of this League shall be to promote voluntarism and to improve the community through the effective action and leadership of trained volunteers. Its purpose is exclusively educational and charitable.

The Junior League of Baton Rouge, Inc., proudly announces that as of August 1, 1991, the combined sales of *River Road Recipes* and *River Road Recipes II, A Second Helping*, have earned $2,000,000 to fund League projects in the Baton Rouge community. Projects supported and sponsored by the Junior League of Baton Rouge, Inc. include, but are not limited to, the following:

BATON ROUGE SPEECH AND HEARING FOUNDATION
LOUISIANA ARTS AND SCIENCE CENTER
BATON ROUGE ASSOCIATION FOR
 RETARDED CHILDREN
CITY BEAUTIFICATION
BATON ROUGE AREA COUNCIL ON ALCOHOLISM
COMMUNITY VOLUNTEER BUREAU
EAST BATON ROUGE PARISH FAMILY COURT VOLUNTEER
 PROGRAM
KEYETTES SPONSORSHIP
ACADEMIC READINESS
ARTS AND HUMANITIES COUNCIL — COMMUNITY
 DEVELOPMENT
BATON ROUGE YOUTH
ORAL HISTORY OF BATON ROUGE
ARTS FOR THE ELDERLY
CHILDREN'S EMERGENCY SHELTER
MAGNOLIA MOUND PLANTATION KITCHEN
RIVER ROAD RECIPES IN BRAILLE
FINE ARTS SERIES
MONTEREY READING
FRIENDS OF LTI
LIBRARY INFORMATION SERVICE
PUBLIC RADIO
BATTERED WOMEN'S SHELTER

CRISIS HOME
HUMAN DEVELOPMENT PROGRAM
PARENTING CENTER
RESPITE CARE
DISCOVERY DEPOT CHILDREN'S MUSEUM
INTERNATIONAL SUMMER SPECIAL OLYMPICS
SYMPHONY AT TWILIGHT
DRUG AWARENESS TASK FORCE
PLAYMAKERS THEATER FOR CHILDREN
ARTISTS IN ACTION
USS KIDD DOCENT PROGRAM
ADOPT-A-SCHOOL
GREATER BATON ROUGE FOOD BANK
HOSPICE
LSU MUSEUM OF NATURAL SCIENCE
PARENTING CENTER OUTREACH
MEDIA LITERACY
TEEN PREGNANCY PREVENTION
VOLUNTEER BATON ROUGE
ARTS IN EDUCATION
EXCELLENCE IN TEACHING
EAST BATON ROUGE PARISH SCHOOL QUIZ BOWLS
PEER HELPERS
SHARED READING EXPERIENCES FOR CHILDREN
 AND PARENTS

Copies may be obtained by addressing *River Road Recipes*, THE JUNIOR LEAGUE OF BATON ROUGE, INC., 5280 Corporate Blvd., Baton Rouge, La. 70808.

Cover Design and Illustrations by
YVONNE PULLEN LEWIS

Illustrations by
EMELIE SNIDER MCLEAN

Printed in the USA by

WIMMER
The Wimmer Companies, Inc.
Memphis • Dallas

# FOREWORD

*River Road Recipes II, A Second Helping* is a second helping only in that the contents reflect the same heritage and influences in cooking as *River Road Recipes*. As its predecessor, *River Road Recipes,* has been so fantastically successful, it was felt that a "second helping" of the same type cooking would be well received. All the entries presented here are entirely different from those in our first book.

Louisiana cuisine—what a story those two words have to tell! Perhaps no other region of the United States has made such a way of life out of the preparation and consumption of food. It is not a matter just for the great restaurants (of which we have many), but even more a concern of the small cafés and seafood establishments, the gourmet and dinner clubs which abound, and particularly the individual homemakers who pride themselves on their own special jambalaya, their succulent shrimp creole or their delectable desserts.

Conversations about food may be reminiscent of a certain perfect dish, once tasted but never forgotten. On the other hand, they may be loudly argumentative—should the gumbo be thickened with okra or with filé, a matter on which reputations have been staked, friendships strained and good taste questioned.

Louisiana's love affair with food began early in its history when colonial settlers arrived from France and Spain. Each brought his own flair with food and adapted it to available local ingredients, thus producing the renowned "Creole Cuisine." In the mid-eighteenth century, the Acadians (French Catholics who were expelled from Nova Scotia) began their long search for a home. Many of them migrated to south Louisiana where their descendants, familiarly called Cajuns, live today. They developed an art of cookery, particularly specializing in the preparation of the myriad seafoods which *le bon Dieu* provided and from which many of them made their living. This style of cooking has survived as the unique legacy of "Acadian Cooking." Also adding flavor to the Louisiana cooking are the German, Hungarian and other European settlers who arrived in this area. Their traditions have been enriched by the African and West Indian influences in the state, giving the cuisine a more exotic flavor than traditional American cookery.

Typical of Louisiana cuisine is the classic dish of jambalaya—that rich amalgamation of rice, onions, meat, seafood, seasonings and imagination—served regularly in so many area homes. There is a famous story, recently recounted by author Harnett Kane, about the good Louisiana Frenchman who died and went to Heaven. On discovering that the celestial kitchens had somehow neglected to include jambalaya in their menu, but that it was available down below, he promptly departed from Paradise—proving that a good Louisianian will gladly go to Hell for a dish of jambalaya.

# INTRODUCTION

As the inspiration for food preparation has changed through the years, so it is still changing today. The scope of available items in the markets, influx of certain convenience foods and the increased pace of life have combined to make great Louisiana cookery easier and more readily attainable everywhere.

So, if you are from Louisiana, we hope that this book will encourage you to try some native recipes you may not have attempted before. If you are from another state or country, we hope you will try the exciting world of Louisiana cuisine.

## RIVER ROAD RECIPES — A SECOND HELPING
## ORIGINAL COMMITTEE

Ann Wilbert Arbour
Margaret Earhart Armstrong
Claire Wilson Bahlinger
Annette Barton
Elizabeth Buckles Bello
Betty Brown Berry
Shelley Turner Bonanno
Rosemary Searcy Campbell
Peggy McCreary Christian
Nancy McLellan Claitor
Patricia Weaver Comeaux
Fannie Samuel Compton
Mary Moseley Daves
Marilyn Rodemacher Davis
Ann Pugh Doherty
Sara Menefee Downing
Jenola Gouge Duke
Estina Brown Field
Michelle Menton Gauthier
Elizabeth Farnsworth Geheber
Kay Long Gilmore
Mary Lynn Grogg Hogeman
Susie Comeaux Hotard
Carolyn Reinhardt Jones

Barbara Olsen Kizer
Emily Robinson Lamont
Ann Mestayer Laville
Jeanne Devall Lowry
Berta Laycock Mayer
Joan Hatcher McCaskill
Ernestine McCoy McConnell
Emelie Snider McLean
Katherine LaCour Miller
Lucy Hanson Nunnally
Linda Barrilleaux Ohmstede
Emily Roberts Robinson
Ann Borron Row
Barbara Gatchell Salmon
Peggy Huddleston Sartain
Donna Maddox Saurage
Anne Gueymard Shirley
Amy Blanche Slowey
Kay Griffon Smart
Mary Elizabeth Wylie Snellgrove
Patricia Toca Thompson
Cathy Semmelman Valentin
Augusta Harper Waggenspack
Mary Scott Wilson

*River Road Recipes II — A Second Helping* was named by Sue Wilbert Turner

# CONTENTS

These recipes represent the favorite ones of our Baton Rouge Junior League members and friends. They reflect our special heritage of French, Spanish and "American" influences. Some of the terms used are in Louisiana Acadian French and may be unfamiliar to those who know standard French.

We have spent four years collecting, testing and proofreading these recipes. It is our greatest hope that this book will live up to your expectations and that it will be as errorfree as possible.

Enjoy experimenting with these recipes and *Bon Appétit* from the Baton Rouge Junior League.

*Trade names of products are used only when necessary.*

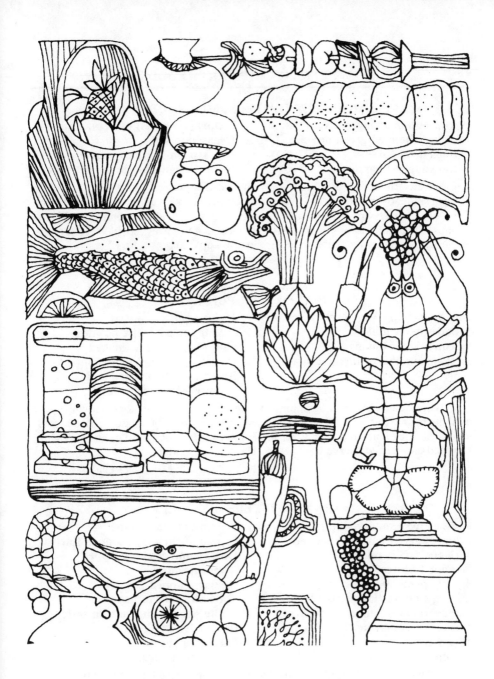

## APPETIZERS AND PARTY FOODS

Parties come in a host of sizes and styles. They all have one thing in common, the serving of food—tasty, interesting and hopefully plentiful. It's a time when guests enjoy trying something different and hostesses take pride in the variety and versatility of their kitchens. At mealtimes, remember that the serving of an appetizer can change dinner into a *dinner party*.

## GOURMET OYSTERS IMPROMPTU

½ cup butter or margarine
1½ cups chopped green onions
  (tops included)
1 cup chopped parsley

2 cups (1½ pints) oysters, drained
1 teaspoon salt
½ teaspoon Tabasco sauce
1 cup Italian-style bread crumbs

Set electric skillet at 350 degrees and melt butter. (If using range, cook in 10-inch skillet over medium heat.) Sauté onions and parsley until limp. Add oysters. Cook until oysters are slightly curled, about 3 minutes. Add seasonings and bread crumbs. Stir lightly to mix ingredients. Reduce heat to lowest position for serving. Serve with crackers or melba rounds. Yield: 6 cups. Serves 8 to 12.

Miss Harriet Babin


## HOT OYSTER PUFFETS

One 8-ounce package cream cheese
6 tablespoons milk
¼ cup minced onions
¼ teaspoon Worcestershire sauce

1 clove garlic, minced, or
  ⅛ teaspoon garlic powder
One 3¾-ounce tin smoked
  oysters drained and chopped
Bread rounds, toasted and
  buttered on one side

Whip cream cheese, milk, onions, Worcestershire and garlic together with a fork until light and fluffy. Fold in oysters. Heap a spoonful of mixture on buttered, untoasted side of bread rounds. Place under low broiler. Toast until mixture is lightly browned and puffed. Serve hot. Makes 1½ cups of mixture.

Mrs. Neel Garland


## MARNA'S OYSTERS BIENVILLE

6 dozen oysters (save liquid)
1 bunch green onions, chopped
4 cloves garlic, minced
¼ pound butter
8 tablespoons flour
1½ cups liquid (Use oyster liquid,
  mushroom liquid and add heavy
  cream to make up the 1½ cups)
Heavy cream
½ cup lemon juice

½ cup dry white wine
½ pound shrimp, chopped finely
One 5¾-ounce can chopped
  mushrooms
¼ cup chopped parsley
Tabasco sauce to taste
White pepper and salt, to taste
Rock salt
Parmesan cheese
Lemon wedges

Open oysters and reserve liquid. Sauté green onions and garlic in butter. Stir in flour and cook, over low heat, until bubbly. Add liquid, a little at a time, and simmer until smooth and creamy. Add remaining ingredients. Simmer this sauce about 15 minutes. Place oysters, in shells, on rock salt and bake until edges curl at 375 degrees. Drain excess liquid from shells and top with sauce. Sprinkle with grated Parmesan cheese and run under broiler until slightly brown on top. Serve with lemon wedges. Serves 6 to 12.

Mrs. Melvin A. Shortess

## SHRIMP MOLD I

One 10-ounce can tomato soup
Three 3-ounce packages cream
  cheese, at room temperature
1 envelope unflavored gelatin
¼ cup cold water
2 cups (about one pound) boiled
  shrimp, seasoned and shredded

1 cup mayonnaise
1 small onion, grated
½ cup finely chopped celery
Dash garlic powder
1 tablespoon lemon juice
Salt, pepper, and red pepper to
  taste

Heat soup and dissolve cheese in it. Soak gelatin in cold water and add to soup mixture. Let cool to room temperature (about ½ hour). Add all other ingredients, pour into an oiled medium-size fish mold and chill overnight.

Mrs. Kip Smith

## SHRIMP MOLD II

Two 4½-ounce cans shrimp, drained
  and mashed (or equivalent fresh
  shrimp)
2 cups mayonnaise
Juice of 1 lemon

2 envelopes gelatin, dissolved in
  ¼ cup water
1 small onion, grated
2 tablespoons horseradish
Salt and pepper to taste

Combine all ingredients and pour into greased ring or fish mold and refrigerate until firm. A few drops of red food coloring may be added to make a pale pink. Serve with Ritz crackers. Makes 1 medium-sized fish or ring mold.

Mrs. Jack B. Adger
Montgomery, Alabama

## SHRIMP PARTY SANDWICHES

One 8-ounce package cream cheese,
  softened
Juice of 1 large lemon
1 small onion, grated
1 stalk celery, minced

Salt to taste
Red pepper, if desired
Worcestershire sauce, if desired
1 pound headless boiled shrimp,
  peeled
Buttered round of bread

Mash cream cheese and add lemon juice, onion, celery, and salt to taste. Red pepper and Worcestershire sauce may be added, if desired. Stir in shrimp, which have been broken into bits. Let stand 1 hour. Spread between buttered rounds of bread. Makes 50 finger sandwiches.

Mrs. Iveson B. Noland, III

## SHRIMP OR LOBSTER DIP

1 cup mayonnaise
¾ tablespoon horseradish
¾ tablespoon capers
¾ tablespoon mustard
2 tablespoons finely chopped onions

2 tablespoons finely chopped celery
2 tablespoons finely chopped dill
  pickles
2 tablespoons finely chopped
  parsley
Salt and red pepper to taste

Mix all ingredients together. Use as a dip for boiled shrimp or canned lobster

Mrs. Millard Byrd, Jr.

## MARINATED SHRIMP

2 pounds shrimp, boiled, peeled and
  cleaned
1 lemon, thinly sliced
1 onion, thinly sliced
½ cup sliced pitted ripe olives
2 tablespoons chopped pimiento
½ cup fresh lemon juice
¼ cup oil

1 tablespoon wine vinegar
1 clove garlic
½ bay leaf
1 tablespoon dry mustard
¼ teaspoon cayenne pepper
1 teaspoon salt
Freshly ground black pepper to
  taste

Boil shrimp. Drain, peel and clean. Add lemon and onion slices, olives and pimiento. Toss. In second bowl combine remaining ingredients and pour over shrimp. Refrigerate overnight, stirring occasionally. Serve in marinade and have toothpicks for spearing the shrimp.

Mrs. W. A. Whitley

## SHRIMP AND BACON BITS

1 pound medium-large headless shrimp
One 12-ounce bottle chili sauce
½ cup water
3 cloves garlic, crushed

½ to ¾ pound thinly sliced
  bacon
Salt and pepper to taste
Tabasco sauce to taste

One to two days before serving, cook the shrimp in boiling salted water until they turn pink, about 5 minutes. Drain immediately and cool. Shell and devein shrimp. Dilute chili sauce with ½ cup of water and add crushed garlic. Add shrimp to the mixture, mix well, cover and refrigerate. The day before, or the morning you plan to serve, broil bacon slices on one side only (they should not be crisp). Drain and cut each slice in half crosswise. Wrap the bacon around the shrimp and secure with a toothpick. Can be marinated longer, if desired. When you wish to serve, broil shrimp and bacon on both sides until bacon is crisp. Serve in chafing dish with marinade. Yield: 3 to 4 dozen pieces.

Mrs. D. W. Huff, Jr.

## HOT SHRIMP DIP

¼ cup onions, finely minced
1 tablespoon butter
One 8-ounce package cream cheese,
  softened
One 8-ounce carton sour cream
One 4½-ounce can deveined shrimp,
  drained

1 tablespoon lemon juice
½ teaspoon salt
¼ teaspoon white pepper
Dash of Tabasco sauce
¼ teaspoon chili powder
¼ teaspoon Worcestershire sauce
¼ tablespoon garlic salt
Paprika to add pink color

Sauté onion in butter. Stir in cream cheese and sour cream. Add shrimp, mashing into bits with rubber spatula. Add lemon juice and seasonings. Serve warm from small chafing dish, accompanied by potato chips or corn chips. Yields about 3 cups.

Mrs. Frank W. Middleton III

## SHRIMP DIP

3 tablespoons butter
½ tablespoon chopped green pepper
1 onion, minced
Two 7-ounce cans shrimp, drained
and mashed

1 tablespoon Worcestershire sauce
3 tablespoons ketchup
Cayenne pepper to taste
¼-pound good yellow cheese or
wine cheese
1 tablespoon sherry

Sauté green pepper and onion in butter until soft, but not brown. Add remaining ingredients and cook in double boiler until thick. Serve hot in a chafing dish with melba rounds.

Miss Kathleen Flanagan

## CRAB MOLD

3 pounds fresh crab meat
1 envelope plain gelatin
½ cup water
2 stalks of celery

¼ bell pepper
2 tablespoons capers
1½ teaspoons seasoned salt
1 teaspoon pepper
1 cup homemade mayonnaise

Drain crab meat well and pick thoroughly. Dissolve gelatin in boiling water. Let cool. Very finely chop celery and bell pepper. Add to crab with capers and salt and pepper. Fold in mayonnaise and cooked gelatin. Chill in a 2-quart mold. Serves 30 to 40.

Mrs. William S. Slack

## CLAM DIP

1 clove garlic
One 8-ounce package cream cheese
2 teaspoons lemon juice
1½ teaspoons Worcestershire sauce
½ teaspoon salt

One 7-ounce can minced clams,
drained (reserve liquid)
3 tablespoons clam broth
Dash of freshly ground black
pepper

Rub a mixing bowl with the clove of garlic which has been cut in half. Place the cream cheese in the bowl and cream it until smooth. Gradually add the remaining ingredients, blending well. If a thinner dip is desired, add more clam broth. Serve with potato chips, corn chips or melba rounds. Yields 1 pint.

Mrs. Norman Saurage III

## JEZEBEL DIP

One 10-ounce jar apple jelly
One 5-ounce jar horseradish

One 12-ounce jar pineapple preserves
or marmalade

Mix all ingredients in a saucepan and heat until melted. Cool to room temperature. Serve with ham cubes, sausage balls or pork bits on toothpicks. Leftover sauce may be stored indefinitely in refrigerator.

Mrs. William T. Heflin

## ARTICHOKE DIP

One 15-ounce can Progresso seasoned
  bread crumbs
Four 14-ounce cans artichoke hearts
2 cups olive oil

Juice of 4 lemons (ReaLemon may
  be used)
2 cups grated Romano cheese
4 pods garlic, puréed
Red pepper to taste

Combine the bread crumbs, water from the artichokes, lemon juice and olive oil. Put the artichoke hearts in the blender and blend on high speed until well blended. Add artichoke hearts to above mixture. Add cheese, garlic and red pepper. Put in buttered 4-quart casserole and bake at 350 degrees 20 to 30 minutes until warm. This may be spooned into a chafing dish and served with melba rounds. Delicious! Yield: 4 quarts.

Mrs. John W. Saladin

## BLACK OLIVE DIP

1 soft, ripe avocado
1 tablespoon minced onions
2 tablespoons mayonnaise
2 tablespoons lemon juice

½ teaspoon salt
¼ teaspoon Tabasco sauce
One 8-ounce package cream cheese,
  softened
½ cup chopped ripe olives

Peel avocado and mash. Stir in onion, mayonnaise, lemon juice, salt and Tabasco sauce. Cream the cheese and blend well. Stir in black olives. Chill. This may also be used as a sandwich filling.

Mrs. Iveson B. Noland, III

## HUMMUS (CHICK PEA PURÉE)

Juice of 2 large lemons
½ teaspoon cumin
Large pinch cayenne pepper
½ teaspoon salt
2 cloves garlic, chopped

1 tablespoon oil
One 20-ounce can chick peas,
  drained (reserve liquid)
3 tablespoons sesame seeds
½ cup parsley, chopped

Garnish: paprika, parsley, chopped eggs, bacon, olives (one or more).

Blend lemon juice, seasonings, garlic, oil and 3 tablespoons chick pea liquid in blender. Add half of the peas and blend. Add remaining peas and purée. Add more chick pea juice if needed for blending. Scoop into a bowl and add remaining ingredients except garnish. Refrigerate several hours.

Mrs. Dean M. Mosely

## DRESSING OR DIP

1 cup sour cream
1 pint Hellman's mayonnaise
1 tablespoon parsley
1 teaspoon monosodium glutamate
1 teaspoon sugar
½ to ¾ teaspoon garlic salt

2 tablespoons Parmesan cheese,
  grated
1 cup Mozzarella cheese, grated
1 tablespoon onion flakes
Lawry's seasoned salt to taste
Pepper to taste

Mix all ingredients thoroughly. Refrigerate in tightly covered jar. Serve with fresh vegetables or chips.

Miss Kathleen Flanagan

## LOADED MEATBALLS

**Meatballs:**

1½ pounds chopped chuck steak
1 egg, beaten
1 teaspoon salt

1 tablespoon catsup
½ cup water
1 slice white bread, crumbled

Mix together the above ingredients. Form the mixture into small bite-sized meatballs.

**Sauce:**

2 tablespoons olive oil
1 small onion, minced
1 clove garlic, crushed
¼ teaspoon salt
2 dashes Angostura bitters
1 beef bouillon cube

1 teaspoon dry mustard
1 teaspoon flour
1 cup water
½ cup bourbon
¼ cup sweet vermouth
¼ teaspoon oregano

Get olive oil good and hot in a frying pan and fry meatballs, shaking pan over heat, until they are well-browned. When they turn a nice mahogany color, take them out of the pan.

Fry onion and garlic until they are soft but not brown. Add all the remaining sauce ingredients to the pan and bring to a boil. Cook over high heat, stirring steadily until liquid is reduced and sauce is thickened.

Put meatballs back in pan and cover. Reduce heat and simmer for five minutes. This can be served immediately, but tastes better if refrigerated for a day and reheated before serving. Can be used as a main course over noodles. Make meatballs larger. Serves 3 to 4 as a main course.

Mrs. Robert Royer

## SWEDISH MEATBALLS
### (Sweet and Sour Sauce)

**Meatballs:**

1 pound lean ground beef
¾ cup minced celery
¼ cup chopped almonds or cashews
1 clove garlic, finely chopped

1 teaspoon salt
½ cup soft bread crumbs
1 teaspoon soy sauce
½ teaspoon monosodium glutamate
2 eggs, slightly beaten

Mix all ingredients. Form into small meatballs and deep-fat fry.

**Sauce:**

1 cup chicken bouillon
½ cup sugar
3 tablespoons cornstarch
½ cup pineapple juice

½ cup vinegar
2 tablespoons soy sauce
1 bell pepper, chopped
One 8-ounce can pineapple chunks

Combine first 6 ingredients. Cook for 3 minutes or until thickened. Add bell pepper, pineapple chunks, and meatballs. Simmer about 15 minutes. Serves 12 to 15.

Mrs. H. J. Walker

## MARINATED MUSHROOMS

⅓ cup salad vinegar
1 cup French olive oil
1 teaspoon garlic, pressed
1 tablespoon Worcestershire sauce
1 teaspoon monosodium glutamate

1 tablespoon Beau Monde
1 tablespoon salad herbs
1 teaspoon pepper
1 teaspoon salt
Three 8-ounce cans large button
    mushrooms

Mix all ingredients except mushrooms. Add mushrooms and let stand 3 to 4 hours. Drain to serve.

Mrs. T. Buffington Beale

## MEATBALLS

3 pounds ground meat
1 cup cracker crumbs
1 teaspoon pepper
1 teaspoon monosodium glutamate
6 drops Tabasco sauce
3 tablespoons cumin

3 eggs
1 teaspoon salt
1 clove garlic, pressed
1 onion, grated
1 tablespoon chili powder
1 small can tomato sauce
1 small can spaghetti sauce

Combine all but last two ingredients and form into small cocktail balls. Brown in oil and place in a large baking pan. Combine last 2 ingredients and pour over meatballs. Bake in 350 degree oven, uncovered, for about 1 hour or until almost dry.

Mrs. Ford S. Lacey

## MUSHROOMS IN SOUR CREAM

¾ pound fresh mushrooms
3 tablespoons butter
2 tablespoons flour

1 tablespoon lemon juice
¼ teaspoon oregano
Salt and pepper to taste
1 cup sour cream

Trim the fresh mushrooms, slice lengthwise and sauté in butter over moderate heat. Cover and cook over low heat 5 minutes longer. Remove from heat and stir in flour. Return to low heat and cook, stirring for two minutes or until sauce thickens. Remove from heat and add remaining ingredients. Return to heat and heat thoroughly, but do not boil. Serve with French bread, thinly sliced, buttered and broiled till brown. Serves 8 to 10.

Mrs. J. Cooper Harrell, Jr.

## ARTICHOKE HORS D'OEUVRES

Two 14-ounce cans artichoke hearts
    (water packed)

1 cup mayonnaise
1 package Italian dressing
    (dry salad mix)

Drain artichokes well. Mix with fork until artichokes are broken up. Add mayonnaise and dry Italian dressing.

Mrs. Fred A. Blanche, Jr.

## STUFFED MUSHROOMS

2 dozen small mushrooms or
  6 large mushrooms
Olive oil
4 tablespoons margarine
1 onion, finely minced
1 stalk celery, finely minced

1 clove garlic, finely minced
1 tablespoon dried parsley flakes
½ teaspoon salt
Dash cayenne pepper
3 slices bread, made into crumbs
  in blender
Parmesan cheese

Wash mushrooms. Remove stems. Trim off and discard dry end of each stem. Chop the remaining stems finely and save. Brush oil on inside and outside of each mushroom cap. Arrange caps in shallow casserole dish. Melt margarine in skillet and sauté onion, celery and garlic until soft. Add finely chopped stems, parsley, salt, pepper and bread crumbs. Stir until well blended. Stuff and mound each mushroom cap with this mixture and sprinkle lightly with Parmesan cheese. Bake at 325 degrees for 25 minutes.

Mrs. Perry T. Chesney

## CHICKEN LIVER PÂTÉ

1 pound chicken livers
1 medium white onion, chopped
½ cup butter
¼ cup water

Salt to taste
Black pepper to taste (generously)
3 hard-boiled eggs
⅓ cup olive oil
2 green onions, finely chopped

Sauté livers and onions in butter. Add water for juice, if needed. When livers and onions are done, season with salt and pepper. Remove livers from juice to cool, reserving juice. Mince livers with egg whites using two knives or a meat grinder. Mash egg yolks into smooth paste with olive oil. Add paste to livers with enough juice to obtain a spread-type consistency. Add to this the finely chopped green onions. Shape into a 2-quart mold and refrigerate. Mold may be garnished with thin slices of green stuffed olives, minced fresh parsley, sieved hard-boiled egg whites, etc. Serves 25 to 30 people when used on wheat thins or other crackers.

Mrs. Robert M. Slowey

## GRILLED REUBEN JUNIORS

One 8-ounce long party rye
Two tablespoons mustard with
  horseradish
Two 4¾-ounce cans corned beef spread

¼ pound Swiss cheese, thinly
  sliced
1 cup sauerkraut, well drained
  (optional)

Spread half of the bread slices lightly with mustard, and then with the corned beef spread. Add two thin slices of Swiss cheese and a dollop of sauerkraut. Top with remaining bread slices and grill slowly in a buttered skillet. Remove when cheese is soft and bread is golden. Yields 18.

Mrs. Ben Thompson, Jr.

## RAW PARTY VEGETABLES

| | |
|---|---|
| 1 cup olive oil | 1 teaspoon pepper |
| 1½ cups wine vinegar | ¼ cup sugar |
| 2 teaspoons salt | 1 clove garlic |
| | Raw vegetables |

Combine all ingredients except raw vegetables, and bring to a boil. Cool for 5 minutes and add raw vegetables: sliced carrots, radishes, bell pepper, celery, zucchini, black olives, small onions (or large ones, quartered), yellow squash and cauliflower. Marinate for at least 24 hours. Pour marinade off before serving. Serve in wooden salad bowl with toothpicks. *Marvelous for a cocktail party.*

Mrs. W. A. Rolston, Jr.

## STUFFED ARTICHOKE LEAVES

| | |
|---|---|
| 4 large artichokes | Two 6-ounce jars marinated |
| 1 lemon | artichoke hearts |
| ½ cup butter | 1 tablespoon Worcestershire sauce |
| 2 tablespoons lemon juice | ⅛ teaspoon dry mustard |
| | ½ cup seasoned bread crumbs |

Wash and trim artichokes. Place in deep pot with enough water to cover. Squeeze lemon and drop rind and juice into pot with water and artichokes. Cook for about 1 hour or until tender and the leaves easily pull out. Select 50 to 60 of the largest leaves and set aside. Melt butter in a skillet. Scrape the meat off the remaining artichoke leaves and remove the hearts from the artichokes and chop. Add these to butter in skillet. Drain marinated hearts, chop and add them to the skillet mixture. Mash all hearts in butter. Add lemon juice, Worcestershire sauce, mustard and bread crumbs and mix together. Place 1 teaspoon of the mixture at the base of each leaf that you have set aside. Place leaves on baking sheet. Just before serving, heat in oven preheated to 350 degrees for about 10 minutes. *The long preparation time is justified by the "compliments to the cook."*

Mrs. W. F. Williamson, Jr.

## PICKLED JERUSALEM ARTICHOKES

20 cups Jerusalem artichokes

| | |
|---|---|
| **Jar Stuffing: (per 1 pint jar)** | **Brine:** |
| 2 cloves garlic | 1 quart apple cider vinegar |
| 2 sprigs fresh dill (or ½ teaspoon dill seed) | 2 quarts water |
| | ½ cup salt |
| 2 red hot peppers (or ½ teaspoon cayenne pepper) | |

Scrub artichokes well. Do not peel. Cut into about one inch pieces, without destroying natural tuber shape. Stuff sterilized one-pint jars with artichokes, garlic, dill and pepper. Boil brine ingredients for 5 minutes. Pour into jars while hot. Seal. Let stand at least 2 weeks before serving. Yields ten 1-pint jars.

Mrs. John S. Terrell
Shreveport, Louisiana

## CHEESE BALLS

1 cup margarine
1 cup self-rising flour
Dash of Tabasco sauce

1 5-ounce jar Kraft Old English
sharp Cheddar cheese

Mash margarine and cheese with fork. Mash in flour and Tabasco sauce. Roll into marble sized balls. Freeze before baking. Bake at 350 degrees for 10 to 12 minutes. Serve hot. Yields 50.

Mrs. M. S. Howie

## SPICY CHEESE BALL

One 1-pound package Cheddar cheese
One 8-ounce package cream cheese
and chives (if unavailable use
regular cream cheese and add
1 tablespoon chives)

One 8-ounce package cream cheese
Small wedge Roquefort cheese,
approximately 3 to 4 ounces
1½ ounces bourbon whiskey
Tabasco sauce to taste
Parsley flakes or pecans, to garnish

Grate Cheddar cheese and let other cheeses reach room temperature. In large mixing bowl, mix the cheeses and add bourbon, Worcestershire sauce and Tabasco sauce. The mixing can be done by hand or with electric mixer. This is rather messy. Chill slightly—an hour or so. Roll into two balls. These balls may be rolled in parsley flakes or pecans. If you are freezing, do not roll the balls in garnish until you have thawed them. Yields 2 medium-sized cheese balls.

Mrs. Calvin S. Moore

## CHUTNEY CHEESE

8 ounces cream cheese, softened
4 ounces Cheddar cheese, grated
¼ teaspoon salt

¾ teaspoon curry powder
4 tablespoons dry sherry
¾ cup chutney, chopped
Green onions, chopped

Thoroughly mix first five ingredients. Form into a flat circle on a serving plate and chill. Just before serving, spread chutney and green onions on top. Serve with bacon flavored crackers to bring out the chutney flavor.

Mrs. C. Bernard Berry

## CHEESE BALL

Two 8-ounce packages cream cheese,
softened
One 13-ounce can crushed pineapple,
drained

¼ cup bell pepper, finely chopped
2 tablespoons onion, finely chopped
¼ cup chopped pecans
1 tablespoon seasoned salt
Additional: 1 cup chopped pecans

Soften cheese and mix all ingredients together. Refrigerate mixture overnight before rolling into a ball. Roll in additional cup of chopped pecans. Decorate with cherries or stuffed olives. Serve with rice crackers. Freezes well.

Mrs. N. J. Swart

## BLEU CHEESE ROLL

½ cup butter
4 ounces Bleu cheese
One 8-ounce package cream cheese
¼ cup minced onion

1 tablespoon fresh parsley
Dash Worcestershire sauce
Dash Tabasco sauce
Chopped pecans to garnish
(optional)

Let butter and cheeses reach room temperature. Cream butter and Bleu cheese. Add softened cream cheese. Mix well. Add minced onion and remaining ingredients except nuts. Chill. Shape cheese into a ball and roll in chopped nuts to coat outside. Wrap in wax paper and chill until ready to serve.

Mrs. John E. Gonce

## SAUSAGE CHEESE BALLS

One 10-ounce package coon cheese

1 pound hot bulk sausage
3 cups Bisquick mix

Melt cheese in double boiler. Add sausage and mix thoroughly. Pour into large mixing bowl and add Bisquick mix gradually. Mix well after each addition. Shape mixture into small balls. Bake on lightly greased cookie sheet at 350 degrees until lightly browned, about 10 to 15 minutes. These may be frozen before cooking. Freeze on a tray or cookie sheet, then place in plastic bags and return to freezer. Thaw before baking. Yield: 130 balls.

Mrs. Thomas H. Campbell, Jr.
Yazoo City, Mississippi

## CHEESE NUT SPREAD

8 ounces sharp Cheddar cold pack
　cheese food
8 ounces cream cheese
½ to 1 cup sour cream
1 tablespoon olive oil
2 teaspoons vinegar
2 teaspoons dried minced onion
½ teaspoon paprika
½ teaspoon chili powder
½ teaspoon dried minced garlic

1 teaspoon salt
¼ teaspoon pepper
½ teaspoon Worcestershire sauce
¼ teaspoon Tabasco sauce
3 heaping tablespoons cottage
　cheese
½ cup grated Parmesan cheese
4-ounce package of shredded sharp
　cheese
1 cup chopped nuts
(cashews or pecans)

Let sharp cheese and cream cheese soften to room temperature. Combine olive oil, vinegar and seasonings and let set. Blend together the sharp cheese, cream cheese and sour cream. Add this to olive oil mixture and blend. Mix in cottage cheese, Parmesan cheese, shredded cheese and nuts. Before serving let soften at room temperature for easier spreading. Serve with crackers or raw vegetables. Serves 50.

Mrs. J. Randall Goodwin

## SAUSAGE BALLS

5 pounds hot bulk sausage
1 medium-sized jar chutney

1 pint sour cream
1 cup dry sherry

Roll hot sausage into small balls. Fry and place on paper towel to drain. Chop chutney into fine pieces, saving juice. Combine chutney, juice, sour cream, and sherry. Heat. Place in chafing dish and add sausage balls. Serve with toothpicks.

Mrs. Ford S. Lacey

## HOT SAUSAGE AND PINEAPPLE BITS

2 pounds hot link sausage
1 pound bulk sausage
1 cup brown sugar, packed

One 12-ounce can pineapple chunks,
cut in half and drained,
reserving juice

Slice link sausage crosswise in pieces ¼ inch thick. Make bulk sausage into balls one inch in diameter. Brown sausages in iron skillet. Drain all but 3 tablespoons of the grease. Add pineapple chunks, brown sugar and the reserved pineapple juice. Cover and cook slowly for 30 minutes. Place sausage in chafing dish. Serve with toothpicks as an appetizer or serve for supper with buttered grits.

Mrs. Vernon P. Middleton

## COCKTAIL HAM

2 to 4 tablespoons light brown sugar
1 cup Kraft hickory flavored
   barbecue sauce

1 pound ham, thinly sliced and
   cut in squares
Cocktail hamburger buns

Dissolve sugar in sauce. Add ham and heat thoroughly. Let cool. Reheat. This improves the flavor. Place in chafing dish and serve with buns.

Mrs. John B. Whitley

## CHINESE SPARERIBS

2 pounds spareribs
3 cloves garlic, sliced
1½ teaspoons salt
½ cup honey

¼ cup soy sauce
¼ cup catsup
¾ teaspoon monosodium glutamate
1 cup chicken stock
½ teaspoon prepared mustard

Have spareribs cut into bite sized pieces. Combine remaining ingredients and marinate ribs in this mixture overnight. Turn ribs occasionally. When ready to bake, place on rack in 325 degree oven for 1 hour and 15 minutes. Baste frequently with marinade. Turn ribs several times for even browning. Serves 8.

Mrs. R. L. Rieger

## EGG ROLLS

**Dough:**

| | |
|---|---|
| 1 egg, slightly beaten | ½ teaspoon salt |
| 2 cups flour | ½ cup cold water |

Reserve 1 tablespoon egg. Mix remainder with flour, salt and water until all dry ingredients are moistened. Knead until smooth. Wrap in plastic wrap and refrigerate 30 to 40 minutes.

**Filling:**

| | |
|---|---|
| 3 tablespoons vegetable oil | 2 cups chopped Chinese cabbage, or |
| ½ pound lean pork, chopped | fresh or canned bean sprouts |
| or finely diced | ½ teaspoon salt |
| ¼ pound shrimp, chopped | ¼ teaspoon monosodium glutamate |
| (raw or cooked) | 1 teaspoon cornstarch |
| 1 cup chopped celery | 1 tablespoon soy sauce |
| 4 green onions, chopped | Oil for frying |

Heat 3 tablespoons oil in a large skillet over high heat. Add pork. Cook, stirring until meat loses its color. Add shrimp and cook 1 minute. Add vegetables and seasonings. Cook 2 minutes, stirring often. Add cornstarch and mix well. Stir in soy sauce. Cook 1 minute. Drain in a colander set in a bowl. Cool completely.

Divide dough in thirds. Roll each piece into a 12-inch square on a surface sprinkled with cornstarch. Trim edges and cut into 4 squares. Place 1 square with a corner pointing toward you. Put 2 to 3 tablespoons filling on dough slightly below center. Brush edges of dough with reserved egg. Fold the corner nearest you over the filling. Fold the left corner, then the right. Roll toward top to form a cylinder. Repeat with remaining squares. Cover with a damp towel until ready to use. Heat 2 inches of oil to 375 degrees. Cook rolls, 3 or 4 at a time, until crisp and golden. Drain. Serve with sweet-sour sauce and hot mustard. Makes 12.

Mrs. William J. Doran, Jr.

## BEVERAGES

There are many ways to toast your health in Louisiana. The cry of *Santé* may be raised over a variety of delicious beverages: rich, French dripped coffee; homemade wines from native fruits and berries; chilled champagne over fresh, Louisiana strawberries; or a myriad of holiday punches. Dating back to the early settlement of the state, when the stirrup cup was all-important to the weary traveler and the medicinal cordial was essential to households far from doctors, beverages have maintained a place of prominence in Louisiana cuisine.

### GOOD COFFEE EVERY TIME

One of the most satisfying pleasures of the day can be found in a pot of good coffee. Despite claims for special grinds and fancy brewers, a simple drip pot and a non-special grind of coffee usually produce the best flavor. Use the freshest, most delicious coffee you can buy, whether you prefer American-style coffee or a dark roast or New Orleans style coffee and chicory. Use no less than ⅔ capacity of a sparkling clean coffee pot that circulates boiling water evenly through the coffee grounds.

    Measurement: For 4 servings, use ½ cup coffee to 3 cups water

                    For 8 servings, use 1 cup coffee to 6 cups water

If your ground coffee basket holds ½ measuring cup of coffee with adequate room for swelling and bubbling, then you have a "four-cup" pot, *even* if it is labeled differently. It will make a maximum of 4 really good servings. So you would use 3 cups boiling water to drench and drip through the coffee grinds for 5 or 6 minutes. Immediately remove spent grinds and swish a spoon through the liquid coffee so each serving tastes the same. Then enjoy the goodness of rich, smooth coffee flavor.

Norman Saurage III
Community Coffee Company, Inc.

### BURNT SUGAR COFFEE

| | |
|---|---|
| **1 tablespoon sugar** | **2 tablespoons French drip coffee,** |
| **¼ cup water** | **already dripped** |
| | **1½ cups milk** |

Mix sugar and water. Cook in small saucepan until mixture is brown, almost burned. Add coffee and milk. Heat together. This makes 2 cups.

Mrs. John B. LeJeune, Sr.

### IRISH COFFEE

| | |
|---|---|
| **1½ teaspoons sugar** | **Strong hot coffee** |
| **2¼ ounces Irish whiskey** | **Whipped cream** |

Add to each prewarmed stemmed glass sugar and Irish whiskey. Stir until sugar is dissolved. Fill glasses with strong hot coffee and top with whipped cream. Be sure to place a sterling silver spoon in each glass while adding coffee to prevent breaking the glass. *So good on a cold night!*

Mrs. Charles Whitehurst

### LOUISIANA COFFEE FLOAT

| | |
|---|---|
| **2½ cups cold milk** | **½ cup chocolate syrup** |
| **4 heaping teaspoons dark roast** | **Ice cream (vanilla)** |
| **instant coffee** | |

Put milk, coffee and chocolate in blender and blend until smooth. Scoop ice cream into glasses, pour milk mixture over it and stir lightly. Top with whipped cream if desired. Yields 3 tall glasses.

Mrs. Norman Saurage III

## SPICED TEA

One 1-pound 11-ounce jar Tang
Two 3-ounce packages sweetened
  lemonade mix
1 cup instant tea

1 cup sugar
½ teaspoon cloves
½ teaspoon cinnamon
Stick cinnamon (optional
  as garnish)

Mix all ingredients, except stick cinnamon, together thoroughly and store in an airtight container. To prepare tea, place 1 or 2 heaping teaspoons of the mix in a cup or mug and add boiling water. Stir and serve. Stick cinnamon may be placed in cup or mug if desired. Mixture will keep up to a year in an airtight container. Makes 80 to 100 cups or 3 pints of the mix.

Mrs. Norman Saurage III

## ICED SPICED TEA

4 tea bags
1 quart boiling water
1 stick cinnamon
½ teaspoon whole cloves

1 cup sugar
Juice of 3 lemons
1 quart cold water
Fresh mint (optional)

Combine the tea bags, boiling water, cinnamon and cloves. Let steep for 3 to 8 minutes. Strain and add remainder of ingredients. Refrigerate and serve over ice. Garnish with fresh mint. Makes ½ gallon.

Mrs. James E. Toups, Jr.

## OLD VIRGINIA WASSAIL

Two quarts sweet apple cider
Two cups orange juice
One cup lemon juice

Two cups pineapple juice
One stick cinnamon
One teaspoon whole cloves
Sugar or honey to taste

Combine ingredients in large pot and simmer a few minutes. Strain and serve hot. Yield: 20 servings.

Mrs. W. J. Oliver III

## EASY PARTY PUNCH

One 46-ounce can unsweetened
  pineapple juice

One 46-ounce can apple juice
Two 28-ounce bottles 7-Up,
  chilled

Freeze pineapple juice and apple juice in their cans. One hour before serving, set out the frozen cans. When ready to serve, mix fruit juices with the chilled 7-Up. No additional ice is needed for the punch. Yields about 30 cups of punch.

Mrs. James R. Douglas

## WEDDING PUNCH

1 cup sugar
1 cup water
One 6-ounce can frozen lemon juice

One 46-ounce can pineapple juice
1 quart ginger ale
⅓ to ½ of a 1-ounce bottle of almond flavoring

Bring sugar and water to boil. Add the lemon juice and pineapple juice. Add ginger ale and almond flavoring just before serving. Serves 25.

Mrs. E. D. Martin

## MILK PUNCH I

1 quart vanilla ice cream or ice milk

½ gallon milk
2 to 3 cups bourbon

In mixer, blend together softened ice cream and milk. Add bourbon and mix. Place mixture in freezer until ready to use. The mixture fits conveniently into two ½-gallon milk cartons. Take from freezer and place in regrigerator 3 or 4 hours before serving. Do not thaw completely—leave icy. Serve from silver pitcher. Makes approximately 1 gallon.

Mrs. William L. Adams

## SANGRIA

Two fifths Burgundy wine
One 6-ounce can frozen orange juice concentrate, thawed

One 6-ounce can frozen lemonade concentrate, thawed
Two quarts club soda
Sugar to taste

Mix fruit juices with wine. Add soda and sugar to taste. Pour over ice and serve. Garnish with slices of orange and lemon in punch bowl. Yield: 32 servings.

Mrs. E. A. Smith, Jr.

## VODKA PUNCH

Eight 6-ounce cans frozen lemon juice
Twelve 12-ounce cans frozen orange juice

Ten 32-ounce cans pineapple juice
4 to 6 fifths vodka (80 proof)
Six to eight 20-ounce cans pineapple chunks (optional)
6 to 8 quarts club soda

Prepare frozen juices as directed on cans. Mix all ingredients together, except club soda. Refrigerate or keep as cold as possible until ready to serve. Pour over large piece of ice and garnish with very thin slices of lemon speared with sprigs of fresh mint. Add club soda just before serving. Serves 125 to 150.

Mrs. Maurice Julius Wilson

## MOCHA COFFEE PUNCH

**Punch:**

⅓ cup strong, brewed coffee

⅓ cup granulated sugar

½ pint vanilla ice cream (1 cup)

1 quart cold, whole milk

In a 2- to 3-quart bowl, blend all ingredients together using an electric mixer. Divide the mixture into two 1-quart ring molds. Freeze. Using the same amounts of ingredients and the same method, make a second and a third batch of the same punch mixture. Refrigerate until ready to serve. Prepare topping immediately before serving.

**Topping:**

½ cup heavy cream

2 tablespoons instant cocoa

1 tablespoon granulated sugar

⅛ teaspoon cinnamon

Shaved chocolate

Whip cream until it thickens. Gradually add cocoa, sugar and cinnamon. Continue whipping until cream holds its shape. Set aside. Unmold one of the frozen rings into punch bowl. Reserve the second ring until needed. Pour ½ refrigerated liquid punch over mold. Reserve rest until needed. Float topping in the center of the ring. Garnish with shaved chocolate. Ladle some of the liquid punch and topping into each cup served. Serves 20.

Mrs. William Adams

## LOUISIANA PEACH BRANDY

1 wide-mouth gallon jar, with top

10 to 12 peaches (washed, unpeeled)

2½-pounds sugar

1 fifth gin

Put peaches in jar. Pour in sugar and gin. Put top on jar. Leave in a secure place. Every couple of days, twist jar around to help dissolve sugar. After about a week, add more gin to cover peaches. (Peaches will shrink.) Taste after a couple of months. You may add more sugar or gin to taste. Remove peaches. (They are good on ice cream.) Strain liquid through several layers of cheese cloth so it will be beautifully clear. Bottle and enjoy. This may be made in July and bottled in November or December for Christmas gifts. Yield: ¾ gallon.

Mrs. Percy E. Roberts, Jr.

## SUREFIRE BLOODY MARY

Two 46-ounce cans V-8 juice

6 ounces lemon juice

4 ounces Worcestershire sauce

20 shakes monosodium glutamate

20 drops Tabasco sauce

20 shakes lemon-pepper

 seasoning

20 shakes seasoned salt

One fifth vodka

Mix thoroughly. Yield: 24 drinks.

Mrs. James R. Ourso

## FROZEN DAIQUIRIS

2 cups water
2 cups sugar
Two 6-ounce cans frozen limeade
  concentrate
Two 6-ounce cans frozen lemonade
  concentrate

One 6-ounce can frozen
  lemon juice
1 fifth rum
6 cups water
Fresh mint for garnish
  (optional)

Combine water and sugar. Heat 10 minutes to make a syrup. Mix all ingredients and freeze overnight. Spoon into small Old Fashion glasses and garnish with mint, if desired. Makes 32 drinks.

Mrs. James E. Toups, Jr.

## PEACH DAIQUIRIS

One 10-ounce package frozen
  peaches, partially thawed
6 ounces light rum

½ of 6-ounce can frozen
  lemonade concentrate
2 cups crushed ice

Combine all ingredients and whirl in blender until peaches are puréed and mixture is uniform. Store in covered plastic container in freezer until ready to serve in small cocktail glasses. *This beverage has a lovely color—pretty and easy to prepare!* Serves 8 to 10.

Mrs. Wallace Sandifer

## MISSISSIPPI GAMBLER

10 lemons
Fifth good bourbon

Fifth water
Approximately 1 cup sugar
Fresh mint to garnish

Squeeze lemons by hand. Remove seeds and reserve 6 rinds. Mix juice and rinds with remaining ingredients and stir well. Store in covered crock or jar for 24 hours. Do not use metal container. Squeeze rinds and remove from mixture. Pour liquid into a covered plastic container and place in freezer 2 days before you wish to serve. Scoop out slush into julep cups or small glasses. Garnish with mint, if desired. This is a good substitute for "whiskey sour type" drinks. Yield: 8 to 12 drinks.

Mrs. C. Bernard Berry

## MAGNOLIA MOUND PUNCH

1 bottle pre-chilled strawberry wine
  such as St. Martin's (not
  strawberry flavored wine)

One 32-ounce bottle pre-chilled
  ginger ale
Fresh strawberries

Mix first two ingredients. Strawberries may be floated in the punch as decoration. Makes 12 to 14 four-ounce servings.

Mrs. Kevin Reilly

## SOUPS AND GUMBOS

Here you will find something for every occasion: a tempting appetizer, a hearty main dish, a convenient after-theater snack, or a delightful luncheon entreé. The possibilities are endless, and all you need are a good and spacious pot, a selection of ingredients, and lots of seasoning. Natives often prefer the black iron pots for gumbo. In Louisiana, a pot of soup or gumbo may be not only the food for a party, but may well be the reason for the party.

## SHRIMP, CRAB AND OKRA GUMBO

5 onions, quartered
2 bell peppers, chopped
6 cloves garlic, chopped
1 bunch green onions, chopped
6 quarts water
6 tablespoons flour

6 tablespoons oil
2½ pounds cut okra
Salt, pepper, onion salt, garlic
   salt and cayenne pepper to taste
6 pounds headless shrimp
6 pounds gumbo crabs
Gumbo file'

In a large pot, boil vegetables in water until the vegetables settle to the bottom. In another pot make a dark brown roux with flour and oil stirring constantly. Add water and vegetables slowly to the roux, stirring constantly. Fry okra with a small amount of grease and salt until okra is soft (avoid sticking). Stir okra into gumbo. Season to taste. Allow this to cook for 3 hours. Seasoning will weaken during prolonged cooking so season periodically. Peel and devein shrimp. Discard feelers from crabs and use claws and body (cut body in half). Add shrimp and sectioned crabs to gumbo and cook for an additional 30 minutes. Serve over rice. Add a small amount of file' to each serving. Serves approximately 20.

Mrs. Julie Dugas

## SEAFOOD GUMBO I

1 cup bacon drippings
1 cup all purpose flour
8 stalks celery, chopped
3 large yellow onions, chopped
1 bunch green onions, chopped
1 green pepper, chopped
2 cloves garlic, minced
½ cup parsley, chopped
1 pound okra, sliced
2 tablespoons shortening
2 quarts chicken stock
2 quarts water
½ cup Worcestershire sauce

Tabasco sauce to taste
½ cup catsup
One 16-ounce can whole tomatoes
2 tablespoons salt
1 large slice of ham, chopped
2 bay leaves
¼ teaspoon thyme
¼ teaspoon rosemary
2 cups cooked chicken, chopped
1 pound claw crabmeat
3 to 4 pounds boiled shrimp
1 pint oysters, optional
1 teaspoon brown sugar
Lemon juice to taste

Heat bacon drippings over medium heat, add flour slowly and stir constantly until roux is a chocolate-like brown. This takes a long time. Add celery, onions, green pepper, garlic, parsley and cook 45 minutes to 1 hour stirring occasionally. Fry okra in shortening until slightly browned. Add to first mixture and stir well for a few minutes. Add chicken stock and water, Worcestershire sauce, Tabasco sauce, catsup, tomatoes with juice, salt, ham, bay leaves, thyme, rosemary. Simmer 2½ hours. Add chicken, crabmeat, shrimp and simmer 30 minutes more. (If using oysters, add with seafood.) Add brown sugar and lemon juice. Serve in bowls over hot rice. Well worth the time! Serves 20.

Mrs. Robert Witcher
Manhasset, New York

## SEAFOOD GUMBO II

½ cup salad oil
½ cup flour
1 large onion, chopped
2 to 3 garlic cloves, minced
One 1-pound can tomatoes, undrained
1½ pounds frozen okra or equivalent fresh
Oil for frying okra
2 quarts hot water
3½ tablespoons salt

¾ teaspoon red pepper
1 large bay leaf
¼ teaspoon thyme
8 to 10 allspice berries
Few grains chili pepper
2 pounds headless raw shrimp, peeled
1 pound claw crab meat, picked
1 pint oysters
½ cup chopped green onions
½ cup chopped parsley

Make a very dark roux in a large heavy pot. Add onions and garlic. Cook slowly until onions are transparent. Add tomatoes and cook on low heat until oil rises to the top (about 30 minutes) stirring frequently. In separate skillet, fry okra in oil on moderately high heat, stirring constantly until okra is no longer stringy. Add the okra to the other mixture, stir and simmer about 10 minutes. Add water, salt and pepper. Simmer partially covered for 45 minutes. Add other seasonings and simmer an additional 20 minutes, then add shrimp—simmer 15 minutes; then add crab meat, simmering 15 minutes more. Add the oysters the last 5 minutes of cooking. Taste carefully for seasoning, adding more if necessary. Remove from fire and stir in green onions and parsley. Serve over rice. Variations may be made by adding different seafoods, sausages or poultry. Serves 8 to 10.

Mrs. R. Boatner Howell, Jr.

## CRAWFISH FILÉ GUMBO

1 cup oil
1 cup flour
1 cup chopped celery
1 cup chopped onions
1 gallon water
One 6-ounce can tomato paste
2 tablespoons butter

One 10-ounce can Rotel tomatoes
1 pound crawfish tails
1 pound crabmeat (claw is better)
½ cup chopped green onion tops
½ cup chopped bell pepper
½ cup parsley
Garlic, salt and pepper to taste
Filé

Heat oil in a large black pot. Add flour to oil. Make a dark roux. Add celery and onions. Sauté 30 minutes. Add water. Brown tomato paste in butter. Cook until it loses its bright red color. Add ½ to ¾ can Rotel tomatoes. Add this mixture to other pot and simmer 1 hour. Add crawfish, crabmeat, green onion tops, bell pepper and parsley. Adjust seasoning and simmer about 20 to 30 minutes. This is a thin gumbo. If it needs to be thickened, add a little cornstarch dissolved in water. Serve on rice and let each person add filé to his own taste. Serves 12.

Mrs. J. Noland Singletary

## GUMBO

1 chicken or leftover carcass
Salt, pepper and cayenne pepper
   to taste
½ to 1 pound sausage, chopped
2 cups okra
1 bell pepper, chopped
3 pods garlic, chopped
1 large onion, chopped

3 bay leaves
1 teaspoon basil
2 teaspoons thyme
2 tomatoes, fresh or canned
3 tablespoons fat or oil
3 tablespoons flour
1 cup stock
Shrimp, oysters, crabs (optional)

Cook chicken in water with salt, pepper and cayenne pepper until tender. Remove meat from bone in slivers. Save stock. You may also use a leftover turkey, ham or duck carcass in place of chicken. In a large pot, sauté sausage. Remove sausage from pot and sauté okra, bell pepper, garlic, onion, bay leaves, basil and thyme in sausage drippings. Stir frequently to prevent burning or sticking. When tender, add tomatoes that have been puréed in blender or finely chopped. Let this simmer 15 minutes, stirring frequently. Add chicken and stock. Let gumbo mixture simmer. The roux is made in a small pan, preferably cast iron. Heat fat or oil over medium heat until it is just about to smoke. Add flour, stirring constantly. It should take 3 to 5 minutes to turn dark brown. Be careful not to burn. When roux is done, remove from heat and let cool 5 minutes. Slowly add 1 cup of hot stock, stirring so it won't lump. Add this to gumbo. You may also add shrimp, gumbo crabs, crab claws or crabmeat and oysters. Season to taste with salt and cayenne pepper. Simmer 2 to 3 hours. Serve over rice. If okra is not used in gumbo, sprinkle 1 teaspoon of file in each bowl after gumbo has been served. Serves 12.

Mrs. Hilary Duchein Hurst

## ARTICHOKE SOUP

½ cup butter
1 large onion, chopped
1 bunch green onions, chopped
2 pods garlic, pressed
2 tablespoons parsley, chopped
2 dozen oysters

Two 1-pound cans of artichoke
   hearts
1 cup oyster liquor or water
One 10¾-ounce can cream of
   mushroom soup
1 bay leaf
Salt and pepper

Melt butter in Dutch oven. Add chopped onions and cook until transparent. Add garlic and parsley and cook 2 to 3 minutes. Add oysters and cook 3 to 4 more minutes. Add drained, quartered artichoke hearts and cook for a few more minutes. Add oyster liquor, cream of mushroom soup and bay leaf. Cook for 20 minutes. Prepare 30 minutes or so before serving to allow flavors to penetrate. Salt and pepper to taste. Serves 4 to 6.

Mrs. Percy Roberts, Jr.

## BETTY'S BRUSSELS SPROUTS SOUP

½ cup butter
½ cup flour
Salt and pepper to taste
1½ cups chopped celery

1 cup chopped onion
1 quart chicken broth
5 cups milk
2½ pounds frozen Brussels sprouts

Melt butter in saucepan. Stir in flour, salt and pepper. Stir until smooth and set over low heat. Sauté celery and onion. Gradually add chicken broth and milk. Add Brussels sprouts that have been cut in half. Cook for 35 minutes. Serves 10 to 12.

Mrs. Roosevelt LeBlanc, Chef
Bocage Racquet Club

## FRENCH ONION SOUP

4 tablespoons butter
2 tablespoons oil
7 cups onion, thinly sliced
1 teaspoon salt

3 tablespoons flour
2 quarts or six 10¾-ounce cans
chicken, beef, or chicken and
beef stock combined
Salt and pepper to taste

In a heavy 4- to 5-quart saucepan or soup kettle, melt butter with oil over moderate heat. Stir in the onions and salt. Cook uncovered over low heat, stirring occasionally for 20 to 30 minutes or until the onions are a rich golden brown. Sprinkle flour over the onions and cook, stirring for 2 or 3 minutes. Remove the pan from the heat. In a saucepan, bring the stock to a simmer, then stir the hot stock into the onions. Return the soup to low heat and simmer, partially covered, for another 30 to 40 minutes, occasionally skimming off the fat. Taste for seasoning. Add salt and pepper if needed. Serve with croutons. Serves 6 to 8.

Mrs. Michael T. Delahaye

## VEGETABLE SOUP

4 meaty soup bones
3 quarts water
Salt, pepper, cayenne pepper
2 teaspoons Worcestershire sauce
4 ribs celery, cut up

5 carrots, cut up
⅓ head cabbage, cut up
3 to 4 medium onions, cut up
2 potatoes, cut up
One 16-ounce can tomatoes or 6 fresh

Combine all ingredients and simmer covered for 3 to 4 hours until meat is tender. Remove meat and vegetables from stock. Debone meat and take out gristle. Push vegetables through colander or sieve. Return meat and vegetables to stock. Adjust seasonings. (You may add any other left over vegetables you have available.) Serves 12 generously.

Mrs. Richard H. Tannehill

## MUSHROOM SOUP

1 cup chopped green onions
5⅓ tablespoons butter
2 cups chopped fresh mushrooms

2 tablespoons flour
One 13¾-ounce can chicken broth
13¾ ounces milk
Salt, pepper, cayenne pepper to taste

Sauté onions in butter until tender, about 5 minutes. Add mushrooms. Cook 2 minutes. Add flour and chicken broth and simmer 5 minutes. Add milk, salt, pepper and cayenne pepper and heat. (You may have to add a little water or milk if soup tastes too rich.) Serves 4 to 6.

Mrs. Richard H. Tannehill

## ONION SOUP

2 tablespoons butter
6 large onions, thinly sliced
7 cups chicken broth
3 tablespoons sherry

Salt and pepper to taste
6 to 8 buttered, toasted French
  bread rounds
Parmesan cheese, grated

Heat large iron pot and melt butter. Add onions and fry slowly until golden brown, stirring often. Gradually stir in chicken broth, add sherry, salt and pepper. Cover pan tightly and simmer 30 minutes. Pour into individual ovenproof bowls. Place slice of toast on soup, buttered side up. Spread heavily with grated cheese dotting on top with butter. Place under broiler about 1 minute or until cheese is golden brown. Serves 6 to 8.

Mrs. Karl E. Boellert

## VICHYSSOISE

Two 14-ounce cans beef broth
Two 14-ounce cans chicken broth
2 bouillon cubes (chicken or beef)
2 cups water
One 2-pound package frozen, whole
  new potatoes
½ teaspoon marjoram
1 teaspoon basil

One 8-ounce package frozen,
  chopped onions
1 teaspoon dehydrated parsley
  flakes
1 teaspoon tarragon
Salt and pepper to taste
Breakfast cream, ¾ to 1 cup per
  serving
Celery salt

Combine all ingredients except cream and celery salt. Cook in an uncovered pot beginning with a hot fire. After boiling point is reached, reduce heat immediately and continue to simmer uncovered until thick. Stir occasionally. While cooking, mash potatoes against side of pot. It takes this about 2 hours to cook down to proper thickness—quite thick. Immediately blend small amounts at a time in electric blender just until smooth. Do not over blend. Chill. This base will keep in the refrigerator for a week if placed in a tightly covered jar and then used as you or your guests can assimilate the "extra pounds." This is very rich, but oh so good! Makes 2 quarts base.

To serve, add ¾ cup of this base to ¾ to 1 cup breakfast cream per serving. Serve very cold. A dash of celery salt should top each serving. Serves 16 to 20 as an appetizer.

Mrs. W. F. Williamson, Jr.

## POTATO SOUP

3 to 4 cups peeled and sliced
  red potatoes,
3 cups sliced leeks or yellow onions
1½ to 2 quarts water, or just
  enough to cover potatoes and onions
1 tablespoon salt

2 to 3 tablespoons powdered
  chicken stock, or 5 to 6 chicken
  bouillon cubes
Black pepper to taste
2 to 3 tablespoons butter
½ pint cream (optional)

Bring potatoes and onions to a boil in salted water. Reduce heat and simmer partially covered for 45 minutes. Put through a food mill (or blender) and return to pot. Add black pepper, 2 to 3 tablespoons butter and ½ pint cream (if desired). Heat and serve. Serves 8 to 10.

Mrs. James W. McCaskill

## BETTY'S OYSTER STEW

1 pint shelled oysters
¼ cup butter
½ cup chopped onion
½ cup chopped celery
⅓ cup chopped bell pepper

3 tablespoons flour
5 cups milk
1½ teaspoons salt
½ teaspoon pepper
½ tablespoon Worcestershire sauce

Drain oysters and save liquid. Melt butter. Add onions, celery and bell pepper. Sauté until tender. Add flour and stir until smooth. Gradually add milk and oyster liquid. Add salt and pepper. Heat to boiling point. Reduce heat and let cook for 15 to 20 minutes. Add oysters and Worcestershire sauce. Let cook until oysters curl, about 3 to 5 minutes. Serves 10 to 12.

Mrs. Roosevelt LeBlanc, Chef
Bocage Racquet Club

## OYSTER STEW I

4 dozen oysters
4 stalks celery
2 large onions
1 pint water
1 teaspoon salt
¼ pound butter

Two 14-ounce cans evaporated milk
¼ teaspoon Tabasco sauce
Salt and cayenne pepper to taste
1 bunch green onion tops (optional)
12 crackers rolled between waxed
  paper

Drain oysters reserving liquid. Boil chopped celery and onion, covered, in salted water until tender. Place vegetables and liquid into blender and blend until smooth. Add water to make 1 quart and pour into a large pot. Add butter, evaporated milk and oyster liquid. Heat mixture, but do not boil. Add oysters, seasonings, green onions (if desired) and cracker crumbs. Heat until oysters curl. Serves 4.

Mrs. D. M. Wellan

## OYSTER STEW II

1 quart milk
1 cup heavy cream
1 bay leaf
3 stalks celery, finely chopped
Salt and black pepper
½ teaspoon monosodium glutamate

¼ pound butter
4 tablespoons finely chopped
  shallots
4 dozen oysters and liquid
1 bunch parsley, chopped fine
Cayenne pepper to taste

Simmer milk and cream with bay leaf, celery, salt, pepper and monosodium glutamate. In another saucepan, melt butter. Add shallots and cook until soft. Drain oysters reserving liquid. Add oysters to butter and shallots and cook until oysters curl (very short time). Combine with milk, oyster liquid, parsley and cayenne. The celery may be simmered whole with the milk, then discarded along with the bay leaf. Serves 6 to 8.

Mrs. Charles F. Duchein, Jr.

## SHRIMP AND CORN SOUP

⅓ cup oil
3 tablespoons flour
2 medium onions, finely chopped
1 large bell pepper, coarsely
  chopped
1 pound medium shrimp, peeled
2 tablespoons parsley

Salt, black pepper and red pepper
  to taste
One 1-pound can whole peeled
  tomatoes, undrained
One 1-pound can whole kernel corn
  (drain off ½ liquid)
1 cup water

Make a roux with oil and flour. When roux is golden brown, add onions. Cook for 10 to 15 minutes. Add bell pepper, shrimp, parsley, salt and pepper. Simmer for 5 to 10 minutes. Add tomatoes, corn, and 1 cup water. Simmer at least 1 hour adding more water gradually until desired consistency. Serves 6.

Mrs. Cora B. Johnston

## BASS SOUP

1 medium onion, sliced thinly
1 bunch chopped green onions
2 stalks celery with tops, chopped
½ cup butter
2 to 3 tablespoons oil

Flour—enough to make a paste
4 cups fish stock (boil fish
  bones an hour to get stock)
4 pounds bass, filéd and skinned
Salt, pepper and garlic salt to taste

Sauté onions and celery in butter until soft. In another pot, make a light roux with oil and flour. Keep stirring until the flour is golden brown. To the roux add fish stock. Stir until thoroughly blended, and let simmer. Add vegetable mixture. Let simmer about 30 minutes, covered. Cut bass into bite size pieces. Season with salt, pepper and garlic salt generously. Add fish to mixture and cook 5 to 10 minutes until bass is done. This is better the day after, warmed over briefly. Serve like this or add small amount of white wine just before serving. For a main meal, add rice as a sort of gumbo.

Mrs Charles W. Wilson III

## TURTLE SOUP

3 pounds turtle meat, cut into
  1-inch cubes
1 cup oil
1 cup flour
1 cup diced onions
1 cup diced celery
6 cloves chopped garlic
One 8-ounce can tomato sauce

2 quarts water
¼ cup beef extract
2 teaspoons celery salt
4 bay leaves
2 lemons, halved
1 teaspoon thyme
½ cup chopped parsley
Salt and lemon-pepper to taste

**Garnish:** sliced lemon, chopped egg, sherry.

    Saute' turtle meat in shortening until brown. Set aside. Brown flour, and add onion, celery and garlic. Cook 10 minutes. Add remaining ingredients and turtle meat. Simmer about 2 hours until meat is very tender. Garnish with sliced lemon, chopped egg and sherry before serving. Yields 1 gallon.

Mrs. Iveson B. Noland, III

## CANADIAN CHEESE SOUP

1 large potato, finely diced
1 large onion, finely diced
¼ cup celery, finely diced
¼ cup carrots, finely diced
1 cup water

2 cups chicken broth
1 cup (¼ pound) grated sharp
  Cheddar cheese
½ cup breakfast cream
Salt and Tabasco sauce to taste
2 tablespoons parsley, chopped

    In a 1½-quart covered saucepan, simmer vegetables in water until tender, about 15 to 20 minutes. Add remaining ingredients except parsley. Heat, do not boil, and serve garnished with parsley. Serves 4 to 6.

Mrs. Fred Parnell

## SPLIT PEA SOUP

One 16-ounce package dry split peas
1 ham bone or 1 cup ham pieces
3 quarts water, beef, chicken or
  vegetable stock
1 cup finely chopped celery
1 cup finely chopped onions
2 chopped carrots (optional)

2 tablespoons lemon-pepper
  seasoning
3 teaspoons salt
1 teaspoon Worcestershire sauce
¼ cup dry sherry (optional)
Lemon thinly sliced (optional)
Parsley (optional)

    Put all ingredients except the last three in a large pot. Bring to a boil, then reduce heat. Simmer about 2 hours. Remove ham bone and chop the meat in small pieces. Return meat to pot. Add sherry, if desired, and cook for 15 minutes. Pour into soup bowls and garnish with lemon pieces sprinkled with parsley. This freezes well.

    To reduce cooking time, the peas may be soaked overnight. Serves 8 to 10.

Mrs. Wray Edward Robinson

## SALADS

Nothing enhances a meal more than a classic green salad: crisp, chilled, and perfectly seasoned with dressing. But a fresh fruit salad has strong points in its favor, too, particularly with certain main dishes, as do tasty gelatin concoctions and marinated vegetable salads. Heartier salads offer a welcome change from hot meals, especially on summer evenings. Whichever you choose to prepare, be sure that it is carefully seasoned and that all ingredients are truly fresh. Luckily, we don't have to emulate homemakers in the early days when salad greens were always picked before sunrise to assure that they retained their fresh flavor.

## SALAD DRESSING-IN-A-JAR

¼ cup lemon juice (fresh)
¼ cup olive oil
½ teaspoon ground pepper
1 teaspoon Worcestershire sauce
½ teaspoon salt

2 cloves garlic, mashed, or
  ½ teaspoon garlic powder
1 egg, beaten
½ cup freshly grated
  Parmesan cheese
4 to 6 anchovies, mashed

Shake ingredients together in a one-pint jar. Shake with vigor. Keep in refrigerator several hours before serving. Pour over salad greens and croutons and toss lightly. Yield: ½ pint.

Mrs. James Hatcher

## SENSATION SALAD DRESSING

½ cup salad oil
½ cup olive oil
2½ tablespoons lemon juice
1½ tablespoons vinegar
2 pods garlic, pressed

¾ teaspoon salt
1 cup Romano cheese, grated
¼ cup Bleu cheese, crumbled
Lettuce
Parsley, chopped (about 1 bunch)
Grated black pepper to taste

Mix first six ingredients thoroughly for dressing. Pour over lettuce to which lots of parsley has been added. Toss greens till well coated. Sprinkle Bleu cheese and Romano cheese over greens and toss again. Grate black pepper over salad. Yield: 1¼ cups. Enough dressing for 2 large or 3 small heads of lettuce.

Mrs. James F. Pierson, Jr.

## TETON SALAD DRESSING

1 cup sour cream
1 cup mayonnaise
1 clove garlic (optional)

1½ teaspoons lemon juice
4 ounces Bleu cheese
½ heaping teaspoon celery salt

Combine all ingredients. Stores well in regfrigerator. Yield: 2 cups.

Mrs. M. Allen Dickson

## SALAD DRESSING
### (Especially for Spinach)

1 cup oil
5 tablespoons red wine vinegar
  or rice vinegar
2 tablespoons sugar (leave out if
  using rice vinegar)
1 clove garlic (or 1 teaspoon garlic
  purée)

2 tablespoons chopped parsley
4 tablespoons sour cream
Coarse black pepper
¼ teaspoon dry mustard
8 strips bacon, fried
4 hard-boiled eggs
Croutons (optional)

Mix all ingredients except bacon, eggs and croutons. This dressing will last for weeks in the refrigerator. Add bacon, hard-boiled eggs, and croutons (if desired) just before serving. Serves 16.

Mrs. Fred A. Blanche, Jr.

## BLEU CHEESE MAYONNAISE DRESSING

1 cup olive oil                          ½ teaspoon dry mustard
⅓ cup white vinegar                      1 teaspoon salt
2 heaping tablespoons mayonnaise         4 ounces Bleu cheese, crumbled

Put all ingredients in blender. Cover. Blend at high speed for 10 seconds. Yield: 1½ cups.

Mrs. Robert Snellgrove

## BLEU CHEESE SALAD DRESSING

¼ cup wine vinegar                       1 hard cooked egg, chopped
½ cup olive or salad oil                 One 4-ounce package Bleu cheese
1 medium onion, chopped                  1 teaspoon salt
                                         1 teaspoon pepper

Mix all ingredients. Pour over washed, dried and chilled salad greens. Yield: 1 cup.

Mrs. Frank M. Woods
Miami, Florida

## ROQUEFORT CHEESE DRESSING

4-ounce wedge Roquefort cheese or        ½ cup buttermilk
  Bleu cheese                            1 teaspoon celery salt (optional)
1 pint mayonnaise                        1 teaspoon onion salt (optional)
                                         1 teaspoon garlic salt

Mash Roquefort cheese with fork. Add cheese to mayonnaise. Add buttermilk, celery, onion, and garlic salts. Mix well with a spoon and store in refrigerator in a jar until ready to serve on lettuce salad. Keeps well for months in refrigerator. Yield: 3 cups.

Mrs. W. D. Wall, IV
Mrs. Gary Heidebrecht

## HOMEMADE BLENDER MAYONNAISE

1 cup salad oil                          1 tablespoon tarragon vinegar
1 whole egg                              1 teaspoon salt
1 tablespoon Worcestershire sauce        1 teaspoon Tabasco sauce
1 tablespoon lemon juice                 1 teaspoon prepared mustard

Put ¼ cup oil and all other ingredients in blender. Blend for several seconds. Add remaining ¾ cup oil slowly while blender is on. Blend approximately 1 minute. Makes 1½ cups.

Mrs. Cheney C. Joseph, Jr.

VARIATION:

Use 1 teaspoon dry mustard in place of prepared mustard and 2 tablespoons wine vinegar or 3 tablespoons lemon juice in place of tarragon vinegar.

Mrs. Ralph Braun
Mrs. R. Lewis Rieger

## POPPY SEED DRESSING

1 cup sugar
2 teaspoons dry mustard
2 teaspoons salt

⅔ cup vinegar
3 tablespoons onion juice
3 tablespoons poppy seeds
2 cups salad oil

Add all ingredients and mix in mixer or shake in jar. This is better if not made in blender. Will keep indefinitely. Yield: 3½ cups.

Mrs. D. J. Daly
Mrs. Randall J. Lamont

## STRAWBERRY DELIGHT SALAD OR DESSERT

One 6-ounce package strawberry
   gelatin
1 cup boiling water
Two 10-ounce packages frozen,
   sliced strawberries, thawed

One 1-pound 4-ounce can crushed
   pineapple, drained
3 medium bananas, mashed
1 cup coarsely chopped nuts
One 8-ounce package cream cheese
1 cup sour cream

In large bowl stir gelatin in boiling water until dissolved. Add strawberries with juice, drained pineapple, bananas and nuts. Pour one-half of this mixture into a 12x8x2-inch container and refrigerate until firm. Soften cream cheese and combine with sour cream. Spread evenly over chilled layer; gently spoon on remaining half of strawberry mixture. Chill. Cut into squares and serve on lettuce leaf for salad. Serves 12.

Mildred Tribble

## UNDER-THE-SEA SALAD

One 3-ounce package orange gelatin
2 cups boiling water
One 3-ounce package cream cheese
½ pound small marshmallows
1 cup mayonnaise

One 8¼-ounce can crushed
   pineapple, undrained
1 cup whipping cream
One 3-ounce package lime gelatin
2 cups boiling water

Dissolve orange gelatin in boiling water. Add cream cheese and marshmallows and stir until dissolved. Set aside to cool. Whip cream. When gelatin mixture is cooled, fold in mayonnaise, pineapple and whipped cream. Put in 9x9-inch dish. When completely set, cover with lime gelatin which has been dissolved in 2 cups of boiling water. If using a mold, put lime gelatin in first, and when set add the other layer. Yield: 12 servings.

Mrs. D. J. Daly

## MANDARIN ORANGE SALAD

One 3-ounce package orange gelatin
One 3-ounce package lemon gelatin
1 cup boiling water
One 6-ounce can frozen orange juice
  concentrate

One 1-pound 13-ounce can crushed
  pineapple
Two 11-ounce cans mandarin
  orange slices
Juice of all the fruit
½ cup chopped pecans (optional)

Dissolve gelatin in boiling water in large mixing bowl. Allow to cool in refrigerator for 15 minutes. Add other ingredients. Pour into ring mold or individual molds and refrigerate. Serve on lettuce leaf topped with homemade mayonnaise or poppyseed dressing. Serves 10 to 12.

Mrs. W. F. Williamson, Jr.

## GINGER PEACH SALAD

½ envelope plain gelatin
1 tablespoon cold water
One 3-ounce package orange gelatin
One 3-ounce package lemon gelatin
1 cup boiling water
Juice of peaches and pineapple
1 tablespoon lemon juice
1 tablespoon orange juice

1 teaspoon (or more) powdered
  ginger
½ teaspoon salt
½ cup chopped nuts
½ cup chopped celery
One 29-ounce jar spiced peaches,
  chopped
One 8¼-ounce can crushed
  pineapple

Dissolve plain gelatin in 1 tablespoon cold water. Dissolve flavored gelatins in 1 cup boiling water. Add plain gelatin and juice from peaches and pineapple. Add lemon and orange juice. Add ginger and salt, stir well to mix seasoning. Add nuts, celery, peaches and pineapple, mixing well to distribute throughout the gelatin mixture. Pour in a greased 2-quart mold. Place in refrigerator for several hours prior to serving. Serves 12 or more.

Mrs. W. C. Nettles, Sr.
Clemson, South Carolina

## GRAPEFRUIT AND AVOCADO SALAD

4 grapefruits
4 avocados

Lettuce
Dressing

Cut the grapefruits in half and section carefully. Remove all sections and place in bowl. Peel avocados and slice about the same size as the grapefruit sections. Arrange on individual salad plates in a lettuce cup, alternating slices of grapefruit and avocado. Pour dressing over and serve.

**Dressing:**

¼ cup salad oil
¼ cup white vinegar

¼ cup sugar
¼ cup catsup

Combine all ingredients in jar and shake vigorously until well mixed. (This may be made ahead and refrigerated until needed.) Serves 8.

Mrs. Richard M. Nunnally

## FROZEN FRUIT SALAD

2 cups sour cream
One 1-pound 4-ounce can crushed
    pineapple

1 cup pecans, chopped
15 maraschino cherries, cut up
½ cup sugar

Mix all ingredients together and pour into cupcake liners in muffin tins. Freeze. After frozen, put the individual salads in plastic bags. Yield: thirteen ½-cup salads.

Mrs. Ronnie Merrill

## CHEESE PARTY SALAD

One 3-ounce package lemon gelatin
Two 3-ounce packages lime gelatin
3 cups boiling water
Pineapple juice and water added
    to make 1 cup

One 8-ounce package cream cheese
One 12-ounce carton cottage cheese
2 cups grated American cheese
One 1-pound 13-ounce can crushed
    pineapple, drained and reserved
2 cups whipped topping

Place all gelatin in large bowl. Add water and pineapple juice with enough water added to make one cup and stir until dissolved. Cut cream cheese into small pieces and add to hot gelatin. Stir and mash with a spoon slightly (will still be somewhat lumpy). Chill until consistency of syrup, about 1 hour. Stir in cottage cheese, American cheese and pineapple. Fold whipped topping into mixture. Pour into 13x9x2-inch pan or into 3-quart mold or individual molds and chill until firm. Serves 20 to 24.

Mrs. C. E. Porter
Gainesville, Texas

## FLORENCE CULPEPPER'S MOLDED SHRIMP SALAD

1 pound fresh or frozen shrimp
2 envelopes (2 tablespoons) unflavored
    gelatin
½ cup cold water
One 10½-ounce can tomato soup,
    undiluted
One 8-ounce package cream cheese,
    softened
1 cup mayonnaise
¼ to ½ cup finely chopped celery

¼ cup finely chopped green onion
¼ cup finely chopped green pepper
¼ cup finely chopped dill and
    sweet pickles
5 stuffed olives, chopped
1 teaspoon salt
Dash red pepper (optional)
2 hearty dashes Worcestershire
    sauce
2 tablespoons Tabasco sauce

Cook and chop shrimp. Dissolve gelatin in the cold water. Let stand while heating undiluted soup. Heat soup to boiling point. Remove from stove and add to gelatin. Cream the cheese with a fork. Stir gelatin mixture well and add the creamed cheese. Blend thoroughly with electric mixer. Allow mixture to cool. Add the shrimp, mayonnaise, celery, onion, green pepper, pickles and olives. Mix well. Add salt, red pepper, Worcestershire sauce and Tabasco sauce. (Add little by little and taste as you go.) Pour mixture into a 5-cup mold which has been greased with butter. Refrigerate until firm. Unmold and serve with garnish of vegetables such as asparagus and cold boiled broccoli. May also serve with potato chips. Yields 8 to 10 servings.

Mrs. Eugene Cazedessus, Jr.

## SALAD LOAF

One 8-ounce package cream cheese
1 cup sour cream
One 16-ounce can dark sweet
  pitted cherries
One 8¼-ounce can crushed pineapple

One 11-ounce can mandarin orange
  sections
½ cup sugar
½ cup chopped pecans
2 cups miniature marshmallows

Let cream cheese stand at room temperature. Cream until fluffy. Fold in sour cream. Drain fruits in colander, add to first mixture. Add sugar, pecans, and marshmallows. Stir until well mixed. Pour in loaf pan or square container. Freeze six hours. Serves 10.

Mrs. M. Robinson

## HOLIDAY CRANBERRY SALAD

One 16-ounce can whole cranberry
  sauce
Juice of ½ lemon
½ pint whipping cream

½ cup sugar
½ teaspoon vanilla
½ cup mayonnaise
½ cup chopped pecans

Mix cranberries and lemon juice. Spread this mixture in shallow pan or ice cube tray. Whip cream. Add sugar and vanilla. Mix in mayonnaise. Spread over cranberries and sprinkle top with nuts. Freeze. Serve on lettuce leaves. Serves 8.

Mrs. Claiborne Dameron

## FROZEN CRANBERRY SALAD

One 1-pound can whole cranberry
  sauce
One 1-pound 4-ounce can crushed
  pineapple, drained

1 cup miniature marshmallows
¼ cup lemon juice
½ cup chopped pecans
1 cup sour cream

Mix ingredients well. Pour in 2-quart pyrex dish and freeze. Remove from freezer 10 to 15 minutes before serving. Serve on lettuce leaf and top with mayonnaise. Serves 12.

Mrs. Harry W. Barber

## PEACH SALAD

Two 3-ounce packages lemon gelatin
2 cups boiling water
1 cup orange juice

One envelope Dream Whip
One 3-ounce package cream cheese
One 1-pound 6-ounce can peach
  pie filling

Dissolve one package gelatin in one cup boiling water. Add orange juice. Prepare Dream Whip as directed on package and blend in cream cheese. Add gelatin mixture. Pour into 9x13-inch container. Chill until firm. Dissolve second package of gelatin in one cup boiling water. Add pie filling and spread over congealed mixture. Cut into squares to serve. Yield: 8 to 10 servings.

Mrs. Horace Waldrup

## CURRIED PEACH HALVES

1 can peach halves (any size can)
1 rounded teaspoon chutney per
    peach half

1 rounded teaspoon brown sugar
    per peach half
Curry powder

Arrange peach halves, cut side up, in shallow pyrex baking dish. Put chutney in center of each. Sprinkle brown sugar over each half. Sprinkle all lightly with curry powder. Place under broiler for a few minutes until sugar is melted and peaches are well heated. Serve with curried dishes, chicken or ham.

Mrs. Weldon Smith

## BAKED FRUIT WITH SHERRY

Fruit:

1 orange
½ cup golden raisins
One 9-ounce can pineapple tidbits

One 1-pound can pears
One 1-pound can peaches
One 1-pound can white cherries

Slice orange thin and cook in boiling water to cover until skin is easily pierced by fork. Plump raisins by soaking in ½ cup boiling water. Meanwhile, drain and mix remaining fruit, reserving ¾ cup juice. Drain orange, discarding juice. Add orange and raisins to other fruit.

Sauce:

3 tablespoons flour
¾ cup sugar
½ teaspoon salt

¾ cup fruit juice
3 tablespoons margarine
½ cup sherry

Mix flour, sugar and salt in sauce pan. Slowly add fruit juice. Cook and stir until sugar dissolves. Remove from heat and add margarine and sherry. Pour sauce over fruit in deep baking dish. Cover and marinate overnight. Remove cover and bake 1 hour at 330 degrees. Delicious served with wild duck or dove. Also good served with ham instead of raisin sauce. Can take place of salad. Serves 8.

Mrs. Weldon Smith

## TWENTY-FOUR-HOUR SALAD

3 egg yolks
2 tablespoons sugar
3 tablespoons vinegar
Dash of salt
2 tablespoons reserved pineapple
    juice
1 tablespoon margarine
2 cups quartered marshmallows

2 cups pitted Queen Anne
    cherries, drained
2 cups pineapple, drained
    and diced
2 cups mandarin orange sections,
    drained
¼ cup blanched slivered almonds
½ pint whipping cream, whipped

Cook egg yolks, sugar, vinegar, salt, pineapple juice and margarine in double boiler, stirring constantly until thick. Let cool. Fold in marshmallows, fruits, almonds and whipped cream. Let stand in refrigerator at least 24 hours. Serves 10 to 12.

Mrs. Weldon Smith

## SPICED PICKLED PEACHES

One 1-pound 13-ounce can
  cling peaches, slices or halves
¼ cup sugar

¼ cup vinegar
1 teaspoon whole cloves
1 teaspoon allspice
1 teaspoon peppercorns

Pour the syrup from the can of peaches into saucepan. Add the sugar, vinegar, cloves, allspice, and peppercorns. Bring to boil, then pour over peaches in a container with a top. Cover and cool. Prepare a day ahead and keep in refrigerator. Gently shake occasionally. I use the peach halves, and use this to complement an entrée, not as a salad. Yield: Depends on number of peaches in can, approximately 10.

Mrs. William H. Lee, II

## BLUEBERRY SALAD

One 15-ounce can blueberries
One 1-pound 4-ounce can pineapple
  chunks

One 6-ounce package raspberry
  gelatin
1 cup chopped pecans.

Drain blueberries and pineapple, measuring combined juices. Add water to juices to make 3½ cups liquid. Bring 2 cups of liquid to a boil. Add gelatin, dissolve and cool slightly. Add remaining liquid; chill until partially set. Stir in fruits and nuts. Pour into mold or 8x8x2-inch container, coated lightly with mayonnaise, and refrigerate until firm. Serve on lettuce leaf with the following topping.

**Topping:**

1 cup whipped topping

½ cup sour cream

Combine and spoon on congealed mixture. Green cherries make an attractive garnish. Serves 8 to 10.

Mrs. J. E. Brown
Iuka, Mississippi

## BRONZE PENNIES CARROTS

**Vegetables:**

Two pounds carrots, scraped,
  thinly sliced and cooked until
  tender

1 medium onion, thinly sliced

**Marinade:**

One 10½-ounce can tomato soup
1 cup sugar
½ cup salad oil

¾ cup vinegar
1 tablespoon prepared mustard
1 tablespoon Worcestershire sauce
Salt and pepper to taste

Mix marinade and heat until sugar is dissolved, then set aside. Place cooked carrots in large dish (7x11-inch). Break sliced onions into rings and place over carrots. Pour marinade over all. Cover and refrigerate overnight. Keeps for 1 week. Serves 6 to 8.

Mrs. Adrian de Montluzin
Mrs. W. E. Edrington, Sr.

## ARTICHOKES IN VINAIGRETTE

⅓ cup cider vinegar
¼ cup tarragon vinegar
1 tablespoon sugar
¾ teaspoon salt
2 tablespoons oil
1 tablespoon lemon juice
1 hard cooked egg, chopped

⅓ cup chopped dill pickle
⅓ cup chopped onion
⅓ cup chopped bell pepper
1 tablespoon chopped pimiento
One 9-ounce package frozen
    artichoke hearts (cooked and
    drained)

Combine vinegars, sugar, salt, oil and lemon juice. Add egg, pickle, onion, bell pepper and pimiento. Mix well. Add artichoke hearts, cover and chill 1 to 2 hours. Serve on lettuce. Garnish with additional hard cooked egg, if desired. Serves 8.

Mrs. J. Noland Singletary

## ITALIAN ROASTED PEPPERS

6 large, firm bell peppers
4 tablespoons olive oil
1 tablespoon lemon juice

¼ cup parsley, chopped
1 clove garlic, chopped
¼ teaspoon oregano
Salt and pepper

Wash and dry peppers. Cut in half and remove seeds. Put on broiler rack, skin side up, and broil about 10 minutes or until skin is medium brown and peppers are soft. Remove and cool. Peel off brown skin and cut lengthwise into 2-inch strips. Mix oil, lemon juice, garlic, parsley and oregano. Place peppers in bowl and pour mixture over them. Add salt and pepper to taste. Store in refrigerator until cold.

Mrs. Anthony DiJohn

## CHINESE SAILOR SALAD

1 cup canned bean sprouts, drained
1 cup canned Chinese or chop
    suey vegetables, drained
1 pound fresh spinach
1 cup sesame seed oil or peanut oil
½ cup soy sauce
4 tablespoons lemon juice

3 tablespoons grated onion
3 tablespoons sesame seeds lightly
    toasted in 350 degree oven for
    about 15 minutes
1 teaspoon sugar
1 teaspoon black pepper
1 cup thinly sliced water
    chestnuts

Soak bean sprouts and Chinese vegetables in cold water for several hours, or until crisp. Drain thoroughly. Wash spinach in several changes of cold water until it is clean. Cut off tough stems. Dry leaves thoroughly. Chill. In bowl, combine oil, soy sauce, lemon juice, grated onion, sesame seeds, sugar and black pepper. Let dressing stand for at least one hour. Arrange spinach leaves in salad bowl, top with bean sprouts and Chinese vegetables. Over these, arrange water chestnuts. Pour dressing over salad and toss thoroughly. This may be prepared a day ahead by keeping spinach in paper towels to absorb moisture. Change towels once or twice a day. Vegetables may also be kept in water-filled container and drained when needed. Serves 12.

Mrs. W. C. Nettles, Jr.

## ONION-ROQUEFORT SALAD

2 large onions
One 4-ounce package Roquefort or
  Bleu cheese
½ cup salad oil
2 tablespoons lemon juice

1 teaspoon salt
⅛ teaspoon pepper
⅛ teaspoon paprika
½ teaspoon sugar
1 large head lettuce (mixed
  greens, if desired)

Slice and separate onions. Crumble cheese with a fork. Mix all ingredients except lettuce in a large bowl. Chill. Just before serving, tear lettuce into bowl and toss. Salad dressing can be made early in the day, or day before. Serves 6 to 8.

Mrs. Roger Davison

## TOMATO SALAD

5 ripe home-grown tomatoes
½ cup olive oil
2 tablespoons wine vinegar
1 teaspoon dried basil
¼ teaspoon finely chopped garlic
1 teaspoon salt

Black pepper
2 tablespoons thinly sliced green
  onions
1 tablespoon finely chopped
  parsley (use flat leaf rather
  than curly)

Cut tomatoes into ¼-inch slices. Arrange in a shallow pyrex dish. Mix the oil, vinegar, basil, garlic, salt and pepper. Combine the green onions and parsley and sprinkle on top of the tomatoes. Pour the dressing over all. Can serve immediately but better to let stand 30 minutes to an hour. Serves 4 to 6.

Mrs. J. D. Guillory

## THREE BEAN SALAD

Vegetables:
One 16-ounce can green beans
One 16-ounce can wax beans

One 15½-ounce can kidney beans
1 bell pepper
1 medium onion

Drain beans. Slice pepper in strips. Slice onion thinly. Combine beans, pepper and onion.

Marinade:
¾ cup sugar
1 teaspoon salt
½ teaspoon pepper, coarse grind

¾ cup salad oil or olive oil
⅔ cup white vinegar or garlic
  wine vinegar

Mix all ingredients. Add to vegetables and stir well. Marinate several hours or overnight in refrigerator. May garnish with artichokes. Serves 8 to 10.

Mrs. John Gonce

## MEXICAN CHEF SALAD

1 pound ground beef
1 can ranch style pinto beans
Salt and pepper
1 onion, chopped (purple adds color)
4 tomatoes, cut in wedges
1 head lettuce

4 ounces cheese, grated
8 ounces Thousand Island or
  French dressing
One 6-ounce package Doritos
  (plain or taco)
1 large avocado, sliced

Brown ground beef with can of drained pinto beans. Season with salt and pepper. Simmer 10 minutes. Mix onion, tomatoes and lettuce. Add cheese and salad dressing and toss. Crumble and add Doritos. Add avocado. Mix hot ground beef and beans with salad and serve immediately. Serves 8.

Mrs. Sterling Gladden, Jr.

## SWEET AND SOUR COLE SLAW

One 4-pound cabbage
3 large white onions
¾ cup sugar
1 cup white vinegar

1 teaspoon salt
1 tablespoon sugar
2 tablespoons dry mustard
1½ teaspoons celery seeds
1 cup salad oil

Shred cabbage into a large container, top with the onions sliced into thin rings, and sprinkle with ¾ cup of sugar. Combine vinegar, salt, sugar, mustard, and celery seeds and bring to a boil. Add the salad oil and pour over cabbage mixture while hot. Cover and refrigerate overnight. In the morning, stir well. Especially good with barbecued chicken. Serves 15.

Mrs. Ben R. Miller, Jr.

## ORIENTAL SALAD

Salad:

One 1-pound package fresh spinach
8 slices bacon

3 hard-boiled eggs
One 1-pound 4-ounce can bean
  sprouts, drained

Wash and remove stems of spinach. Break into bite size pieces. Drain well. Fry bacon crisp, drain and break into pieces. Peel eggs and cut up. Put all ingredients in salad bowl and toss. Cover with dressing. Serves 4 to 6.

Dressing:

1 cup salad oil
¼ cup vinegar
¼ cup sugar

⅓ cup catsup
1 teaspoon Worcestershire sauce
1 medium onion, grated
Salt to taste

Mix all together.

Mrs. Henry Sabatier

## RAW SPINACH SALAD AND DRESSING

**Salad:**

⅓ cup finely chopped celery
⅓ cup finely chopped onion
2 hard-boiled eggs, diced

½ cup cubed cheddar cheese
2½ cups spinach, torn into
   bite-size pieces

Combine the first four ingredients. Add spinach and toss lightly.

**Dressing:**

⅔ cup mayonnaise
1 teaspoon vinegar

¼ teaspoon Tabasco sauce
¼ teaspoon salt
2½ tablespoons horseradish

Mix ingredients well. Add dressing to salad just before serving. Serves 6 to 8.

Mrs. James M. Pelton

## SPINACH SALAD

**Dressing:**

1 egg
½ cup sugar

½ cup white vinegar
¾ teaspoon salt
1½ teaspoons bacon fat

Beat egg. Combine egg, sugar, vinegar, salt and bacon fat in pan. Cook over low heat, stirring constantly, until mixture reaches boiling point. Cool and then chill in refrigerator until ready to serve.

**Salad:**

One 10-ounce package fresh spinach
6 slices bacon

6 green onions
2 oranges
½ cup peanuts (optional)

Remove spinach stems. Clean and drain. Cook bacon. Chop green onions and bacon. Peel oranges and section. When ready to serve, combine all ingredients. Serves 6 to 8.

Mrs. Fred R. Hogeman

## HOT POTATO SALAD

1 package instant scalloped potatoes
3 cups water
1 teaspoon salt
1 tablespoon instant minced onion
4 slices bacon

1 cup milk
⅓ cup mayonnaise or salad dressing
2 tablespoons vinegar
1 teaspoon prepared mustard
2 tablespoons bacon fat

Cook potatoes in water with salt and onion for 5 minutes (until almost tender). Drain well. Fry bacon until crisp and crumble. Mix seasoned sauce mix, milk, mayonnaise, vinegar and mustard until smooth. Add sauce, bacon and bacon fat to potatoes. Stir just enough to mix. Cover and bake at 350 degrees for 45 minutes.

Mrs. Leon Gary, Jr.

## GERMAN POTATO SALAD

**Salad:**

6 medium white potatoes
3 medium kosher style dill pickles,
   finely chopped

Yellow onions, finely chopped
   (use same volume as pickles)
6 slices bacon fried crisp,
   crumbled
Salt and pepper to taste

**Dressing:**

½ cup cooking oil

¼ cup vinegar
1 tablespoon bacon grease

Boil potatoes; peel and pare as you would for any potato salad. Toss potatoes, pickles, onions and bacon lightly with salt and pepper. Pour as much dressing as needed to barely coat all the potato mixture and toss lightly again. Serve hot or cold. Serves 6 to 8.

Mrs. Raymond Post, Jr.

## CREOLE RICE SALAD

3 cups cooked rice
4 hard-boiled eggs, chopped
1 cup imitation bacon bits
½ cup chopped pickles

½ cup chopped celery
½ cup chopped onions
½ cup mayonnaise
2 tablespoons French dressing

Mix all ingredients. Chill. Serves 12.

Mrs. William D. Wilkinson

## RICE SALAD

1⅓ cups uncooked rice
½ cup chopped onion
2 tablespoons vinegar
½ teaspoon curry powder

1 cup chopped celery
One 4-ounce can English peas,
   drained
Mayonnaise

Cook rice according to directions on package. Add onion, vinegar, and curry powder. When cool, add celery, peas and enough mayonnaise to hold together. Chill. Serve cold.

Mrs. Dan Flint, Sr.
Gainesville, Texas

## MACARONI SALAD

¾ cup macaroni
2 hard-cooked eggs, diced
1 cup ripe olives, sliced
One 6¼- or 7-ounce can white tuna,
   drained

2 cups cabbage, finely shredded
½ cup mayonnaise
1 teaspoon creole mustard
2 teaspoons vinegar
1 teaspoon salt

Cook macaroni until tender. Drain and rinse in cold water. Combine macaroni with all other ingredients. Serves 6.

Mrs. Louis H. Faxon

## ELBOW MACARONI SALAD

One 12-ounce package elbow macaroni
8 ounces grated sharp Cheddar cheese
1 ounce pimiento
½ cup chopped green onions
½ cup chopped celery
½ teaspoon pepper
2 teaspoons seasoned salt
1 tablespoon lemon juice
Mayonnaise

Cook macaroni. Mix all ingredients except mayonnaise while macaroni is warm. Add enough mayonnaise to moisten. Serves 6 to 8.

Mrs. Gerald W. Shelton

## SPAGHETTI SALAD

One 12-ounce package spaghetti, boiled
One 8-ounce package sharp cheese, diced
8 kosher dill pickles, diced
1 large onion, finely chopped
6 to 8 medium tomatoes, diced
Mayonnaise
Salt and pepper to taste

Boil spaghetti, drain and cool. Cut cheese and pickles in small cubes. Chop the onion fine and dice the tomatoes. Combine in large bowl with mayonnaise, salt and pepper as for potato salad. Allow to marinate overnight in refrigerator before serving. Serves 10 to 12.

Mrs. John Saladin

## EXOTIC CHICKEN SALAD

4 cups chopped cooked chicken
Two 5-ounce cans water chestnuts, sliced
1 cup finely chopped celery
1 pound fresh seedless grapes
1 cup toasted slivered almonds
1 cup mayonnaise
1½ teaspoons curry powder
1 tablespoon soy sauce
1 tablespoon lemon juice
One 16-ounce can pineapple chunks

Combine chicken, water chestnuts, celery, grapes and almonds. Mix mayonnaise, curry powder, soy sauce and lemon juice. Add seasoned mayonnaise to chicken mixture and chill for several hours. Serve on a lettuce leaf and top with pineapple chunks. Serves 10 to 12.

Mrs. Wayne T. Davis

## BAKED CHICKEN SALAD

1½ cups cooked diced chicken
1 cup cream of chicken soup
1 cup finely diced celery
½ teaspoon salt
2 tablespoons chopped green onions
½ cup slivered almonds
1 cup cooked rice
3 teaspoons lemon juice
¾ cup mayonnaise
3 hard-boiled eggs, diced
One 2-ounce jar chopped pimiento
1 cup bread crumbs, buttered

Mix all ingredients except bread crumbs. Place in greased casserole. Top with buttered bread crumbs. Bake 30 to 40 minutes at 375 degrees. Serves 8.

Mrs. Wylie C. Barrow

### SUMMER CRAB RING

2 cups Watercress Mayonnaise Colle
2 cups cooked, flaked crabmeat
¾ cup finely chopped celery

Lemon juice
Dijon style mustard
Salt and pepper to taste

Thoroughly fold crabmeat into Watercress Mayonnaise Colle. Add chopped celery. Season to taste with lemon juice, mustard, salt and pepper. Pack into ring mold. Chill 4 hours or longer. Turn out and serve garnished with watercress, lettuce and hard-boiled egg wedges. Serves 6.

**Watercress Mayonnaise Colle:**

½ cup mayonnaise
¾ cup chopped watercress
1 tablespoon chopped fresh dill
1 teaspoon lemon juice
1 teaspoon grated onion

3 tablespoons fish stock or clam
   juice
1 tablespoon tarragon vinegar
1 tablespoon white wine vinegar
2 teaspoons plain gelatin

In blender, combine first five ingredients. Blend until smooth. Correct seasoning by adding a little salt or lemon juice if needed. Set aside. In a small bowl, combine stock and vinegars. Sprinkle with gelatin and let soften five minutes. Set bowl over pan of hot water. Stir until gelatin is dissolved and mixture is clear. Let mixture cool and beat in the watercress-mayonnaise mixture.

Mrs. Percy Roberts, Jr.

## BREADS

In Louisiana, as in all the world, homemade breads remain a symbol of warm hospitality and a good cook in the kitchen. Whether it's hot, crusty French bread with a bowl of gumbo or delicate breakfast biscuits spread with preserves, these homemade breads consistently nourish and delight us.

## WHIPPING CREAM BISCUITS

**1½ cups self-rising flour**                    **½ pint whipping cream**

Mix flour and cream only until well blended. Butter hands well and form dough into ping-pong size balls, or smaller if desired, for brunch or luncheon. Place on baking sheet 1 inch apart. Bake in 425 degree oven for 10 to 12 minutes or only until golden. Recipe will double successfully. The method for freezing is to prepare dough and shape. Place balls on cookie sheet in freezer. When frozen, remove balls from cookie sheet and store in plastic bags. Makes 2½ dozen large or 3½ dozen small biscuits.

Mrs. George K. Gilbert, Jr.

Mrs. Jake Netterville

## BISCUITS

| | |
|---|---|
| **2 cups flour** | **2 heaping teaspoons baking powder** |
| **½ teaspoon salt** | **4 tablespoons shortening** |
| | **1 cup milk** |

Sift flour with salt and baking powder; cut in shortening with pastry blender until mixture resembles coarse crumbs. Make a well in the flour mixture and add milk all at once. Stir with fork until mixed. Turn out on lightly floured surface. Knead gently ½ minute. Roll with lightly floured rolling pin or pat ½ inch thick and cut with biscuit cutter. Bake on cookie sheet in preheated 450 degree oven for 12 to 15 minutes. For freezing, bake until fully risen and lightly browned—about 7 to 8 minutes. Freeze on cookie sheets and then put in bags. When ready to use, bake 5 to 7 minutes and serve. Makes 20 to 24 medium-sized biscuits.

Mrs. Rivers Wall, Jr.

## BROWN BREAD

| | |
|---|---|
| **3 cups raisins** | **½ cup molasses or dark Karo** |
| **4 cups boiling water** | **2 eggs, beaten** |
| **4 teaspoons soda** | **1 teaspoon salt** |
| **2 tablespoons margarine** | **1 cup chopped nuts** |
| **2 cups sugar** | **5½ cups flour** |

Simmer raisins in boiling water for 5 minutes. Cool. Add remaining ingredients and mix well. Bake at 350 degrees for 30 minutes in 5 or 6 greased and floured 1-pound coffee cans.

Mrs. D. J. Daly

## CARROT BREAD

| | |
|---|---|
| **1 cup sugar** | **1 teaspoon soda** |
| **¾ cup vegetable oil** | **½ teaspoon salt** |
| **2 beaten eggs** | **1 teaspoon cinnamon** |
| **1½ cups flour** | **1 cup grated carrots** |
| | **1 cup chopped pecans** |

Mix sugar, oil and eggs. Sift in flour, soda, salt and cinnamon. Add grated carrots and nuts. Carrots may be grated in a blender. Pour in floured, ungreased loaf pan (9x5x3 inches). Bake at 325 degrees for 1 hour or until done. Cool. May be frozen. Makes 1 loaf.

Mrs. Ronnie Merrill

## CHEESE BATTER BREAD

1 cup corn meal
1½ teaspoons salt
½ teaspoon dry mustard

3 cups scalded milk
1 cup grated sharp cheese
3 eggs, beaten

Mix meal, salt and mustard. Add milk. Cook and stir until thick. Remove from heat and blend in cheese. Let cool. Add meal mixture to beaten eggs and bake 40 minutes in 350 degree oven. Serves 6.

Mrs. G. Ross Murrell, Jr.

## EGG BREAD

1 cup shortening
⅓ cup sugar
2 teaspoons salt
2 cups milk

3 packages yeast
½ cup warm water
6 eggs, beaten
8 cups flour

Heat shortening, sugar, salt and milk until hot and blended. Do not boil. Cool. While mixture cools, dissolve yeast in warm water. When shortening mixture is lukewarm, stir in dissolved yeast. Add beaten eggs and flour alternately. Beat well after each addition. Use only enough flour to make a soft dough. All 8 cups may not be necessary. Let rise in a greased bowl until dough has doubled in size. Place dough on a floured board and knead until smooth, about 10 minutes. Make into 4 loaves. Place in well greased bread pans (9x5x3 inches). Let rise until dough has doubled in size. Bake at 350 degrees for about 1 hour or until loaves sound hollow when thumped with the thumb and index fingers. Cool on a wire rack. Butter tops.

Six smaller loaves may be made by dividing dough into 6 loaves and using loaf pans that are 7⅜x3⅝x2¼ inches. Loaves may be frozen. Makes 4 large or 6 small loaves.

Mrs. Edward E. Trippe
Mansfield, Louisiana

## HONEY BREAD

1¼ cups boiling water
1 cup sugar
¾ cup honey
2½ teaspoons baking soda
Pinch of salt

3 tablespoons rum
2 teaspoons cinnamon
4 cups sifted flour
½ teaspoon finely grated orange
rind (optional)

Stir together the boiling water, sugar, honey, baking soda and salt until the sugar dissolves. Mix in, thoroughly, the rum and cinnamon. Stir the flour in slowly to make a smooth batter. Add the grated orange rind, if desired. Pour the batter into a well buttered loaf pan (9x5x3 inches). For the first 10 minutes, bake in a very hot oven, 450 degrees, then reduce the temperature to moderate, 350 degrees, for one hour longer, or until it tests done. Turn the bread out on a wire rack to cool. Slice bread thinly and spread with butter. It is even more delicious the second day. May be baked in two smaller pans (7½x3½x2¼ inches). In this case, reduce the total cooking time by 15 minutes, or until they test done. Makes one large or two small loaves.

Mrs. L. Scott Curtis

## GINGERBREAD

¾ cup sugar
¾ cup cane syrup, or dark Karo
¾ cup oil
2 eggs
2½ cups unsifted flour
2 teaspoons soda

½ teaspoon baking powder
2 teaspoons ginger
1½ teaspoons cinnamon
¼ teaspoon cloves
¼ teaspoon nutmeg
1 cup boiling water

In mixer, place sugar, syrup, oil and eggs and beat until well mixed. In sifter, put flour, soda, baking powder, ginger, cinnamon, cloves and nutmeg. Sift together 3 times. Add to above mixture. When the two are well mixed, add the cup of water. Pour into a greased and floured 10x14x2-inch pan and bake at 350 degrees, 25 minutes or until done.

Mrs. Norman Saurage, Jr.

## HOLLAND CARROT BREAD

2 cups sifted flour
2 scant teaspoons soda
2 teaspoons cinnamon
½ teaspoon salt

1½ cups sugar
1½ cups corn oil
3 eggs
2 teaspoons vanilla
2 cups grated carrots

Sift together the flour, soda, cinnamon and salt. Add sugar, oil, eggs and vanilla to the dry mixture, and beat on medium speed with electric mixer until well blended. Fold in the carrots. Pour mixture into 2 well greased and floured 9x5-inch loaf pans. Bake at 300 degrees for 1 hour or until bread tests done. Good with coffee.

Mrs. James R. Douglas

## DILL BREAD

1 package or 1 cake yeast
¼ cup warm water
1 cup cottage cheese, lukewarm
2 tablespoons sugar
1 tablespoon onion flakes

1 tablespoon butter
2 teaspoons dill seed
1 teaspoon salt
¼ teaspoon soda
1 unbeaten egg
2¼ to 2½ cups flour

Dissolve yeast in warm water. Combine all ingredients except flour. Mix well, then add flour and make a stiff dough. Let rise until doubled. Punch down and make into a small loaf. Put in a greased loaf pan (9x5x3 inches). Let rise 30 or 40 minutes. Bake 40 or 50 minutes at 350 degrees. Remove from oven and brush with butter, sprinkle with salt. Freezes well. Yield: 1 loaf.

Mrs. Culbert Lee
Monroe, Louisiana

## LEMON BREAD

½ cup shortening
1 cup sugar
2 eggs, slightly beaten
1¼ cups flour
1 teaspoon baking powder
¼ teaspoon salt

½ cup milk
½ cup finely chopped walnuts
  or pecans
Grated rind and juice of 1
  lemon
¼ cup sugar

Cream together the shortening and sugar. Stir in the slightly beaten eggs. Sift together the flour, baking powder, and salt. Stir this mixture into the creamed mixture alternately with the milk. Add the walnuts and grated lemon rind. Bake at 350 degrees for about 1 hour in a 9x5-inch loaf pan. Remove the bread from the oven and pierce surface with a small skewer or toothpick to make small holes. Combine the sugar and lemon juice. Pour over hot bread very slowly.

Mrs. J. Buffington Maguire, Jr.
Pampa, Texas

## GOLDEN CAKE BREAD

4 to 4½ cups flour*
½ cup sugar
1 teaspoon salt
1 package active dry yeast

1 cup milk
½ cup butter or margarine
2 eggs
2 teaspoons vanilla

*On humid days, use maximum amount of flour

In large mixer bowl, combine 2 cups of the flour, sugar, salt and dry yeast. In sauce pan, heat milk and butter until milk is warm. (Butter does not need to melt.) Add eggs, vanilla and warm milk to flour mixture. Mix at lowest speed until moistened. Beat 2 minutes at medium speed. By hand, stir in remaining flour to form a stiff batter. Cover. Let rise in warm place until light and double in size (about 1 hour). Punch down batter. Spread in well greased 9x5-inch loaf pan. Cover. Let rise in warm place until light and double in size (about 45 minutes). Bake at 350 degrees for 40 to 45 minutes or until golden brown. Cool 5 minutes and then remove from pan.

Mrs. James Hatcher

## BANANA MOLASSES BREAD

3 ripe bananas
1 egg, unbeaten
⅔ cup sugar
2 tablespoons light molasses
2 tablespoons melted shortening

2 cups sifted flour
1 teaspoon baking powder
1 teaspoon baking soda
½ teaspoon salt
1 cup chopped walnuts

Mash bananas until no lumps remain. Add unbeaten egg. Mix well. Beat in sugar, molasses and shortening. Mix and sift flour, baking powder, baking soda, and salt. Add to banana-egg mixture. Stir in walnuts. Bake in greased loaf pan (9x5x3 inches) in moderate oven, 325 degrees, for about 1 hour.

**Hint:** Banana bread is like all quick breads and muffins. It doesn't like beating. Once you begin to add the dry ingredients, stir, but do not beat. Stir only enough to blend. The texture will reward you.

Mrs. Heidel Brown

## BANANA NUT BREAD

½ cup margarine
1½ cups sugar
2 beaten eggs
1 teaspoon vanilla
2 cups cake flour, measured after
   sifting

½ teaspoon salt
½ teaspoon baking soda
¼ cup milk
3 small or 2 large bananas,
   mashed to a pulp
1 cup chopped pecans

Cream margarine and sugar. Add eggs and vanilla. Beat until fluffy. Add sifted dry ingredients alternately with milk, bananas and nuts. Beat well after each addition. Bake in waxed paperlined 6½x10½-inch pan in a 350 degree oven for 50 minutes or until brown and an inserted toothpick comes out clean. This bread keeps well in plastic wrap and also freezes well.

Mrs. William Barth
New Orleans, Louisiana

## BRAN BANANA MUFFINS

¼ cup shortening
½ cup sugar
1 egg
4 mashed bananas

1 cup bran
1½ cups flour
2 teaspoons baking powder
½ teaspoon soda
½ teaspoon salt

Cream shortening and add sugar. Add beaten egg, then mix in mashed bananas and bran. Add flour, baking powder, soda and salt which have been sifted together. Mix only enough to moisten dry ingredients. Bake in greased muffin cups at 375 degrees for 15 to 20 minutes. Makes 12 large muffins.

Mrs. Norman Saurage, Jr.

## POCKET BOOK ROLLS

½ cup shortening
½ cup sugar
2 cups milk
1 package yeast

5 to 5½ cups flour, sifted
1 teaspoon salt
½ teaspoon soda
½ teaspoon baking powder

Place shortening, sugar and milk on the stove to melt shortening. Remove from heat just before the mixture boils. Let cool until lukewarm. Add yeast and stir until yeast is dissolved. Add 2 cups flour, enough for a soft batter. Cover the batter. Allow it to rise for 2 hours. Beat down with a large spoon. Stir in salt, soda, baking powder and enough flour for a heavy dough, 3 to 3½ cups. Knead on a floured surface until dough is smooth and no longer sticky, about 3 to 5 minutes. Roll out dough to a thickness of approximately ¼ inch. Make rounds using a floured biscuit cutter. Put a small piece of butter or margarine in the center of each round. Fold rounds almost in half and press firmly with the palm of your hand. Place the rolls fairly close together on a greased cookie sheet. Let rise for 2 hours. Bake in a preheated 400 degree oven for 10 to 15 minutes or until golden. Cool on a wire rack. The dough may be refrigerated for several days. The baked rolls may be frozen. Makes 3 to 4 dozen rolls.

Mrs. Robert M. Coleman, Sr.
Clarksdale, Miss.

## PUMPKIN BREAD

**Bread:**

3 cups sugar
1 cup salad oil
4 eggs
2 cups pumpkin
3⅓ cups flour, unsifted
2 teaspoons soda
2 to 3 teaspoons salt
⅔ cup water

1 teaspoon baking powder
1 teaspoon nutmeg (freshly
　ground is best)
1 teaspoon cinnamon
2 teaspoons pumpkin spices
2 teaspoons vanilla
1 cup chopped dates or pecans, or
　½ cup of each (optional)

Combine sugar and oil in large bowl. Add eggs one at a time, beating after each addition. Add vanilla. Sift dry ingredients together. Set aside. Add dry ingredients alternately with water. Add pumpkin. Add dates, pecans or both at this time. Pour into 3 well greased and floured 9x5x3-inch loaf pans. Bake in preheated 325 degree oven for 1 hour or until they test done. Remove from pans when barely warm.

**Frosting:**

One 8-ounce package cream cheese
4 tablespoons butter or margarine
1½ teaspoons vanilla

1½ cups powdered sugar
Dash salt
½ cup finely chopped pecans

Cream margarine or butter with cream cheese. Add vanilla. Add sifted sugar and salt. Fold in nuts last. Frost cooled bread.

Mrs. Gerald W. Middleton

## QUICK BEER PARTY ROLLS

3 cups biscuit mix

3 tablespoons sugar
One 10-ounce can cold beer

Mix all ingredients. Fill small party muffin tins. Do not double recipe. Bake 10 to 12 minutes at 450 degrees. Makes 2½ dozen rolls.

Mrs. A. Knight Lavender

## ICE BOX ROLLS

¾ cup shortening
¾ cup sugar
1 cup mashed potatoes
2 eggs

1 teaspoon salt
1½ cups lukewarm water
1 package dry yeast
7½ cups flour, sifted

Cream shortening and sugar. Add potatoes, beaten eggs and salt. Dissolve yeast in lukewarm water and add to mixture. Beat well and add to flour a little at a time until all is used. Mix thoroughly and let stand until the dough has doubled in size. Punch down, cover and place in refrigerator. When ready to use, pinch off the amount desired and allow to rise again in a warm room. Pinch off small pieces and place on well greased pan. Let stand for 2 hours or until the rolls have doubled in size. Bake at 450 degrees about 20 minutes.

Mrs. Don R. McAdams

## YEASTED BREAD

6 cups warm water
2 packages yeast
1 cup dry milk
2 cups whole wheat flour

¾ cup sweetening (honey, cane syrup, or maple syrup, not granulated sugar)
6 cups unbleached white flour

Dissolve yeast in water. Stir in sweetening, milk and flour to form thick batter. It is important to stir it for at least 100 strokes. Let rise 60 minutes.

2½ tablespoons salt
¾ cup oil

4 cups whole wheat flour
6 cups unbleached white flour

Fold the salt and oil into the batter. Fold in the whole wheat and white flour until the batter becomes too thick to stir. Turn the batter onto a floured board. Sprinkle a little white flour into the bowl and scrape out the rest of the batter. Knead for about 15 minutes. The amount of flour used for the second part can be measured by cups but also by feeling the texture of the dough. Keep adding flour to the surface of the dough until the dough no longer sticks to the board. When the dough is ready, it will have a smooth, even consistency and bounce back when pressed. Let rise for 50 minutes. Punch the dough down into the bowl with fist about 7 times all along the surface. Let rise 40 minutes. Cut the dough into 4 parts. Shape each into a loaf. Place in oiled loaf pans (9x5-inch) pressing the top of the loaf into the pan, then turning the loaf and pressing the bottom into the pan. This way, the entire surface will be slightly oiled. Let rise for 20 minutes. Bake in 350 degree oven for one hour. Let it cool for at least 45 minutes before cutting.

Anne McKay
Potomac, Maryland

## HUSH PUPPIES

1 cup cornmeal
½ cup flour
2½ teaspoons baking powder

1 small onion, finely chopped
1 egg
½ cup milk
½ teaspoon salt

Mix all ingredients. Cook in hot cooking oil* (375 to 400 degrees) until golden brown on one side. Then turn and cook until brown on other side. Makes about 20 hush puppies.
*Especially good fried in oil in which fish has been fried.

Mrs. Frank Duke

## OLD FASHIONED SPOON BREAD

1 cup cornmeal (white or yellow)
2 cups boiling water
1 cup milk

¼ cup shortening
1 teaspoon salt
2 eggs, beaten

Pour boiling water over cornmeal, stirring to make smooth. Add shortening and salt. Stir well and let cool slightly. Add milk and eggs. Pour into greased 1-quart casserole and bake at 400 degrees for 35 minutes. Serves 5.

Mrs. Louis C. Christian

## HOMEMADE ROLLS

1 cup boiling water
1 cup shortening
1 cup sugar
1½ teaspoons salt

2 eggs, beaten
2 packages yeast
1 cup warm water
6 cups flour, unsifted

Pour boiling water over shortening, sugar and salt. Blend and cool. Add eggs. Dissolve yeast in warm water. Stir and add to mixture. Add flour and blend well. Cover and place in refrigerator at least 4 hours. Roll out on floured board and cut with biscuit cutter. Fold over and put on greased pans. Let rise 3 hours before baking. Bake at 450 degrees for 12 to 15 minutes. You can freeze before letting them rise or after baking. Makes 7 dozen.

Mrs. James R. Douglas

## A QUICK ROLL RECIPE

1 package yeast
2 cups warm milk
1 egg, unbeaten
2 tablespoons shortening, melted

2 tablespoons margarine, melted
6 cups flour
4 tablespoons sugar
1 tablespoon salt

Dissolve 1 package yeast in 2 cups warm (not hot) milk. Stir in unbeaten egg when milk and yeast mixture is slightly cooled and add the shortening and butter which have been melted together. Sift the flour with the sugar and salt and add this to the above mixture. Stir to blend and let rise (covered) until double in bulk. Roll out and cut with biscuit cutter and fold over. Place in greased cake pans and cover again and let rise until light. Bake at 425 degrees for 15 minutes. Makes 3 dozen rolls.

Mrs. J. W. Saladin

## ALL BRAN REFRIGERATOR ROLLS

1 cup shortening
1 cup boiling water
¾ cup sugar
1 cup All Bran cereal

1 teaspoon salt
2 eggs, well beaten
2 packages yeast
1 cup warm water
6 cups flour or more

Mix shortening and boiling water, sugar, All Bran and salt. Let cool until lukewarm. Add eggs. Add yeast that has been softened in warm water. Add flour. Make into rolls. Let rise 2 hours. Bake at 425 degrees for 12 to 15 minutes. The dough may be put in covered bowl and kept in refrigerator for three to four days. Punch down occasionally. Two hours before baking, remove from refrigerator and shape and let rise 2 hours. Makes 3½ dozen.

Mrs. William C. Nettles, Jr.

## RUSSIAN NUT ROLLS

**Rolls:**

| | |
|---|---|
| 2 packages dry yeast | 1 tablespoon salt |
| ½ cup warm water | 1 tablespoon sugar |
| 6 egg yolks | 2 cups shortening |
| 10 cups flour | Two 14½-ounce cans evaporated |
| 1 tablespoon baking powder | milk, minus 1 cup |
| | 1 tablespoon vanilla |

**Filling:**

| | |
|---|---|
| 2 pounds English walnuts | 4 tablespoons butter |
| 2 cups sugar (more if desired) | Approximately ¼ cup milk |

Dissolve the yeast in ½ cup warm water, let rest. Beat the egg yolks. Mix together the dry ingredients and cut the shortening into the flour mixture with two knives or pastry blender until coarse. Add the yeast mixture, egg yolks and the evaporated milk. Mix well and knead 1 minute. Place in a greased bowl and cover. Let rise until double in bulk—3 or 4 hours. Meanwhile, using a food mill or blender, grind finely 2 pounds of English walnuts. Add sugar, softened butter and enough milk to make a dry paste. When dough is ready, divide into 6 to 8 parts. Roll each one on a sugared board. *Sprinkle board with sugar, not flour.* Roll into a rectangle. Spread with nut mixture and roll up as you do a jelly roll. Seal edge well and place on greased cookie sheet with the seal on the bottom. Bake in 350 degree oven about 30 minutes or until brown. Cool and slice. Makes 6 to 8 rolls that slice into numerous servings. If desired, the roll can be sliced prior to baking and cooked individually like cookies. This keeps and freezes well. The recipe can be cut in half if desired.

Mrs. Stephen Glagola

## MEXICAN CORNBREAD I

| | |
|---|---|
| One half of a 4-ounce can diced green chillies | One 8½-ounce can yellow cream style corn |
| One 6½-ounce packet Mexican cornbread mix | ½ cup chopped green onion |
| ¾ cup milk | 1 tablespoon chopped bell pepper |
| 1 egg, slightly beaten | 1 cup grated sharp Cheddar cheese |
| | 2 tablespoons bacon drippings |

Rinse chilies under cool running water. Dry between paper towels and set aside. Put cornbread mix in a bowl. Pour in milk and slightly beaten egg. Add corn, onion, bell pepper, green chilies and cheese. Place bacon drippings in a 9-inch square pan and heat in oven. Stir half of the heated grease into cornbread mixture. Pour batter into remaining hot grease in pan. Bake in 400 degree oven for 30 minutes. Let stay in pan for a few minutes before cutting. If you like hot, spicy food, use the whole can of green chilies. It is not necessary to butter this cornbread. May be kept in refrigerator and reheated. Makes nine 3-inch squares.

Mrs. Manch Cadwallader

## MEXICAN CORNBREAD II

1 cup sour cream
2 eggs, beaten
1 cup cream style corn
⅓ cup Wesson oil
1½ cups white cornmeal

3 teaspoons baking powder
1 teaspoon salt (or a bit more)
2 tablespoons chopped bell pepper
2 chopped jalapeño peppers
1 cup grated sharp cheese

Mix all ingredients except for cheese. Pour half of the batter, then half of cheese, then remaining batter and top with other half of cheese in 2-quart baking dish. Bake at 375 degrees for 30 minutes. If you want to use as hors d'oeuvres, place in a larger pan to make thinner bread and shorten baking time.

Mrs. Fred A. Blanche, Jr.

## OLD FASHIONED SOUTHERN CORNBREAD

1 cup white cornmeal
½ cup flour
1½ teaspoons salt
1 teaspoon sugar

½ cup milk
½ cup boiling water
3 tablespoons corn oil
1 egg
1½ teaspoons baking powder

Combine cornmeal, flour, salt, sugar and corn oil in mixing bowl. Use a cutting motion with spoon so that oil will be well blended with other ingredients: Stir in the boiling water. Mix well. Add cold milk. Stir and let stand, if necessary, until batter has cooled to at least room temperature. Mix in egg and then baking powder. Beat briskly. Pour (or "spoon" if making sticks) into preheated greased pan and bake at 425 degrees until well browned (approximately 20 minutes). This recipe will make the correct amount of batter to fill an 11-stick iron cornbread pan or a 9-inch square pan.

Mrs. A. B. Cross, Jr.

## IRENE'S MUFFINS

2 cups All Bran
2 cups boiling water
One 1-pound box golden raisins
1 cup oleo
3 cups sugar (white or brown)

4 eggs
1 quart buttermilk
5 cups flour
5 teaspoons soda
2 cups All Bran Buds

Put All Bran and golden raisins in a large bowl and pour in boiling water. Cream oleo and add sugar. Add eggs one at a time, beating well after each addition. Add the buttermilk, flour, soda and All Bran Buds. Mix well. Stir in All Bran and raisin mixture. Put in a covered container and refrigerate. This will keep well for 2 weeks. When ready to serve, spoon batter into greased muffin tins and bake at 400 degrees for 15 minutes. This makes a gallon of dough, so may be reduced. Makes about 200 muffins.

Mrs. W. D. Kimbrough

## PAW PAW'S PANCAKES

½ cup flour
½ cup milk
2 eggs, lightly beaten

Pinch of nutmeg
¼ cup butter
2 tablespoons powdered sugar
Juice of ½ lemon

Combine flour, milk, eggs and nutmeg. Beat lightly. Leave batter a little lumpy. Melt butter in a 12-inch skillet. When hot, pour batter into skillet. Place the skillet in a preheated 450 degree oven for 15 to 20 minutes, or until golden brown. Take out and sprinkle the pancake with sugar. Return to oven briefly. Remove the skillet from the oven. Sprinkle the pancake with lemon juice and serve with jelly. Yields 2 large or 4 small servings.

Mrs. Arthur P. Stover

## SUNDAY MORNING PANCAKES

3 cups flour
¼ cup sugar
4 teaspoons baking powder

1½ teaspoons salt
2 eggs
3 cups milk
½ cup oil

Sift together flour, sugar, baking powder and salt. Beat together eggs, milk and oil in a small bowl. Add all at once to flour mixture and stir just until mixed. It should be lumpy. Drop by large spoonfuls on a hot, greased griddle and cook until surface of pancake is bubbly. Turn and cook on other side until golden. Makes 2½ dozen 3-inch pancakes.

Mrs. Norman Saurage, III

## WAFFLES

3 cups flour
1 tablespoon baking powder
1 teaspoon soda
1 tablespoon sugar

½ teaspoon salt
2 eggs, beaten
3 cups buttermilk
⅔ cup shortening

Sift together flour, baking powder, soda, sugar and salt into large bowl. Mix together eggs and buttermilk in small bowl. Add to flour mixture. Add shortening and mix all ingredients with large spoon until well combined, but not smooth. You will still have lumps of shortening about the size of small marbles. Bake in a preheated and well greased waffle baker until crisp and golden. Makes 8 waffles 11x6 inches.

Mrs. Kelly Maddox

## DUMPLINGS

¾ cup sifted flour
2½ teaspoons baking powder

½ teaspoon salt
1 egg
⅓ cup milk

Sift flour, baking powder and salt together. Beat egg. Add milk to egg and mix with dry ingredients. Drop by spoonfuls into boiling gravy or stock. Cover tightly and cook for 15 minutes. Do not remove cover while dumplings are cooking. If the steam escapes, they will not be light. Serves 6.

Mrs. Charles Garvey, Sr.

## YORKSHIRE PUDDING

4 tablespoons butter or margarine     1 cup milk
1 cup flour     2 eggs, beaten lightly
¼ teaspoon salt     Drippings from roast

Preheat oven to 450 degrees. Prepare 2 bread pans 9x5x3 inches by putting two tablespoons of butter in each one. Put the pans into the hot oven so the butter will melt but not burn. Mix together the flour and salt. Add the milk, blending into a smooth paste. Add the beaten eggs and beat mixture with an electric mixer at medium speed for 2 minutes. Pour the batter into two hot pans. Spoon 4 or 5 tablespoons of beef drippings over each pan of batter. Bake 25 minutes or until puffed up and golden brown. Cut into small squares and serve. More drippings may be spooned over each piece to give additional flavor.

Mrs. Nat A. Maestri, Jr.

## POPOVERS

1 cup sifted flour     2 eggs, well beaten
1 teaspoon salt     1 tablespoon melted butter
    1 cup milk, minus 1 tablespoon

Generously grease 12 muffin tins or custard cups and put in a preheated 450 degree oven until you have finished mixing the ingredients. Sift flour and salt together. Combine eggs, butter and milk. Add slowly to flour mixture, stirring with a spoon. Beat thoroughly until free from lumps. Pour into sizzling muffin tins or custard cups, filling only half full. Place immediately into 450 degree oven. Bake for 20 minutes or until browned, then lower temperature to 350 degrees and bake 15 minutes longer. Makes 12 popovers.

Mrs. Randall J. Lamont

## VEGETABLES

Every region has its own special vegetables which abound, and supermarkets have many different varieties available year 'round. Prepared with care and a delicate touch, they are not only important to our diets but satisfying to our palates.

In Louisiana, vegetable dishes are cooked to stand on their own, not as mere adjuncts to the main course. In fact, with the liberal use of ham, sausage, seafood, and other seasonings, they are often a meal in themselves.

## ARTICHOKES SUPREME

Two 14-ounce cans artichoke hearts, quartered
Two 2-ounce cans sliced mushrooms
¼ cup butter
3 tablespoons flour
1 clove garlic
Salt and pepper to taste
¾ cup grated sharp cheese
1½ cups Pepperidge Farm herbed seasoned dressing mix
½ of an 8-ounce can water chestnuts, sliced
¼ cup Parmesan cheese
¼ cup sliced almonds

Drain artichokes and mushrooms, reserving liquid. Melt butter. Blend in flour. Slowly add ½ cup artichoke liquid and ¼ cup mushroom liquid. Simmer until slightly thick, stirring occasionally. Add garlic, salt and pepper and then sharp cheese. When cheese is melted, set sauce aside. In 2-quart casserole, layer 1 cup dressing mix, artichoke hearts, sliced mushrooms and water chestnuts. Pour cheese sauce mixture over this. Mix together ½ cup Pepperidge Farm dressing, Parmesan cheese and almonds and sprinkle over top. Bake at 350 degrees for 20 to 25 minutes. Serves 8.

Mrs. Robert I. Comeaux, Jr.

## ASPARAGUS SOUR CREAM

Two 10½-ounce cans asparagus spears, drained
8 ounces sour cream
¼ cup mayonnaise
Juice of one lemon
¼ cup bread crumbs
2 tablespoons margarine, melted
Paprika

Place asparagus in a shallow 1½-quart casserole. Combine and heat sour cream, mayonnaise and lemon juice. Pour over asparagus. Toss bread crumbs in margarine. Sprinkle crumbs and paprika over sauce. Bake at 325 degrees for 20 minutes or until bubbly. This sour cream sauce is also good on broccoli or string beans. Serves 6 to 8.

Mrs. Harry W. Barber, Jr.

## ASPARAGUS SOUFFLÉ

One 10½-ounce can of cream of asparagus soup
¾ cup grated sharp cheese
4 well beaten egg yolks
4 stiffly beaten egg whites

Heat soup and cheese in top of double boiler over hot water until cheese is melted. Remove from heat. Add a little of this soup mixture to egg yolks, stirring well and pour all back into soup and cheese mixture. Allow to cool slightly and fold into beaten egg whites. Pour into 1½-quart soufflé dish or straight-sided casserole that has been greased and dusted with flour. Place dish in a pan with 1 inch hot water. Bake at 300 degrees for 1 hour. Serve immediately. Serves 4 to 6.

Mrs. Robert D. Erwin
Nashville, Tennessee

### WRAPPED GREEN BEANS

1 slice bacon
12 to 14 whole green beans, canned

Onion salt
1 teaspoon brown sugar
1 teaspoon butter

Place whole green beans on a slice of bacon. Sprinkle with onion salt, brown sugar and dot with butter. Wrap bacon around beans and bake on cookie sheet 15 to 20 minutes at 400 degrees. This is one serving.

Mrs. E. Donald Moseley

### ITALIAN GREEN BEANS

½ cup olive oil
1 onion, thinly sliced
1 cup canned Italian plum tomatoes
½ green pepper, chopped
½ cup chopped celery
¼ cup water

1 teaspoon salt
¼ teaspoon black pepper
2 cloves
1 bay leaf
6 sprigs parsley
1 pound cooked green beans

Heat oil, add onion and cook until soft. Add tomatoes, green pepper, celery, water, salt and pepper. Tie cloves, bay leaf and parsley in a small cheesecloth bag and add to the tomato mixture. Simmer about 25 minutes. Can set aside here until ready to serve. Just before serving, add green beans and heat until very hot. Remove cheesecloth bag and serve. Serves 6.

Mrs. J. D. Guillory

### GREEN BEANS À LA LEMON

2 tablespoons butter
1 tablespoon parsley flakes
⅓ cup chopped onions
2 tablespoons flour
1 teaspoon salt
¼ teaspoon garlic salt
½ teaspoon pepper

Dash red pepper
1 teaspoon grated lemon peel
1 cup sour cream
Two 16-ounce cans French style
  green beans, drained
Bread crumbs and crumbled bacon
  (optional)

Melt butter. Add parsley and onions and then blend in flour. Add salt and pepper, lemon peel and sour cream. Mix into beans. Put into 2-quart casserole and top with bread crumbs and bacon, if desired. Dot with butter. Bake in 350 degree oven until brown and bubbly. Freezes well. Serves 6 to 8.

Mrs. Jo Eva Hannaman

### GREEN BEAN TOSS

Three 9-ounce packages frozen cut
  green beans (or 2 cans)
½ cup canned French fried
  onion rings

10 bacon slices, fried
One 2-ounce jar pimientos, cut up
1 teaspoon salt
½ cup sour cream

Cook beans as label directs. Drain. Use blender to crumble bacon and onion rings together. Toss bacon-onion ring mixture with beans, pimientos and salt. Pour into serving dish. Spoon sour cream in center. Serves 8 to 10.

Mrs. E. Whitehead Elmore

## GREEN BEANS ROTEL

¾ pound bacon
2 medium onions, chopped

1½ cans Rotel tomatoes
5 cans French style green beans, drained

Fry bacon in a three-quart dutch oven. Remove bacon and set aside to drain. Pour out some of the grease. Sauté onions in remaining grease. Add tomatoes (cut large ones) and drained beans. Crumble bacon and add. Let simmer on top of stove about 30 minutes. Freezes well. Serves 14.

Miss Arabelle Woodside

## SWISS GREEN BEANS

Two 1-pound cans French style
green beans
2 tablespoons margarine
2 tablespoons flour
1 teaspoon salt
¼ teaspoon black pepper

1 teaspoon sugar
1 cup sour cream
½ teaspoon grated onion
¼ pound grated Swiss cheese
1 to 1½ cups crushed corn flakes
1 tablespoon melted margarine or butter

Drain green beans. Melt 2 tablespoons of margarine and add flour, salt, pepper, sugar, sour cream and grated onion. Fold the beans into the above mixture. Spread in a 2-quart buttered casserole. Sprinkle top with Swiss cheese and finally top with buttered crushed corn flakes. Bake in 375 degree oven for 30 minutes. Serves 8.

Mrs. R. Wendel Foushee

## GREEN BEAN CASSEROLE WITH SOUR CREAM

2 medium onions, sliced
1 tablespoon minced parsley
¼ cup margarine
2 tablespoons flour
1 teaspoon salt
½ teaspoon pepper
½ teaspoon grated lemon peel

1 cup sour cream
Two 1-pound cans French sliced
green beans, drained
One 4-ounce can mushrooms, drained
½ cup grated cheese
½ cup seasoned bread crumbs
2 tablespoons melted margarine

Cook onions and parsley in margarine until tender, not brown. Add flour, salt pepper and lemon peel. Add sour cream and mix well. Stir in beans and mushrooms. Place in a 7x11-inch casserole. Top with grated cheese. Combine seasoned bread crumbs with 2 tablespoons melted margarine and sprinkle over all. Bake at 350 degrees for 30 minutes. Frozen beans may be used. Cook and drain, then use as above. Serves 8.

Mrs. Norman Saurage III

## BROCCOLI WITH ALMOND BUTTER

Two 10-ounce packages frozen broccoli    ½ cup butter or margarine
or equal amount fresh broccoli    ½ teaspoon salt
1 cup slivered almonds    1½ tablespoons lemon juice

Cook broccoli according to package directions or use fresh cooked broccoli. In separate saucepan, simmer almonds in butter over low heat until golden, stirring occasionally. Remove from heat and add salt and lemon juice. Pour over broccoli. This recipe for almond butter is good with asparagus, brussels sprouts, or cauliflower. Serves 6.

Mrs. Lewis Olen White

## BROCCOLI AU GRATIN

Two 10-ounce packages frozen    ½ cup tomato juice
broccoli spears    ¼ cup bread crumbs
One 10½-ounce can cream of    3 tablespoons melted margarine
shrimp soup    1 cup grated sharp cheese
½ cup breakfast cream    Paprika

Cook broccoli as directed on package; drain, put into a 10-inch Pyrex pie plate. Heat soup, cream and tomato juice until hot and pour over broccoli. Brown bread crumbs in melted margarine, sprinkle over broccoli. Top with grated cheese and paprika. Bake uncovered in 400 degree oven for 15 minutes or until cheese is melted. Serves 6.

Mrs. Harry W. Barber, Jr.

## ZESTY CARROT STRIPS

8 carrots    1 teaspoon salt
2 tablespoons grated onion    ¼ teaspoon pepper
2 tablespoons horseradish    ⅓ cup buttered bread crumbs
½ cup mayonnaise    Dash of paprika

Clean and cut carrots into strips. Cook until tender in salted water. Place in large baking dish in an even layer. Mix together remaining ingredients. Spread this mixture over the surface of carrots. Bake 15 minutes in 375 degree oven. Serves 6.

Mrs. Michael T. Delahaye

## PEPPERED CORN CASSEROLE

1 large onion, chopped    One 16-ounce can whole kernel
½ cup margarine    corn, yellow
One 16-ounce can Rotel tomatoes    One 16-ounce can shoe peg corn,
with chili peppers    white
   One 16-ounce can cream style
   corn, yellow

Sauté onion in margarine. Add tomatoes, drained whole kernel corn, drained shoe peg corn and creamed corn. Regrigerate at least 8 hours. Bake at 325 degrees for 2 hours. Serves 8.

Mrs. Carl Maddox

## CORN PUDDING

4 tablespoons bacon drippings
1 large onion, chopped
¼ bell pepper, chopped
One 16-ounce can cream style corn
⅔ cup yellow corn meal
1 can milk (measure in corn can)
1 egg
1 teaspoon salt

Tabasco sauce
¼ teaspoon monosodium glutamate
  (optional)
1 teaspoon sugar (optional)
1 teaspoon Worcestershire sauce
  (optional)
One can French fried onion rings
  or paprika

In bacon drippings, sauté onions and pepper. Add corn and cornmeal. Stir in milk and egg that have been beaten together. Bring to a boil, stirring constantly. Add salt and pepper and optional ingredients if desired. Pour into greased 2-quart casserole and bake uncovered at 300 degrees for 50 minutes. Cover with can of onion rings or paprika just before serving. Serves 6 to 8.

Mrs. James Sylvest

## EGGPLANT PAYSANNE

1 large eggplant, diced
2 large onions, sliced
1 cup green beans
4 cups peeled tomatoes

½ cup olive oil
2 cups grated cheese
Salt, pepper, pinch of thyme to
  taste

Layer a greased 2½-quart casserole with eggplant, onions, green beans, and tomatoes. Top with the seasonings. Pour olive oil over all. Bake for 2 hours at 325 degrees. Save some of the grated cheese to put on top of casserole after it has been cooked. Brown and serve. Serves 6 to 8.

Mrs. Charles F. Duchein, Jr.

## EGGPLANT GROUND MEAT CASSEROLE

4 large eggplants
1 large onion, chopped
3 stalks celery, chopped
1 large bell pepper, chopped
4 pods garlic, chopped
3 medium slices baked ham, cut in
  small pieces
1 cup butter

1½ pounds mixed ground beef
  and pork
6 to 8 slices stale bread
½ cup cream
1 cup milk
5 eggs
Salt and pepper to taste
Bread, cracker, or potato chip
  crumbs to top

Peel, dice and simmer eggplants in small amount of water until tender. Does not take long. Sauté together onion, celery, bell pepper, garlic and ham in butter until soft. Add all meat and cook until done. Combine bread with cream, milk and beaten eggs. Add this mixture to cooked meat and vegetables. Season to taste with salt and pepper. Mix thoroughly. Pour into ungreased but wet, not too deep, large casserole. Bake in 350 degree oven for about 35 minutes. When done, sprinkle top with your choice of bread or cracker crumbs or crumbled potato chips. Allow 2 to 3 minutes to heat. Remove from oven and serve. Serves 10.

Mrs. Arthur Keller

## EGGPLANT PARMESAN CASSEROLE

| | |
|---|---|
| 1 large eggplant | ½ cup vegetable or olive oil |
| 3 eggs, slightly beaten | 8 ounces Parmesan or sharp ched- |
| 2 cups Italian seasoned bread crumbs | dar cheese, grated |
| | One 8-ounce can tomato sauce |

Peel eggplant and slice thinly, dip in egg, then in bread crumbs. In a large skillet, fry eggplant until tender and brown. Drain on paper towels. Place alternate layers of eggplant, grated cheese and tomato sauce in 2-quart casserole. Bake at 350 degrees until bubbling hot, about 30 minutes. Serves 10.

Mrs. William Barth
New Orleans, Louisiana

## MUSHROOMS PARMESAN

| | |
|---|---|
| 1 pound mushrooms | 2 tablespoons grated Parmesan |
| 3 tablespoons chopped parsley | cheese |
| ¼ teaspoon chopped garlic | Salt and pepper to taste |
| ¼ cup bread crumbs | ¼ cup olive oil |
| | 2 tablespoons dry white wine |

Wash and dry mushrooms. Place in baking dish. Sprinkle with parsley, garlic, half of bread crumbs and grated cheese. Add salt and pepper to taste. Pour oil and wine over this. Turn once and sprinkle with rest of bread crumbs. Bake at 350 degrees for about 20 minutes or until tender. Serve hot. Serves 6.

Mrs. Anthony DiJohn

## GRAMMIE'S OKRA

| | |
|---|---|
| 2 pounds fresh young okra | 1 clove garlic, chopped |
| 2 tablespoons salad oil | Salt and pepper to taste |
| 1 large onion, chopped | 1 cup tomatoes, canned |

Do not use an iron skillet or okra will darken. Wash whole okra and dry thoroughly with paper towels. Slice into ⅛-inch rounds. Sauté in oil over medium heat until okra stops "stringing." This usually takes 20 to 30 minutes, sometimes longer. Don't let it brown. Stir very frequently. Add onion and garlic and sauté until they soften. Then add seasonings and tomatoes and a little liquid from the tomatoes. Allow to simmer for another 5 minutes. Serves 4.

Mrs. V. L. Roy, Sr.

## FRIED OKRA

| | |
|---|---|
| 1 quart young okra | Salt and pepper |
| Boiling water | Yellow cornmeal |
| | Cooking oil |

Wash okra. Discard stems and cut okra into ¼-inch pieces. Par boil for 5 to 7 minutes in salted water. Drain in colander. Sprinkle with salt and pepper and roll in cornmeal. Let rest for 20 to 30 minutes so that cornmeal will stick to okra when ready to fry. Fry in deep fat until golden. Drain on paper towels and serve hot. Serves 4.

Mrs. Richard M. Nunnally

## STEWED OKRA AND TOMATOES

1 pound fresh or frozen okra
3 tablespoons bacon grease or
cooking oil
1 cup chopped onions

1 cup chopped green pepper
One 16-ounce can tomatoes
1 teaspoon salt
¼ teaspoon Tabasco sauce
2 strips crisply fried bacon

Wash fresh okra. Remove stems and cut okra into ½-inch rounds. Cook the okra in 2 tablespoons of melted bacon grease or cooking oil over medium low heat in skillet, stirring constantly, for about 15 minutes until it is not very stringy. In another skillet, sauté onions and green peppers in 1 tablespoon of bacon grease or cooking oil. Combine the cooked ingredients. Add tomatoes, salt and Tabasco sauce. Mix and simmer for 10 minutes. Add more seasoning, if necessary, for taste. Pour in serving dish and crumble bacon on top. Serves 4.

Mrs. Lewis Bannon

## SPINACH AND ARTICHOKE CASSEROLE

Three 10-ounce packages frozen
chopped spinach
One 8-ounce package cream cheese
½ cup margarine

Two 8½-ounce cans artichoke hearts
Salt and pepper to taste
Dash Worcestershire sauce
½ cup buttered bread crumbs or
Italian bread crumbs

Cook chopped spinach. Drain well. Mix with cream cheese and margarine while hot. Season to taste. Place layer of spinach in 2-quart cassrole, then layer of artichokes. Repeat. Cover with buttered bread crumbs or Italian bread crumbs. Bake at 350 degrees for 30 minutes. May be prepared early in the day and refrigerated or frozen. Serves 6 to 8.

Mrs. W. A. Rolston

## MAMA'S SPINACH

Six 10-ounce packages frozen
chopped spinach
½ cup margarine or butter
½ cup flour
4 chopped green onions
3 cups milk

2 teaspoons salt
½ teaspoon pepper
1 teaspoon dry mustard
½ pound American cheese,
coarsely grated
Tabasco sauce
Bread crumbs

Cook spinach and drain. Melt butter and sauté green onions. Add flour. Slowly add milk, then salt, pepper and mustard to make cream sauce. Cook until sauce thickens. Add cheese, then spinach and a few drops of Tabasco sauce to taste. Pour into buttered 3-quart casserole. Sprinkle with bread crumbs and dot with butter. Bake at 350 degrees for 30 minutes. Serves 16 to 18.

Mrs. Jean Frey Fritchie

## QUICK CREAMED SPINACH

One 10-ounce package frozen
chopped spinach
1 tablespoon mayonnaise

2 tablespoons melted butter or
margarine
Parmesan cheese

Cook spinach according to package directions. Drain well. Mix mayonnaise and butter together and fold into drained spinach. Garnish with Parmesan cheese. Serves 2 to 3.

Mrs. Bruce C. Garner

## SPINACH CASSEROLE

Three 10-ounce packages frozen
chopped spinach
½ cup butter
8 ounces cream cheese
½ teaspoon garlic powder
1 tablespoon lemon juice

2 tablespoons Worcestershire
sauce
1 teaspoon salt
3 shakes Tabasco sauce
1 cup Pepperidge Farm Herb
Dressing

Cook spinach and drain in a colander. In same pot used for spinach, melt butter and cream cheese. Add seasoning and mix. Add drained spinach and mix. Pour into a 2-quart casserole and top with herb dressing. Bake at 350 degrees for 30 minutes or until hot. May be made ahead and reheated. Serves 8 to 10.

Mrs. Frank Simoneaux

## SPINACH PAULINE

Two 10-ounce packages frozen chopped
spinach, cooked and well drained
6 tablespoons finely minced onion
¼ cup melted margarine
1 teaspoon salt
¾ teaspoon black pepper

6 tablespoons heavy cream or
evaporated milk
6 tablespoons grated Parmesan
cheese
2 tablespoons cream cheese
Tabasco sauce, if desired
Italian bread crumbs

Cook spinach according to package directions in unsalted water. Drain. Saute' onions in margarine. Add drained spinach, salt and pepper to taste. Pour in milk. Add cheeses and Tabasco sauce. Mix well. Before serving, place in baking dish and top with buttered Italian bread crumbs and bake at 375 degrees for 10 to 15 minutes. Freezes well. Serves 4 to 6.

Mrs. R. A. Herrington

## BAKED PEPPER-CHEESE SQUASH

2 pounds fresh summer squash, or
two 10-ounce packages frozen squash
8 slices bacon

1 large onion, cut in rings
1 roll jalapeño cheese, cut up
Bread crumbs.

Boil squash. Fry bacon until crisp and remove from pan. Brown onion rings in some of the bacon drippings. Crumble bacon. Layer one half of squash, bacon, onion rings, and cheese in 9x9-inch shallow baking dish. Repeat. Sprinkle with bread crumbs. Bake in 325 degree oven for 40 minutes. Serves 10.

Mrs. William A. Atkinson

## MIMI'S ZUCCHINI

3 or 4 zucchini
½ onion, chopped
  finely
2 tablespoons margarine

1 to 1½ cups grated sharp
  cheese
Italian flavored bread crumbs
Margarine

Wash and slice zucchini (not too thinly). Add very little water and salt. Par boil on low heat until tender. Drain well. Put back into pot. Add 2 tablespoons margarine and onion. Simmer until onion is soft. Put in 12x8x2-inch pyrex casserole. Add grated cheese and bread crumbs. Dot with margarine. Bake at 350 degrees for 20 minutes. Serves 8.

Mrs. Robert I. Comeaux, Sr.

## SQUASH CASSEROLE I

2 to 2½ pounds fresh yellow squash
½ cup margarine or bacon drippings
¾ cup chopped onion
15 Ritz crackers, crumbled
2 eggs, beaten

Salt and pepper
½ teaspoon Tabasco sauce
1 cup grated sharp cheese
1½ cups Ritz cracker crumbs
½ cup margarine, melted

Slice and cook squash until tender. Drain. Sauté onions in margarine or bacon drippings. Mix with squash. Add 15 Ritz crackers, eggs, seasonings and cheese. Put in 2-quart casserole. Cover with buttered Ritz cracker crumbs. Bake at 350 degrees for 35 minutes. Serves 8 to 10.

Mrs. Robert I. Comeaux, Jr.

## HERBED SAUTÉED SQUASH

8 small firm yellow squash
3 tablespoons margarine
Pinch of thyme, rosemary and
  marjoram

2 green onions, chopped
2 tablespoons beef extract or
  soy sauce
¼ cup dry white wine
Salt and pepper to taste

Scrub squash and slice thinly. Sauté in margarine over medium heat until translucent and slightly limp, but not mushy, about 10 minutes. Add thyme, rosemary, marjoram and green onions. Sauté for another 2 minutes. Add beef extract and wine. Season to taste. Stir until blended. Can be gently reheated. Serves 4.

Mrs. Bodo Claus

## HELEN'S SQUASH

4 pounds yellow squash, sliced
3 tablespoons margarine
12 ounces sour cream

1 envelope dry onion soup mix
Salt and pepper to taste
Bread crumbs, optional

Boil squash until tender. Drain. Mash with remaining ingredients. Put in 2-quart casserole, top with bread crumbs and bake 30 minutes at 350 degrees. Serves 8.

Mrs. Frank Foil

## SQUASH CASSEROLE II

1½ pounds squash
½ cup chopped onions
¼ cup chopped bell pepper
¼ cup butter or margarine
½ cup mayonnaise
Red pepper to taste

1 cup water chestnuts, thinly
  sliced
½ cup grated sharp yellow cheese
1 teaspoon sugar, optional
2 eggs, beaten
¼ cup bread crumbs

Boil squash, onions and bell pepper until squash is tender. Drain liquid and place the three cooked vegetables into a 2-quart casserole. Add softened margarine, mayonnaise, red pepper, sliced water chestnuts, grated cheese, sugar, and eggs. Blend mixture and cover with bread crumbs. Bake at 350 degrees for 30 minutes. Serves 4 to 6.

Mrs. William Asher Whitley

## SUMMER SQUASH 'N TOMATO

¼ cup margarine
4 cups thinly sliced yellow squash
1 sliced onion, optional
1 teaspoon salt

Dash pepper
¼ cup water
2 tomatoes, peeled and cubed
½ cup grated American cheese
Soy sauce

Melt margarine in skillet. Add squash, onion, salt, pepper, water and tomatoes. Cover, simmer 12 minutes. Sprinkle with soy sauce and cheese. Stir. Cover and simmer another minute or two. Serves 4 to 6.

Mrs. Eugene H. Owen

## RATATOUILLE

1 medium eggplant, peeled and cubed
2 zucchini, cut in ½-inch slices
2 teaspoons salt
½ to 1 cup olive oil
2 onions thinly sliced
2 green peppers cut in thin strips
1½ teaspoons garlic chips or 2 to
  3 fresh garlic cloves, pressed
3 tomatoes peeled and diced

Pepper to taste
¼ teaspoon basil
  (fresh if possible)
½ teaspoon bouquet garni, or
  ¼ teaspoon thyme
½ teaspoon Italian seasoning, or
  ¼ teaspoon parsley
½ teaspoon McCormick's
  Salad Supreme seasoning

Toss eggplant and zucchini with 1 teaspoon salt and let stand 30 minutes. Drain and dry on paper towels. Heat ¼ to ½ cup olive oil in large skillet and lightly brown eggplant and zucchini slices. Remove with slotted spoon and set aside. Add remaining oil to skillet; cook onions and green peppers until tender. Stir in garlic. Put tomatoes on top; cover and cook 5 minutes. Gently stir in eggplant, zucchini, and remaining seasonings. Simmer, covered, until desired tenderness. Uncover and cook 5 minutes, basting with juices from bottom of pan. Serve hot or cold. Serves 8 to 10.

Mrs. Oran Ritter

## BROILED TOMATOES

½ tomato per person
Salt and pepper to taste
½ teaspoon Parmesan cheese per
　serving

1 teaspoon bread crumbs per
　serving
⅛ teaspoon oregano per serving
1 teaspoon butter per serving

Wash firm tomatoes, cut into halves—crosswise. Sprinkle each half with salt and pepper to taste. Mix Parmesan cheese, bread crumbs and oregano together and cover top of each half tomato. Place a teaspoon of butter on top of bread crumbs. Place tomatoes in baking pan; add enough hot water to cover bottom of pan. Preheat broiler and broil 10 to 15 minutes or until bread crumbs are brown.

Mrs. Robert M. Slowey

## OLD FASHIONED BAKED TOMATOES

One 1-pound 13-ounce can tomatoes
Salt and pepper to taste
½ to ¾ cup sugar
3 tablespoons butter

1 medium onion, chopped
　and sautéed
3 slices bread, toasted and
　well buttered

Butter a 2-quart casserole dish well. Put can of tomatoes in casserole. Cut up tomatoes in bite size pieces. Sprinkle with salt, pepper and sugar. Spread chopped onion over all. Cut up butter and dot over all. Cut toasted bread into small pieces and stir in gently. Bake at 325 degrees uncovered about 1½ hours until most of the juice is absorbed and dish looks brown and candied. Serves 4.

Mrs. Frank M. Woods

## BROCCOLI RICE CASSEROLE

½ cup chopped onion
½ cup chopped celery
4 tablespoons margarine
1 cup uncooked rice
One 10½-ounce can cream of
　mushroom soup

Two 10-ounce packages frozen
　chopped broccoli, barely
　cooked and drained
One 8-ounce jar Cheese Whiz
One 4-ounce can water
　chestnuts, diced

Sauté onions and celery in margarine. Cook rice according to package directions. Mix all ingredients. Put in 2-quart baking dish. Bake at 350 degrees for 25 minutes or until bubbly. Serves 8 to 10.

Mrs. Charles McCowan

## SOUTHERN CUSHAW

4½ cups parboiled cushaw
⅔ cup brown sugar
⅔ cup white sugar

½ cup butter
½ teaspoon salt
⅓ teaspoon nutmeg
1 teaspoon vanilla

Cut cushaw (with peel) in pieces, scrape out seed, and boil until tender. Remove peel and drain cushaw well. Mix with the rest of the ingredients. Cook in heavy skillet on top of stove until excess moisture evaporates. Put in 2½-quart rectangular casserole and bake at 350 degrees until lightly browned or very hot. (It should not be watery.) Serves 8. This freezes well.

Mrs. Robert J. Bujol

## VEGETABLE CASSEROLE

6 medium potatoes
4 bell peppers
4 medium onions
1 large eggplant
Olive oil
Red pepper

Salt
Garlic powder
Two 16-ounce cans Italian
   tomatoes (drained and
   coarsely chopped)
Buttered bread crumbs

Peel and slice potatoes as thinly as possible. Remove seeds and cut peppers into wide strips. Peel and thinly slice onions. Cut eggplant (with or without peel) into ½-inch slices or cubes. Fry each vegetable separately in ¼ inch olive oil until soft and just beginning to brown. Do not fry the tomatoes. In a large pyrex casserole(11¾x7¼ inches), layer the vegetables after sautéeing: first potatoes, then onions, peppers and eggplant. Season each layer with salt and red pepper. Sprinkle garlic powder lightly over all. Cover with tomatoes. Sprinkle lightly with bread crumbs. Bake at 400 degrees for 15 to 20 minutes before serving. Serves 6 to 8.

Mrs. Hubert Waguespack

## SAVORY GREEN BEANS WITH RICE

One 1-pound can green beans, drained
1 tablespoon margarine
1 teaspoon salt
¼ teaspoon pepper
⅓ cup chopped onion
2 cups hot cooked rice

1 cup sour cream
1 teaspoon dill weed
Dash salt
1 tablespoon lemon juice
1 tablespoon Worcestershire sauce
6 slices crisp bacon

Heat green beans with margarine, seasoning and onion until onion is wilted. Combine with rice. In a small sauce pan, blend sour cream, dill weed, salt, lemon juice and Worcestershire sauce. Heat. Serve sauce over beans and rice. Sprinkle with crumbled bacon. Serves 6.

Mrs. Duffy Porche

## SWEET AND SOUR BEANS

One 14-ounce can kidney beans,
   drained
One 14-ounce can lima beans, drained
One 14-ounce can white beans, drained
One 28-ounce can pork and beans

6 or 8 slices bacon
3 medium onions, sliced
½ cup vinegar
¾ cup brown sugar
2 tablespoons prepared mustard

Mix all beans. Fry bacon and drain. Turn grease low and sauté onions. Mix vinegar, sugar and mustard. Stir well and add to onions and simmer. Chop bacon into beans and pour onion mixture on beans. Bake in 3-quart casserole for 30 minutes at 350 degrees. This freezes well. Serves 12.

Mrs. F. W. Fidler
Carrollton, Georgia

## RED BEANS

1 pound dried kidney beans
1 ham bone or left over ham
6 cups water
2 pounds link sausage, cut in 1-
   inch pieces

1 teaspoon salt
½ teaspoon hot pepper sauce
1 teaspoon Worcestershire sauce
1 teaspoon onion powder
1 bay leaf
3 cups cooked rice

Soak beans overnight. Drain. In a large Dutch oven or kettle, add all ingredients (except rice) and bring to a boil, stirring frequently to prevent sticking. Reduce heat to low and cook slowly for several hours,* stirring occasionally. If necessary, add water if beans are not tender. If you prefer a thick gravy, mash a few beans and cook longer.* Serve over rice. Serves 6.

*Your personal taste will determine exactly how long the beans should cook.

Mrs. Thomas E. Robinson

## GREEN PEPPER CASSEROLE

½ cup butter
½ cup flour
½ teaspoon salt
1 to 1½ cups milk
¼ teaspoon pepper

½ teaspoon dry mustard
1 cup Old English cheese spread
3 large green peppers
2 hard-boiled eggs
Ritz cracker crumbs

Melt butter. Add flour slowly and stir well. Add salt and milk stirring slowly. Add pepper, dry mustard and cheese. Stir until well blended. In 1½-quart casserole, put ½ green peppers cut in ½-inch pieces, ½ sliced hard-boiled eggs and ½ of cheese sauce. Repeat, then cover top with Ritz cracker crumbs and dot with butter. Bake at 350 degrees for 30 to 40 minutes. This may be made the day before and cooked when needed. Serves 4 to 6.

Mrs. Charles Wylie
Lexington, Kentucky

## STUFFED MIRLITONS

4 large mirlitions
½ cup diced onion
¼ cup chopped celery
3 tablespoons cooking oil
½ cup Italian bread crumbs
1½ teaspoons seasoned salt

1 cup cooked, chopped shrimp, or 1
   pound cooked bulk sausage,
   drained
⅛ teaspoon cayenne pepper
½ cup bread crumbs (plain or
   Italian)

Cut mirlitons in half lengthwise. Remove seeds in center. Boil until tender. Scoop out meat, reserving shell for stuffing. Mash the meat. Saute onion and celery in oil in 9- to 10-inch skillet until tender. Add mashed mirlitons, shrimp (or sausage), ½ cup Italian bread crumbs, seasoned salt and cayenne pepper. Fill shells. Cover with bread crumbs. Bake at 350 degrees for 30 minutes or until browned. Freezes well. Can be served as a main dish. Serves 8.

Mrs. Dean M. Mosely

## GUMBO* VERT

| | |
|---|---|
| 1 small head cabbage | 1 tablespoon cooking oil |
| ½ pound pickled pork | 2 large onions, chopped |
| 1 cup water | 2 tablespoons flour |
| One 16-ounce can spinach | Salt and pepper to taste |

Wash and chop cabbage. Put into pot with pickled pork meat. Add 1 cup water. Let boil until cabbage is tender. Drain in colander, reserving liquid and meat. Chop cabbage and spinach together on chopping board. Cut pickled pork into cubes and fry in small amount of cooking oil with chopped onions for about 5 minutes. Add chopped cabbage and spinach. Cook for about 10 minutes on low heat. Add reserved liquid plus enough water to make 1 cup. Cook 5 more minutes. Mix 2 tablespoons flour and ½ cup cold water. Add flour mixture to pot a little at a time stirring constantly. Cook slowly for about 15 minutes longer. Serve over rice. Serves 6 to 8.

*This is not a form of soup as one would think of as gumbo. It is called gumbo due to the fact that it is a mixture of things—in this case green vegetables.

Mrs. James Hymel, Jr.
Convent, Louisiana

## FLUFFY WHITE RICE

| | |
|---|---|
| 1 cup long grain rice | ½ teaspoon shortening |
| 1½ cups cold water | 1 teaspoon salt |

Wash rice thoroughly unless instructed otherwise on package. Put rice, water, shortening and salt in 1½- to 2-quart saucepan with tight-fitting cover. Leave cover off pan, and cook on high heat until water boils. Immediately cover and turn to low heat and cook for 30 minutes. Do not remove cover during cooking. Rice will be dry and fluffy. Serves 4 to 6.

Mrs. Wayne T. Davis

## DIRTY RICE

| | |
|---|---|
| 1 pound chicken gizzards | 3 tablespoons bacon drippings |
| 1 pound chicken livers | 1 bunch green onions, chopped |
| 6 cups water | 1 bunch celery, chopped |
| 1 tablespoon salt | 2 bell peppers, chopped |
| 1 tablespoon Worcestershire sauce | 1 pound lean ground meat |
| 1 teaspoon red pepper | 2 pounds hot bulk sausage |
| | 2 cups rice, uncooked |

Cook gizzards and liver in water to which the seasonings have been added. Boil 20 to 30 minutes until tender. Grind and set aside. Retain the broth. In a large Dutch oven (preferably iron), sauté the chopped vegetables in the bacon drippings until golden brown. In a separate pot, brown the ground meat and sausage. Remove the excess grease. Mix in the iron pot, the vegetables, gizzards, livers, meat and sausage. Simmer slowly about 15 minutes. Add 4 cups of the broth and cook slowly about an hour. It it becomes too thick, add additional broth. This mixture freezes very well. Simply thaw before proceeding. Prepare 2 cups uncooked rice your favorite way. When done, mix with the meat mixture. This is better if prepared several hours before serving so that the rice absorbs the meat flavor. Bake in a covered dish at 325 degrees for about 30 minutes (over-heating does not hurt the flavor). If you prefer a less meaty dish, add more rice. Serves 15 to 20.

Mrs. Wray Edward Robinson

## WILD RICE SUPREME

| | |
|---|---|
| 12 ounces wild rice | 2 tablespoons butter |
| 6 stalks celery, chopped | 1 teaspoon salt |
| 1 green pepper, chopped | ¼ teaspoon pepper |
| 1 large onion, chopped | 1 cup cream |
| 1 pint sliced mushrooms | 1 cup grated cheese (optional) |

Prepare rice as package directs. Brown celery, pepper, onion and mushrooms in butter. Combine with rice, salt and pepper in 3-quart casserole. Cover with cream. Sprinkle with cheese (if desired). Bake at 325 degrees about 1 hour or until rice absorbs cream and cheese. Serves 6 to 8.

Mrs. E. D. Bateman, Jr.

## WILD RICE CASSEROLE

| | |
|---|---|
| One 6-ounce package long grain and wild rice | One 16-ounce can tomatoes, mashed |
| 1 cup cubed Cheddar cheese | One 4-ounce can mushrooms, minced |
| 1 cup chopped ripe olives | ½ cup chopped onions |
| | ½ cup olive oil |

Soak above ingredients in 2½-quart casserole overnight. The next day, add 1½ cups boiling water. Bake one hour at 350 degrees, covered. Serves 6 to 8.

Mrs. Charles F. Duchein, Jr.

## CURRIED WILD RICE

| | |
|---|---|
| ¾ cup uncooked wild rice | 2 egg yolks |
| 6 slices bacon, diced | 1 cup light cream |
| ½ cup chopped onions | ½ teaspoon curry powder |
| ½ cup grated raw carrots | ½ teaspoon salt |
| | 4 tablespoons butter |

Cook wild rice according to directions on package. Fry bacon. Add onions and carrots to bacon and sauté until onions are soft. Drain and mix with rice. Beat eggs and add cream and seasonings. Add rice mixture to egg mixture. Top with butter. Cook in a buttered 2-quart casserole in a 325 degree oven, covered, for approximately one hour or until custard is set. Serves 6 to 8.

Mrs. James H. LaRoche

## SAVORY RICE

| | |
|---|---|
| 1 cup long grain white rice | 1 rounded tablespoon McCormick's chicken seasoned stock base |
| 2 tablespoons margarine | |
| 2 cups boiling water | 2 pinches thyme |
| 1 pinch basil | 2 pinches rosemary |

Sauté rice in margarine. Add boiling water and stock base. Let simmer a minute. Stir in spices. Turn into 2-quart casserole. Bake, covered, for about 45 minutes in preheated 350 degree oven, until rice is fluffy and slightly moist. Serves 6.

Mrs. Michael H. Mayer

## RICE JALAPEÑO

2⅓ cups raw rice
½ cup margarine
¾ cup chopped green onions,
    tops and bottoms

½ teaspoon oregano
¼ cup Parmesan or Romano cheese,
    grated
1 roll jalapeño cheese
Salt to taste

Cook rice according to package directions. Melt margarine, add chopped onions and simmer until soft. Add oregano and Parmesan or Romano cheese. Pour over cooked rice and toss lightly with a fork. Cut half the roll of jalapeño cheese into small cubes and toss with rice. Put in greased 2-quart casserole. Arrange slices of remaining jalapeño cheese on top. Bake in 400 degree oven until cheese melts. This may be made the day before and heated right before serving. Serves 10 to 12.

Mrs. Raymond G. Post

## RICE WITH GREEN CHILIES AND CHEESE

1 cup raw rice
Salt and pepper to taste
¾ pound Monterey Jack cheese

8 peeled green chili peppers, or
    One 6-ounce can
2 cups sour cream
¼ cup butter

Cook rice in boiling salted water about 15 minutes or until just tender. Drain, wash with cold water and drain again. Season with salt and pepper. Cut each chili pepper into 3 lengthwise strips. Cut ½ pound of the cheese into 24 oblong pieces and wrap a chili strip around each piece. Line buttered 1½-quart casserole with half the rice. Add half the stuffed peppers and cover with 1 cup of sour cream. Repeat the three layers. Top with remaining ¼ pound grated cheese and dot with butter. Bake at 350 degrees for 30 minutes. Serves 6 to 8.

Mrs. David F. Agnew
Mrs. John L. Glover

## RICE CASSEROLE

½ cup margarine
1 cup white rice
½ cup chopped green onion
1 small onion, chopped
One 4-ounce can mushrooms, stems
    and pieces
One 10½-ounce can beef broth

1 cup boiling water in which 3
    beef bouillon cubes are
    dissolved
One 6-ounce can water chestnuts,
    slivered (optional)
½ cup chopped green pepper
    (optional)
Tabasco sauce, salt, pepper to
    taste

Melt margarine and brown rice in it. Add onions. Cook until wilted. Mix in mushrooms, beef broth, water with bouillon cubes, water chestnuts, and green peppers. Season highly. Place in a 1½-quart casserole. Bake for 45 minutes in 350 degree oven. Stir occasionally. Serves 6 to 8.

Mrs. Richard Hummel

## LAS VEGAS RICE

½ cup margarine
2 cups uncooked rice
1 medium onion, chopped

4 cups water
1 teaspoon salt
1 can ripe olives, chopped

Melt margarine. Put in rice. Cook over medium heat until rice begins to brown. Add chopped onion. Continue to cook until rice is very brown, about 20 minutes after onion has been added. Add water and salt. Boil over high heat until water has almost evaporated and is just bubbling on top of rice. Cover and reduce heat. Allow to simmer until thoroughly cooked. When ready to serve, mix in ripe olives. Serve immediately. Serves 6 to 8.

Mrs. Edwin W. Edwards

## RICE SAUSAGE

1 cup rice
1½ cups water
1 package onion soup mix
1 pound smoked sausage, cubed
½ cup chopped onions

⅓ cup chopped bell pepper
1 cup chopped celery
1 ounce of pimiento, sliced
Salt and pepper
¼ cup chopped parsley (optional)

Cook rice with water and onion soup mix in usual manner. Fry sausage. Remove sausage when done and sauté all vegetables except pimiento in small amount of sausage drippings. When rice is cooked, mix in sautéed vegetables, sausage and pimiento. Season with salt and pepper if needed. Parsley sprinkled on top makes a nice garnish. Serves 6 to 8.

Mrs. George Berger
Shades Plantation
Wilson, Louisiana

## SWEET POTATO SUPREME

12 medium sized sweet potatoes, or
    equivalent amount of canned yams
2 large red apples
1 16-ounce bottle white corn syrup
4 tablespoons butter

1 cup sugar
3 tablespoons water
3 tablespoons cherry juice
12 maraschino cherries, chopped
½ cup chopped pecans
¼ cup raisins

Cut sweet potatoes lengthwise after they have been boiled, peeled and cooled. Core apples and cut into ¾ inch thick lengthwise pieces. In a buttered 9x13-inch pan, alternate apples (with the red peeling on top) with the wedge of sweet potatoes. Arrange one side, then the other. If center is empty, arrange potatoes and apples lengthwise in the middle of the dish until it is filled. Cover with foil. Place baking dish of potatoes and apples in 350 degree oven. Bake until all moisture disappears, about 20 minutes. In a quart saucepan, combine the next five ingredients. Cook about 30 minutes or until mixture is very thick. Stir occasionally to keep from sticking. Pour sauce mixture over apples and potatoes. Bake 30 minutes uncovered. Sprinkle with cherries, pecans and raisins. Glaze by basting with pan syrup and bake for 5 more minutes. Serves 8 to 10.

Mrs. F. E. LeBlanc
Donaldsonville, Louisiana

## PRALINE YAM CASSEROLE

**Casserole:**

| | |
|---|---|
| 4 medium yams cooked and peeled, or two 1-pound 4-ounce cans | ½ cup dark brown sugar |
| | ⅓ cup melted butter |
| 2 eggs, beaten | 1 teaspoon salt |
| | ½ cup pecan halves |

Peel and quarter yams. Boil until tender. Drain and mash. Combine yams with eggs, ¼ cup of the brown sugar, 2 tablespoons of the melted butter and salt. Place mixture in a 1-quart casserole. Arrange pecan halves in a pattern over the top. Sprinkle with the remaining ¼ cup brown sugar and drizzle with remaining butter. Bake uncovered in a 375 degree oven for 20 minutes. Serve with orange sauce. Prepared yams freeze well. Serves 8.

**Orange Sauce:**

| | |
|---|---|
| ⅓ cup granulated sugar | 1 teaspoon lemon juice |
| 1 teaspoon cornstarch | 2 teaspoons butter |
| ⅛ teaspoon salt | 1 tablespoon orange liqueur (optional) |
| 1 teaspoon grated orange peel | |
| 1 cup orange juice | 3 dashes aromatic bitters (optional) |

Put first six ingredients in the top of a double boiler. Bring to a boil over medium heat, stirring constantly until sauce thickens. Remove from heat. Stir in butter. Add orange liqueur and/or bitters if desired.

Mrs. J. Garner Moore, III

## CREAMY POTATO BAKE

| | |
|---|---|
| 4 large Irish potatoes | 2 cups half and half |
| 1 teaspoon salt | ½ cup grated onion |
| 1 teaspoon pepper | 3 teaspoons butter |

Scrub, peel and halve potatoes. Cook in boiling water 10 minutes only. Drain well, cool and grate. Combine all ingredients, except butter. Pour into buttered 2-quart casserole. Dot with butter and bake uncovered at 300 degrees for 2 hours. Serves 6.

Mrs. Ron Wagner
Fond du Lac, Wisconsin

## BRENNAN'S STUFFED BAKED POTATOES

| | |
|---|---|
| 2 large Idaho potatoes | 2 tablespoons grated Parmesan cheese |
| 4 strips bacon, quartered | |
| ¼ cup chopped shallots | ½ teaspoon salt |
| ½ cup sour cream | ½ teaspoon black pepper |

Scrub potatoes well and bake 1 hour at 400 degrees. Grill bacon pieces until crisp. Drain off bacon fat except for 3 tablespoons. Add shallots and sauté slowly. Cut potatoes in half lengthwise and scoop out into a skillet, taking care to retain shells intact. Add bacon, shallots, cream, cheese, salt and pepper, mixing and mashing to blend thoroughly. Stuff mixture into potato skins. Bake 15 to 20 minutes at 350 degrees. Serves 4.

Mrs. Randall J. Lamont

## GOLDEN CRUSTED POTATOES

3 cups cooked instant mashed     1 tablespoon finely chopped green
  potatoes (very stiff)            onions
1½ cups creamed cottage cheese   ¼ teaspoon nutmeg
½ cup sour cream                 4 tablespoons melted margarine
¼ teaspoon white pepper          ½ cup slivered almonds

Prepare instant mashed potatoes in usual way using less liquid because of adding other ingredients. Combine the potatoes, creamed cottage cheese, sour cream, pepper, green onions, and nutmeg. Check to see if more salt is needed. Place in a shallow buttered 1½-quart casserole. Cover the top with melted margarine and sprinkle with slivered almonds. Bake in oven at 350 degrees for 20 to 25 minutes or until bubbling hot and golden crusted. Serves 6.

Mrs. W. A. Whitley


## SHIRLEY'S AU GRATIN POTATOES

4 potatoes                       3 cups milk
Salt and pepper                  Butter or margarine
5 tablespoons flour              1 pound Cheddar cheese

Peel and slice potatoes into a large bowl. Salt and pepper generously. Combine 2 tablespoons of flour with milk. Mix well so flour dissolves. Pour over potatoes. Let potatoes soak in milk and seasonings while grating cheese. In a greased 2-quart casserole, put a layer of potatoes and dot with butter. Sprinkle with 1 tablespoon of flour. Cover with cheese. Repeat layers, ending with 3 layers of potatoes and cheese. Stir seasoned milk and pour over casserole. Bake at 400 degrees uncovered for 30 to 45 minutes or until cheese is brown. Then cover and bake until potatoes are tender, about 30 more minutes. Serves 4 to 6.

Mrs. Walter Christy
New Orleans, Louisiana


## GARLIC CHEESE GRITS

2 cups water                     ½ cup butter
Salt                             2 eggs, separated
1 cup quick grits                Salt and pepper
1 roll garlic cheese             Worcestershire sauce
                                 Tabasco sauce

Bring water and salt to a soft boil. Add grits slowly, stirring constantly, as it will thicken quickly because of the small amount of water. After a few minutes of cooking, remove from heat and add cheese (which has been cut in 4 or 5 pieces) and butter. After cooking a few more minutes, add egg yolks, salt, pepper, Worcestershire sauce and Tabasco sauce. Mix well. Fold in stiff egg whites with a fork. Put mixture in a greased baking dish. Bake 30 minutes at 350 degrees, or until golden brown. This dish should be served immediately, as it will rise.

Mrs. Fred A. Blanche, Jr.

## DELICATE GRITS
## (GNOCCHI À LA ROMAINE)

| | |
|---|---|
| **1 quart milk** | **1 cup grated Swiss cheese** |
| **½ cup butter** | **Salt and pepper to taste** |
| **1 cup of 3-minute grits** | **⅓ cup grated Parmesan cheese** |

Bring milk and butter to slow boil and stir in grits slowly. Stir often, until mixture looks like farina. Put in large bowl and beat with electric mixer until grits become creamy, about 5 minutes. Add grated cheese and salt and pepper. Mix well with a wooden spoon. Pour mixture into a greased 2-quart casserole. Put a large piece of butter on top and sprinkle with Parmesan cheese. Bake at 375 degrees for 35 to 40 minutes. This is excellent with grillades or game. Serves 6 to 8.

Mrs. Fred A. Blanche, Jr.

## CHEESE AND EGGS

The long tradition of Lenten abstinence from meat in Louisiana has led to an unusually large selection of cheese and egg recipes used by area cooks. As in the case of gumbos, these foods are found as appetizers, luncheon specialties, main dishes and party fare. Another Louisiana tradition is that of the elaborate breakfast or brunch, at which egg dishes *extraordinaire* are served with style and imagination.

## EGG AND SAUSAGE BREAKFAST DISH

1 pound cooked, drained sausage     1 teaspoon dry mustard
6 eggs, slightly beaten     2 slices crushed, day old bread
2 cups milk     1 cup grated Cheddar cheese
1 teaspoon salt     3 tablespoons chopped onion

Mix ingredients and let sit overnight in a 11x7x1½-inch pyrex dish. Bake at 350 degrees for 45 minutes. This is great for a Sunday brunch. Serves 6.

Mrs. Michael T. Delahaye

## SAUCY EGGS IN SPINACH

One 10-ounce package frozen chopped     One 10¾-ounce can cream of
    spinach     shrimp soup
Nutmeg to taste     2 tablespoons milk
Pepper to taste     4 eggs

Cook spinach according to package directions. Drain well. Add nutmeg and pepper. Blend ¼ cup soup with milk. Mix remaining soup with spinach. Heat. Place spinach mixture in four greased 1-cup individual baking dishes. Break an egg into each dish. Spoon the soup-milk mixture over eggs. Bake in a 350 degree oven for 15 to 20 minutes or until eggs are set. Serves 4.

Mrs. Cheney C. Joseph, Jr.

## MARNA'S EGGS BENEDICT

Eggs Benedict:
4 rounds English muffins     4 poached eggs
4 slices lean ham     Hollandaise sauce
4 thin slices tomato     Paprika

Heat muffins in oven. Top with slice of ham, then tomato, then poached egg. Cover this with hollandaise sauce and sprinkle with paprika. Serves 4.

Hollandaise sauce:
½ cup butter (divided into 4 parts)     ¼ cup lemon juice
4 egg yolks, beaten     White pepper, salt and red pepper
    to taste

In top of double boiler (do not let water boil or touch bottom of pan) place egg yolks and beat in lemon juice slowly and add ¼ of the butter. Stir with wooden spoon until butter is melted. Add second amount of butter and continue this process, stirring constantly, until all of the butter is used. When well mixed, remove pan from the heat and continue stirring until thick and creamy. Add white pepper, salt and red pepper. Use immediately. If the mixture should curdle, beat in one tablespoon of boiling water or cream, beating constantly in order to rebind. (This may be repeated several times.)

Mrs. Melvin A. Shortess

## WAVERLY'S EGGS WITH SOUR CREAM SAUCE PIQUANT

2 cups sour cream
Juice of 2½ lemons
1 teaspoon Worcestershire sauce

4 dashes Tabasco sauce
4 eggs
4 English muffin halves
4 slices ham or Canadian bacon

In a saucepan, heat sour cream, lemon juice, Worcestershire sauce and Tabasco sauce. Poach eggs. Toast muffins and lightly fry ham. Place ham on muffin, then add egg and cover with sour cream sauce. Serve immediately while hot. Serves 4.

Mrs. William M. Simmons

## CHEESE AND SPAGHETTI CASSEROLE

One 12-ounce package very thin
  spaghetti
½ cup butter, melted
1 medium onion, chopped

¼ cup flour
1 teaspoon pepper
1 teaspoon dry mustard
2 cups milk
1 pound American cheese, grated

Partially cook spaghetti in salted water. Drain. Melt butter in top of double boiler. Add onions and cook until wilted. Combine flour, pepper and dry mustard with butter mixture. Add milk and grated cheese, setting aside 1¼ cups cheese to top casserole. Heat until cheese is melted. Mix cheese sauce with spaghetti in a 4-quart dish. Sprinkle remaining grated cheese on top. Bake at 375 degrees for 30 to 45 minutes.

Mrs. Lloyd T. Leake

## SUPER-DUPER SCRAMBLED EGGS

5 eggs
3 green onions with tops
¼ teaspoon chopped bell pepper
2½ ounces sharp Cheddar cheese
1 teaspoon salt

¼ teaspoon dried minced garlic
⅛ teaspoon black pepper
⅛ teaspoon chili powder
⅛ teaspoon paprika
3 tablespoons water or milk
2½ tablespoons bacon drippings

Beat eggs. Add green onions, bell pepper and cheese which has been cut into bite size pieces. Add seasonings and liquid, mix well. Pour into hot bacon drippings and scramble. Serves 3 to 4.

Mrs. J. Randall Goodwin

## DELICIOUS HIGH PROTEIN PANCAKES

4 eggs
1 cup cottage cheese
2 tablespoons oil

½ cup oatmeal (or ¼ cup wheat
  germ and ¼ cup oatmeal)
¼ teaspoon salt

Place all ingredients in a blender and mix thoroughly. Drop by tablespoons onto hot, greased frying pan. Serves 3 to 4.

Mrs. Ross Munson

## QUICHE LORRAINE

½ pound bacon
1 large onion, chopped
3 eggs
One 13-ounce can evaporated milk
½ teaspoon salt

½ teaspoon dry mustard
Black pepper and cayenne pepper
  to taste
One 10-inch unbaked pie shell
½ pound Swiss cheese, grated
2 tablespoons butter

In skillet, brown bacon. Remove and crumble. In bacon grease, sauté onion until clear. Remove with slotted spoon. With fork, beat together eggs, milk and seasonings. Put bacon in bottom of pie shell. Put onions on top and then put a layer of Swiss cheese. Pour milk mixture over all and dot with butter. Bake at 375 degrees for 35 minutes or until brown and bubbly and crust is golden brown. Let stand 15 to 20 minutes before cutting. Good served either hot or cold. It is a perfect luncheon dish. Also good served in small wedges as an appetizer or baked in an oblong pan and cut into small squares as an hors d'oeuvre. Serves 6 as a main dish or 10 as an appetizer.

Mrs. Norman Saurage, III
Mrs. Percy Roberts, Jr.

## QUICHE LORRAINE WITH HAM

4 thin slices onion
Margarine
10-inch pie shell, partially baked
4 slices crisp bacon, chopped
8 paper-thin slices ham, shredded

8 paper-thin slices imported
  Swiss cheese
3 eggs
¼ teaspoon dry mustard
1 cup light cream, heated
Garlic powder to taste
Nutmeg to taste

Sauté onion in margarine until soft. Sprinkle drained onion and bacon over bottom of pie crust. Add half the ham, then 4 slices of cheese. Repeat layer using remaining ham and cheese. Beat eggs and mustard together. Add heated cream and continue beating. Pour over pie and let stand 10 minutes. Sprinkle tiny bit of garlic powder and nutmeg on top. Bake in 350 degree oven 25 to 30 minutes or until custard is set. Serves 6.

Variation: Use 1 to 1½ cups lump crabmeat instead of ham.

Mrs. James Hatcher

## EGGS MORNAY

2 cups white sauce
⅔ cup mayonnaise
1 cup shredded sharp cheese
½ cup grated Parmesan cheese

2 tablespoons sherry
Two 10-ounce packages frozen
  chopped spinach, cooked
6 eggs

Prepare white sauce. Combine mayonnaise, sharp cheese, Parmesan cheese and sherry. Gradually add white sauce to this mixture. Cover the bottoms of 6 individual casseroles with cooked spinach. Place an egg in the center of each. Top with sauce. Bake at 350 degrees for 25 minutes. Serves 6.

Mrs. W. A. Rolston, Jr.

## ENCHILADAS

2 large onions, chopped
2 large bell peppers, chopped
3 tablespoons salad oil
2 cans enchilada sauce
1 cup sour cream

Salt to taste
One package corn tortillas (12)
1 pound Monterrey Jack cheese,
    cut in strips
2 cups Cheddar cheese, shredded

Cook onions and peppers in oil until soft but not brown. In a skillet, blend enchilada sauce and sour cream. Salt to taste. Heat just to simmer. Dip tortillas in enchilada sauce and let stand to soften. Put tortillas in baking dish. Top each tortilla with the onion and pepper mixture and the Monterrey Jack cheese. Roll. Pour remaining sauce over all. Top with shredded cheese. Bake at 375 degrees for 20 to 25 minutes. Serves 6.

Mrs. Margo Robertson

## MOCK SOUFFLÉ

10 slices white bread
½ cup softened butter
1 pound grated sharp Cheddar cheese
4 eggs, slightly beaten

3 cups milk
1½ teaspoons salt
1 teaspoon dry mustard
1 tablespoon Worcestershire sauce

Remove crust from bread. Spread butter on each slice. Cut each slice into four strips. Butter a 2-quart casserole and lay alternate layers of bread strips and grated cheese, ending with grated cheese. Beat eggs well. Add seasonings and milk to eggs. Spoon egg mixture over cheese. Refrigerate for 24 hours. Bake at 350 degrees for 45 minutes. Serves 6 to 8.

Mrs. Dennis L. Judice

## CANADIAN BACON SOUFFLÉ

½ cup shortening
½ cup flour
2 cups milk
6 egg yolks, well beaten
1 cup grated Cheddar cheese
½ teaspoon salt

¼ teaspoon pepper
¼ teaspoon Tabasco sauce
⅔ cup lightly cooked Canadian
    bacon cubes
7 egg whites
4 paper-thin slices Swiss cheese

Preheat oven to 375 degrees. Grease a 2-quart casserole. Blend shortening and flour together until crumbly. Stir in milk and bring to a boil. Stir until mixture is very thick and pulling away from the sides of the pan. Remove from heat. Let stand two minutes and add egg yolks. Stir in grated cheese, salt, pepper, Tabasco sauce and bacon. Beat egg whites until they peak. Fold in gently. Spoon mixture into greased casserole. Cover with Swiss cheese. Bake for 25 to 30 minutes. Serves 4.

Mrs. John B. Nolan

## CRÊPES FLORENTINE

**Crêpes:**

| | |
|---|---|
| **1 cup flour** | **2 cups milk** |
| **Salt and pepper to taste** | **6 eggs** |

Sift flour, salt and pepper. Mix with milk. Add eggs and beat. Let stand for at least 4 hours, covered. A medium sized frying pan may be used and heated until very hot. Grease lightly with margarine or salt pork. Ladle a scant ¼ cup batter to thinly cover bottom of skillet. When slightly brown and edges curl, turn and lightly brown other side. Each crêpe takes about 1 minute on the first side and ½ minute on the other. Crêpes may be placed on a dry dish towel until all are made. Or, as they cool, they may be stacked between wax paper. Crêpes freeze beautifully, wrapped in foil, if one wishes to make them ahead.

**Filling:**

| | |
|---|---|
| **1 pound chopped, frozen spinach** | **1½ pound Ricotta cheese** |
| **¼ pound Swiss cheese, cut into** | **3 egg yolks** |
| **very tiny cubes** | **Pinch of nutmeg** |
| **¼ pound Mozzarella cheese, cut** | **Salt and pepper** |
| **into very tiny cubes** | **½ cup grated Parmesan cheese** |

Cook spinach according to directions on package. Drain and cool. Combine cold spinach with other ingredients, but use only ½ of the Parmesan cheese. Place filling on crêpes and roll.

**Bascemeli sauce:**

| | |
|---|---|
| **½ cup butter** | **1 quart milk** |
| **½ cup flour** | **Salt, pepper and nutmeg to taste** |

Melt butter. Add flour and stir constantly for 15 minutes. Heat milk, but do not boil. Add milk slowly to flour mixture, stirring constantly. Cook until fairly thick. Add salt, pepper and nutmeg.

**Tomato sauce:**

| | |
|---|---|
| **1 onion, finely chopped** | **1 whole clove garlic** |
| **Olive oil** | **One 40-ounce can peeled tomatoes,** |
| | **chopped** |

Sauté onion in small amount of oil. Cook garlic with onion until the latter is golden brown. Discard garlic. Add tomatoes to onion and simmer about 20 minutes, or until thickened.

In a baking dish, place a thin layer of both sauces on bottom. Place rolled crêpes side by side, and pour remainder of both sauces over them. Sprinkle with remainder of Parmesan cheese and bake in 250 degree oven for about 20 minutes. Serves 6.

Mrs. Charles F. Duchein, Jr.

## CHEESE STRATA

12 slices white bread, buttered
6 ounces sharp cheese, sliced
One 10-ounce package chopped
  broccoli
2 cups diced ham

6 eggs, slightly beaten
3½ cups milk
1 medium onion, minced
1 teaspoon salt
½ teaspoon dry mustard
Shredded cheese

Cut bread into rounds and set aside. Remove and discard crusts from remaining bread and fit scraps in bottom of a 13x9x2-inch greased baking dish. Layer cheese slices over bread followed by a layer of broccoli, then the ham. Put rounds on top. Combine remaining ingredients except shredded cheese and pour over bread. Cover and refrigerate overnight or for six hours. Bake uncovered at 325 degrees for 55 minutes. Sprinkle with shredded cheese 5 minutes before taking from oven. Let stand for 10 minutes before cutting. Serves 6.

Mrs. Charles F. Duchein, Jr.

## PIMIENTO CHEESE SANDWICH FILLING

1 pound mild Cheddar cheese
One 4-ounce jar pimiento
1 teaspoon lemon juice

2 tablespoons grated onion
2 tablespoons sugar
¼ teaspoon salt
1 cup mayonnaise

Allow cheese to soften at room temperature. Carefully wipe the oil from the cheese. Run the cheese through a food chopper, using a fine blade. Drain and dry the pimiento and run through chopper. Add to the cheese. With a fork, mash the cheese and pimiento until completely blended and free of lumps. Add rest of ingredients and blend with a fork until mixture has consistency of heavy cream. Yields 2 cups.

Mrs. Claude Wynne Eubanks

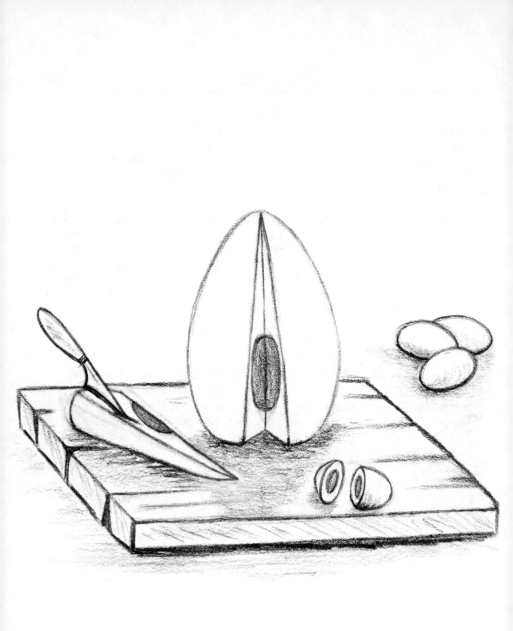

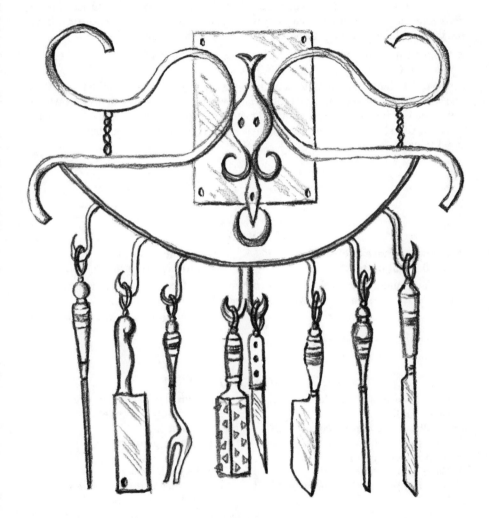

## MEATS

The most varied of all recipe categories must surely be meat. It includes everything from roasts to ribs and from ham to hamburgers. To most of us, meat remains the starting point around which we plan our meals. Described here are some of your favorite dishes and some surprises we think you'll like to try.

## FIRST, YOU MAKE A ROUX

As the statement, "First, you make a Roux!" so often opens a Louisiana French cook's recipe, we felt it necessary to give a basic roux recipe for your use. A basic roux does take a long time to make, so don't expect instant cooking.

**2 tablespoons butter, shortening or       2 tablespoons flour
   bacon fat**

Melt the butter, shortening, or bacon fat in a heavy, thick pot or skillet. Add flour and stir constantly over low heat until *dark* brown. The trick is to get it dark brown but not burned. If it is over browned, it will taste bitter so it should be discarded. To this basic roux, add seasoning and stock to make sauces, gravies, gumbos and all sorts of good things.

The Editors


## CARPETBAG STEAK

**1 pound or more beef steak          2 slices bacon
8 to 10 small oysters                Salt and pepper to taste**

Have butcher cut steak at least 1 inch thick and then slit steak all around. Stuff with small oysters; surround with bacon and broil. Season to taste. Serves 3.

Miss Ellen Roy Jolly


## ROLLED ROAST ALEXANDER

**One 4- to 6-pound shoulder roast    1 cup grated Parmesan cheese
1 clove garlic, cut                  ½ cup chopped parsley
One 10½-ounce can chicken broth      1 teaspoon salt
3 tablespoons, butter or margarine   ¼ teaspoon pepper
¼ cup minced onion                   ⅛ teaspoon basil
1 clove garlic, crushed              2 tablespoons flour
2 cups bread crumbs, unseasoned      One 8-ounce can mushrooms
                                     ½ cup dry white wine**

Place roast in a roasting pan and rub with cut garlic. Add chicken broth. Roast at 325 degrees for 40 minutes per pound, basting occasionally. Meanwhile, melt butter in skillet; add onion, crushed garlic, and slightly brown. Stir in bread crumbs, cheese, parsley, salt, pepper, and basil. Remove roast from oven, cut off string, and brush meat generously with pan drippings. Roll roast in crumb mixture, being sure to coat all sides completely. Pour off drippings from pan and reserve. Return roast to oven and bake at 350 degrees for 20 minutes. Heat 1½ cups pan drippings in skillet. Gradually stir in flour, mushrooms, and wine. Cook until thick, stirring constantly. Serve this sauce with the roast. Serves 6 to 8.

Mrs. James H. Alexander, Jr.

## BOEUF EN CROÛTE or
## BEEF WELLINGTON

**Roast:**

| | |
|---|---|
| **4- to 4½-pound tenderloin** | **Salt and pepper** |

Roast ahead of time a trimmed, seasoned beef tenderloin at 425 degrees until desired doneness is reached, 45 minutes for rare, or use a meat thermometer. Reserve roasting juices for later use.

**Pastry:**

| | |
|---|---|
| **¼ pound cream cheese** | **1 cup flour** |
| **¼ pound butter** | **Sprinkle water as needed** |

Vary above amount to have dough easy to manage. Cream together cream cheese and butter. Cut in flour as in pie dough. Sprinkle water until dough is easy to manage. Rest the dough in refrigerator 2 hours.

**Forming Wellington:**

| | |
|---|---|
| **1 recipe dough (from above)** | **Mushrooms, sliced and broiled** |
| **French pâté (optional)** | **in butter (optional)** |
| **1 teaspoon Cognac (optional)** | **1 egg yolk** |
| | **1 teaspoon water** |

Roll out pastry in a rectangle large enough to wrap around the roast. You may cover cooled roast with any of the above optional ingredients or leave the roast plain. Place roast on dough and completely encase meat in the dough, overlapping the dough on the bottom side. Any extra dough may be made into decorative small cut-outs (as with small cookie cutters). These may be made to adhere in decorative pattern by moistening with water. Make small incisions in dough for the steam to escape. Paint entire surface with mixture of egg yolk and water. Place seam side down on roasting pan and bake at 400 degrees for 30 minutes or until crust is golden brown. Serve in ½ inch slices with sauce.

**Sauce:**

| | |
|---|---|
| **Reserved cooking juices** | **1 tablespoon flour or thickener** |
| **½ cup port wine** | **Salt** |
| **½ cup beef bouillon** | **Pepper** |

Make sauce while pastry rests so it will be ready when meat is finished cooking. Mix reserved juices with wine and bouillon. Season with salt and pepper to taste. Let simmer up to 2 hours until sauce is thick and reduced in volume. Make a paste of 1 tablespoon flour or your favorite thickener and some of the sauce. Gradually return to sauce stirring constantly. Simmer until sauce thickens.

This is a recipe that is both expensive and time-consuming to fix. However, it is beautiful and very impressive, as well as delicious, for extra special company or occasions.

Mrs. Charles H. Ramsey

## TENDERLOIN FOR TWO

2 tablespoons butter
1 clove garlic, minced
¾ to 1 teaspoon dried basil,
  crushed
Salt and pepper

Two 4-ounce slices beef
  tenderloin
2 large fresh mushrooms, fluted
2 slices French bread, buttered
  and toasted

Melt butter in a heavy skillet. Stir in garlic and basil. Sprinkle meat with salt and freshly ground pepper; add to skillet along with mushrooms. Pan broil over medium-high heat (4 minutes each side for rare, 6 minutes each side for medium). Serve on toast, pour on pan drippings, and top with mushrooms.

Mrs. C. Bernard Berry

## PANBROILED SIRLOIN STEAK

1 sirloin steak
Salt and pepper
2 tablespoons butter
2 teaspoons olive oil
1 teaspoon dry mustard

2 teaspoons frozen chives,
  chopped
Juice of ½ lemon
2 teaspoons Worcestershire sauce
Parsley, chopped

Trim steak and pound thin with a mallet or rolling pin. Season with salt and pepper, and brush lightly with olive oil. Put 2 tablespoons butter and olive oil in a skillet, add the dry mustard and chopped chives. Heat skillet until oil is sizzling, and cook the steak until it is done the way you like it. Place the meat on a warm platter. Quickly add to the skillet the lemon juice, Worcestershire sauce and a little warm water. Boil quickly for just a minute, scraping up all the brown bits in the pan. Add the parsley. Pour over steak and serve immediately. Do *not* use a non-stick skillet. Serves 4.

Mrs. J. D. Guillory, Jr.

## SWISS STEAK SAUTERNE

2 pounds round steak, cut ½ inch
  thick
1 teaspoon salt
⅛ teaspoon pepper
Flour

Oil
½ medium onion, chopped
1 cup sauterne (or other white
  dinner wine)
One 6-ounce can sliced mushrooms,
  undrained

Pound steak, and cut into 6 serving size pieces. Sprinkle with salt and pepper, dip in flour. In a heavy skillet brown meat and onions in heated oil. When well browned, add wine and mushrooms. Cover and cook over low heat for 1 to 1½ hours or until meat is tender. Serves 4.

Mrs. J. William Carr

## BARBECUE BEEF

One 3-pound chuck roast
One 18-ounce bottle catsup
2 onions, diced
2 tablespoons liquid hickory smoke

1 teaspoon lemon juice
2 tablespoons wine vinegar
2 tablespoons Worcestershire sauce
2 teaspoons salt

Cover roast with water. Cook until tender, approximately 4 hours. (3 to 5 cups of water are sufficient if cooked in covered container.) Cool meat and pull into slivers. To the cooking water, add slivered meat and remaining ingredients. Simmer for 1 hour or until desired consistency. Serve on toasted buns or noodles. This yields 2 quarts and can be frozen.

Mrs. Rollo C. Lawrence

## MARINATED CHUCK ROAST

1 cup prepared Italian salad dressing
2 cups beer
¼ cup lemon juice
2 bay leaves
1 teaspoon salt
1 teaspoon pepper

1 teaspoon dry mustard
1 teaspoon basil
1 teaspoon oregano
1 teaspoon thyme
One 3- to 10-pound chuck steak
or roast

Combine the above and pour over meat. Refrigerate for several hours or overnight. Place roast in roasting pan and brush with marinade. Roast in a 325 degree oven for 2½ hours for rare roast. The same procedure adapts quite well for outdoor barbecue cooking, adjusting cooking time with heat of fire.

Mrs. R. W. Valentin
Houston, Texas

## BEEF BRISKET

One 4- to 5-pound beef brisket
Salt, black pepper and red pepper

1 large onion, sliced
2 cloves garlic
6 tablespoons sherry or claret wine

Place brisket in large heavy pot. Cover with water and seasonings. Bring to boil. Then reduce heat and let simmer to desired doneness (approximately 3 hours). Serve with new potatoes and hot horseradish.

Mrs. William S. Slack

## MARINATED BRISKET

5 or 6 pounds beef brisket
Meat tenderizer
Garlic salt

Celery salt
Seasoned salt
3 tablespoons liquid smoke
¼ cup Worcestershire sauce

Sprinkle meat with tenderizer and salts. Combine liquid smoke and Worcestershire sauce and pour over meat. Marinate in refrigerator for 24 hours. Bake in covered casserole (in marinade) at 225 degrees for 5 to 6 hours. Serves 5 to 6.

Mrs. Tom Phillips

## BEEF-KA-BOB MARINADE

Top round or sirloin steak
1½ cups salad oil (preferably
   olive oil)
¾ cup soy sauce
¼ cup Worcestershire sauce
2 tablespoons dry mustard
2¼ teaspoons salt

1 tablespoon black pepper,
   course and freshly ground
½ cup wine vinegar
1½ teaspoons dried parsley
   flakes
2 garlic cloves, crushed
⅓ cup fresh lemon juice

Combine all ingredients except steak. Marinate steak (1½-to 2-inch cubes) for at least 4 hours. This sauce can be used as a basting sauce while the beef-ka-bobs are cooking, and it can be re-used. It will keep for several days in the refrigerator or indefinitely in the freezer.

Mrs. Michael H. Mayer
Mrs. Gerald W. Shelton

## BEEF AND OLIVE RAGOÛT

1 pound round steak, cubed
2 tablespoons butter
½ cup minced celery
½ cup sliced onion
1 medium green pepper, sliced
1 large clove garlic, minced

One 10¾-ounce can tomato soup
¼ cup dry red wine
¼ cup stuffed olives, sliced
¼ teaspoon salt
⅛ teaspoon pepper
One 4-ounce can mushrooms,
   sliced (save liquid)

Brown meat in butter on low medium heat. Add celery, onion, green pepper and garlic. Cook until almost tender. Stir in soup, wine, mushroom liquid, olives, salt and pepper. Cover and simmer 1 hour or until meat is tender. Add mushrooms. Serve over hot buttered cooked noodles. Serves 4.

Mrs. Rolf Schroeder

## WILD RICE AND BEEF CASSEROLE

1½ to 2 pounds ground chuck
One 6-ounce package Uncle Ben's
   Wild and Long Grain Rice
1 large onion, chopped
One 8-ounce can mushrooms, stems
   and pieces

One 10½-ounce can cream of
   mushroom soup, undiluted
One 10½-ounce can cream of
   chicken soup, undiluted
Salt and pepper to taste
Kellogg's herb seasoned crouettes

In a large skillet or Dutch oven, brown the meat and onion. Drain. Prepare rice according to directions on package. Add rice, mushrooms, and soups to meat. Salt and pepper lightly. Mix well. Transfer to a 3-quart casserole. Top with crouettes, cover, and bake 45 minutes to 1 hour at 350 degrees. This freezes well and serves 8 to 10.

Mrs. Fred R. Hogeman

## MEXICAN SANDWICH

One 13-ounce package regular size
Fritos
4 cups hot cooked rice
Two 1-pound 3-ounce cans chili
without beans, heated
4 cups shredded crisp lettuce

2 tomatoes, chopped
2 green onions, chopped
¼ to ½ pound Velveeta cheese,
grated
One 2-ounce jar stuffed olives,
chopped

Place ¼ package Fritos in bottom of 4 dinner plates. Top Fritos with remaining ingredients in order given above. Serve immediately.

Mrs. Ira Woodfin

## CARBONNADE DE BOEUF

6 slices bacon
Salt and pepper
3 pounds lean boneless beef chuck
or rump, cut into 2-inch chunks
5 tablespoons butter
5 tablespoons flour
4 large onions, coarsely chopped

1½ cups beef stock
Two 10-ounce cans beer
1½ teaspoons sugar
1 tablespoon vinegar
1 large bay leaf
3 large cloves garlic
4 or 5 parsley sprigs, finely
chopped

In a heavy black iron Dutch oven fry bacon until crisp and set aside. Pour off almost all the fat, leaving just enough to have a thin film on the bottom. Salt and pepper meat lightly. Heat fat until smoking hot, and brown meat, a few pieces at a time. If needed, add a little more bacon fat. When all the meat is browned remove and add butter to the pot. When the butter melts stir in flour until well blended and light brown. Add onions and sauté until soft and lightly browned. (You may need a little more bacon fat.) Add beef stock and beer. Stir constantly over low heat until well blended and mixture begins to boil. Add sugar, vinegar, bay leaf, and garlic. Simmer for 2 to 3 minutes; then taste the sauce to see if salt and pepper are sufficient. Stir in parsley. Return meat to the pot. There should be enough sauce to cover, but if you are a little short, add beer. Stir gently; cover and place in the lower part of oven at a temperature to keep it simmering for 1½ to 2 hours. The meat should be fork-tender when ready. Serve with noodles.

Mrs. R. E. Couhig
Asphodel Plantation

## FAVORITE MEATLOAF

1½ pounds ground meat
1 envelope dry onion soup
One 6-ounce can evaporated milk
1 egg, slightly beaten

1 teaspoon salt
1 teaspoon Worcestershire sauce
Pepper to taste
Sharp cheese slices (optional)

Mix all ingredients together, except cheese, and form into a loaf. Bake in lightly greased shallow pan at 350 degrees for 1 hour. Slices of cheese may be placed on top of meatloaf to melt just before serving. Serves 4 to 6.

Mrs. Charles Mittendorf

## BEEF STROGANOFF

| | |
|---|---|
| 1 large round or sirloin steak | Two 10¾-ounce cans beef bouillon |
| ½ cup butter | Salt and pepper to taste |
| 1 bunch green onions, chopped | One 6-ounce can mushrooms, |
| ½ cup flour | undrained |
| 2 tablespoons Dijon style mustard | ½ cup sauterne |
| | 1 cup sour cream |

Cut steak into strips, ½x3 inches. Melt butter in skillet and sauté chopped onions until limp. Push to one side and add meat. Sauté quickly until brown. Add flour and mustard; stir. Add bouillon, salt, and pepper. Cover and simmer until tender (1 to 1½ hours.) Add mushrooms, sauterne, and sour cream. Heat, but do not boil. Thicken with flour and water if necessary, or thin with a little water if too thick. Serve over rice or noodles and pass extra sour cream. Serves 6 to 8.

Mrs. Norman Saurage, III

## STUFFED BELL PEPPERS

| | |
|---|---|
| 1 tablespoon bacon grease | 8 sprigs parsley, chopped |
| 1 onion, chopped | 1 cup diced, cooked ham |
| 1 small bell pepper, chopped | 5 to 6 pieces toast |
| 2 stalks celery, chopped | Salt and pepper |
| | 3 bell peppers, cut in half |

Put bacon grease in skillet, add vegetables and cook until limp. Add ham. Wet toast in a colander and break up. Put in skillet. Salt and pepper mixture. Mix well. Put halves of bell pepper into pot of water and cook until limp. Stuff peppers with mixture and put into shallow baking dish with small amount of water. Bake in oven at 350 degrees for 20 minutes. These freeze well! Serves 6.

Variation: Can substitute ground beef and pork sausage for ham.

Mrs. Rivers Wall, Jr.

## BEEF PARMIGIANA

| | |
|---|---|
| 1 large thin round steak (2 pounds) | 1 teaspoon salt |
| 1 egg, beaten | 1½ teaspoons pepper |
| ½ cup grated Parmesan cheese | 1½ teaspoons marjoram |
| ½ cup dry bread crumbs (seasoned | Two 6-ounce cans tomato paste |
| is best) | 4 cups hot water |
| ½ cup cooking oil | ½ pound Mozzarella cheese, |
| 1 large onion, chopped | sliced |

Put steak between pieces of wax paper; place on a board and pound until thin. Trim all gristle and fat. Cut into serving size pieces (about eight to ten 3x4-inch pieces). Dip meat in egg and roll in mixture of Parmesan and crumbs. Heat oil in skillet or iron pot. Brown steak on both sides over medium heat. Lay in single layer in 13x9-inch baking pan. In same skillet, cook onions until soft. Stir in seasonings and tomato paste. Add hot water. Cook 5 minutes. Pour most of sauce over meat. Place cheese slices on meat and add remaining sauce. Bake uncovered at 350 degrees for 1 hour. Serve over spaghetti. Can be made in the morning, covered, and refrigerated uncooked. Serves 6-8.

Mrs. Norman Saurage, III

## STROGANOFF AU PERRY

2 pounds lean boneless sirloin
¼ pound butter or margarine
3 to 4 medium onions, thinly sliced
1½ pounds canned or fresh
  mushrooms, thinly sliced
2 tablespoons tomato paste

2 cups dairy sour cream
1½ teaspoons salt
½ teaspoon pepper
½ cup Marsala wine
3 cups cooked wild rice, or white,
  or mixture of both

Slice steak at angle into ¼ inch strips. (Partially freeze steak for easier slicing.) Melt half the butter in extra large skillet; sauté the beef until brown. Remove beef. Melt half of the remaining butter in skillet; sauté onions for 10 minutes over medium heat. Remove onions. Melt remaining butter; sauté mushrooms for 5 minutes over medium heat. Return beef and onions to skillet. Add tomato paste, sour cream and seasonings; mix thoroughly. Cover and cook over low heat 30 minutes or until beef is tender. Add wine; simmer 5 minutes longer. Serve over a bed of rice. May be prepared early in the day, but save wine and add when warming. Serves 6.

Mrs. William H. Lee, II

## POPPY SEED NOODLES FOR STROGANOFF

Boil medium noodles in large container of salted water for 12 minutes. Drain, butter, and sprinkle generously with poppy seeds. Turn gently and serve immediately.

Mrs. Weldon Smith

## CARRIE'S STUFFED PEPPERS

8 medium to large bell peppers
Water
5 slices bacon, fried and drained
¼ cup butter
1 large onion, chopped
4 green onions, chopped
4 stalks celery, chopped
1 pod garlic, minced
4 bell pepper tops, chopped
3 pounds ground beef

1 cup bread crumbs
2 eggs
¾ cup milk
2 tablespoons parsley, chopped
Salt and pepper to taste
Pickapeppa sauce or Worcestershire
  sauce to taste
5 slices raw bacon, cut into
  thirds
Water

Cut the tops off the peppers, and clean out pulp and seeds. Reserve tops. Steam peppers in a large covered pot (with a small amount of water) until color has changed to dull green. Drain and set aside. Fry 5 slices of bacon; drain, crumble, and set aside. Sauté the onions, celery, garlic, and pepper tops in butter. Add the ground meat, and cook until thoroughly browned. (If there seems to be too much liquid, remove some with a large spoon.) Add bread crumbs and mix. Add eggs and milk, which have been mixed together. If preferred, add more bread crumbs to make the mixture thicker. Add crumbled bacon and parsley. Season to taste with salt, pepper, and sauce. Spoon mixture into peppers so that each one is full (a little over the top.) On top of each pepper, make an X with bacon strips, and put a toothpick in each one. Place stuffed peppers in a casserole or pan with a small amount of water in the bottom. Bake at 350 degrees for approximately 40 minutes. These freeze well. Serves 8.

Carrie Winzy

## MEATLOAF

1 small onion, chopped
2 stalks celery, chopped
½ cup chopped bell pepper
2 small cloves garlic, minced
1 egg
½ cup evaporated milk
½ cup bread crumbs

1 to 1½ pounds ground chuck
Salt and pepper to taste
Flour
4 tablespoons oil
2 tablespoons flour
One 15-ounce can tomato sauce
1 sauce can water
1 tablespoon Worcestershire sauce

Chop onion, celery, bell pepper and mince garlic, and set aside. Mix egg, milk, and bread crumbs. Add meat to this, and mix thoroughly with hands. Add chopped ingredients and mix thoroughly. Add salt and pepper; mix; then shape into a loaf. Flour the loaf and brown it on all sides in hot oil in a large iron pot. Remove loaf. Make a roux by adding about 2 tablespoons flour to remaining oil. When flour is dark brown, add tomato sauce, water, and Worcestershire sauce. Return loaf to gravy. Bake uncovered at 350 degrees for 1 hour. Baste loaf at beginning and in middle of cooking time with the gravy. Serves 4 to 6.

Mrs. Jesse Coates, Jr.

## SPEEDY LASAGNA

One 8-ounce package macaroni
  dumplings
1 pound ground meat
2 tablespoons margarine
1 teaspoon salt
¼ teaspoon pepper

One 16-ounce jar Progresso Meat
  Flavored Spaghetti Sauce
2 tablespoons parsley flakes
1 teaspoon oregano
½ pint cottage cheese (optional)
One 6-ounce package Mozzarella
  cheese

Cook dumplings according to package directions. Preheat oven to 325 degrees. Brown ground meat in margarine. Add salt, pepper, spaghetti sauce, parsley flakes, and oregano. In a 2-quart casserole layer dumplings, meat sauce, cottage cheese, and Mozzarella cheese. You have enough to do this twice. Place uncovered in oven until cheese on top melts. This freezes well and serves 6.

Mrs. Raymond Post, Jr.

## PORK CHOP CASSEROLE

1 box Uncle Ben's Seasoned Long
  Grain and Wild Rice
One 10¾-ounce can cream of
  mushroom soup

One 16-ounce can fancy Chinese
  vegetables, drained
1½ cups water
4 to 6 pork chops
Salt and pepper

Mix the rice, soup, vegetables, and water; place in a greased 3-quart casserole. Arrange pork chops on top. Sprinkle with salt and pepper. Bake at 375 degrees for 1 hour and 20 minutes. Serves 4 to 6.

Mrs. Robert Singer

## ITALIAN MEAT ROLL

2 eggs, beaten
¾ cup soft bread crumbs
½ cup tomato juice
2 tablespoons snipped parsley
½ teaspoon oregano
1 teaspoon salt
½ teaspoon pepper

1 small clove garlic, minced
2 pounds lean ground meat
8 thin slices ham
6 ounces Mozzarella cheese, shredded
3 slices Mozzarella cheese, halved diagonally

Combine eggs, bread crumbs, tomato juice, parsley, oregano, salt, pepper, and garlic. Stir in meat. Mix well. On foil, pat meat mixture into a 12x10-inch rectangle. Arrange ham slices on top of meat, leaving small margin around edges. Sprinkle with shredded cheese. Starting from short end, roll up meat (like jellyroll) using foil to lift. Discard foil. Seal edges and ends by pinching meat together. Place in a 13x9x2-inch pan, seam side down. Bake at 350 degrees for 1 hour and 15 minutes or until done. (Center will be pink.) Place cheese wedges over top and return to oven for 5 minutes or until cheese melts. Serves 6 to 8.

Mrs. Gerald W. Shelton

## ITALIAN EGGPLANT

1 large eggplant, peeled and sliced
1 egg, slightly beaten with a little milk
Flour, seasoned
Cooking oil
1½ pounds ground beef
1 onion, chopped
One 1-pound 4-ounce can tomatoes

One 8-ounce can tomato sauce
1 tablespoon parsley
1 bay leaf
½ teaspoon thyme
1 pinch basil
1 teaspoon sugar
Salt and pepper to taste
½ pound Mozzarella cheese, sliced

Dip eggplant slices in egg and milk. Shake in seasoned flour. Sauté in oil until lightly browned. Meanwhile, brown meat and onion. Add tomatoes, tomato sauce, and seasonings. Simmer slowly for 30 minutes. Arrange alternate layers of eggplant, meat sauce, and cheese in a baking dish. Bake 30 minutes at 400 degrees.

Mrs. Jack B. Adger
Montgomery, Alabama

## ROMAN HOLIDAY

1 large onion, chopped
4 tablespoons bacon grease
1½ pounds ground beef
½ pound bulk sausage
One 16-ounce can tomatoes
One 10½-ounce can tomato soup
One 17-ounce can creamed corn

One 4-ounce can green chili peppers, chopped
One 2-ounce bottle stuffed olives, cut in half
½ cup chili sauce
1 pound yellow cheese, grated
2 pounds spaghetti

Sauté onion in bacon grease. Add ground beef and sausage; cook until done. Add tomatoes, soup, corn, chili pepper, olives, and ½ the cheese. Cook spaghetti, drain, and add to the mixture. Top with remainder of cheese. Cover and bake at 350 degrees for about 30 minutes or until cheese is melted. This freezes well and serves 15.

Mrs. Charles C. Brown, III

## LASAGNA

8 ounces lasagna noodles
1 cup finely chopped onion
1 clove garlic, minced
3 tablespoons olive or salad oil
1 pound ground meat
1½ teaspoons salt
¼ teaspoon pepper

1½ teaspoons oregano
2 cups tomatoes
One 8-ounce can tomato sauce
One 12-ounce carton creamed
   cottage cheese or Ricotta cheese
One 6-ounce package Mozzarella
   cheese, sliced thin
½ cup grated Parmesan cheese

Cook noodles according to package directions. Drain. Preheat electric skillet to 350 degrees. Brown onion and garlic lightly in oil. Add ground meat and cook until brown. Stir in seasonings and tomatoes. Reduce heat to 225 degrees. Arrange lasagna noodles on top of meat sauce, then cottage cheese and Mozzarella. Sprinkle Parmesan cheese on top. Make deep gashes through surface with sharp knife. Cover and cook 25 minutes. Uncover and cook 15 minutes until cheese melts and sauce is bubbly. Serves 8.

Oven cooking: In a 7x11x2-inch baking dish alternate layers of cooked meat sauce, cottage cheese, and lasagna noodles. Place slices of Mozzarella cheese on top; then sprinkle with Parmesan cheese. Bake at 350 degrees for 30 minutes. Serves 8.

Miss Harriet Babin

## STUFFED TUFOLI

2 tablespoons flour
2 tablespoons margarine
½ bunch green onions, chopped
¼ cup chopped parsley or
   dehydrated may be used
1 tablespoon Worcestershire sauce
1 tablespoon Italian seasoning mix
1 tablespoon salt
Dash red pepper to taste

1 pound ground meat
6 slices bread, toasted
2 cups water and 3 cubes bouillon
   or one 10¾-ounce can bouillon
   soup and 1 cup water
1 tablespoon Parmesan cheese
1 egg
One 6-ounce package tufoli
*Tomato gravy or white sauce

Brown flour in margarine. Add vegetables and seasonings. Cook until wilted. Add ground meat and brown about 15 minutes. Remove the excess grease. While meat mixture is cooking, moisten bread with the bouillon mixture. Add water if too dry. Mix the meat, bread, cheese, and egg. Cook about 10 to 15 minutes. Follow the directions on the tufoli package, but reduce cooking time. Cook about 10 minutes or until the pasta is still firm and easy to handle. Stuff each tufoli with the meat mixture. (At this point they freeze beautifully; just place on cookie sheet; freeze and package later in the desired quantity to be used—about 3 to 4 per person.) When ready to serve pour a small amount of tomato gravy in a rectangular casserole. Add the stuffed tufoli. Cover and bake 25 to 35 minutes in a 325 degree oven. Serve in separate containers and pour additional gravy over tufoli when serving. Serves 4 to 6.

*Use your favorite recipe or canned tomato gravy or, if you prefer, a simple white sauce may be used.

Mrs. Wray Edward Robinson

## MANICOTTI

Sauce:

| | |
|---|---|
| 1 package Lawry's spaghetti sauce mix | One 8-ounce can tomato sauce |
| One 1-pound 13-ounce can tomatoes | 2 tablespoons garlic spread |
| | 1½ teaspoon seasoned salt |

Mix all ingredients, cover, and simmer for 20 minutes.

Stuffing:

| | |
|---|---|
| 1 pound ground beef | 1 tablespoon salad oil |
| ½ cup chopped green pepper | 8 ounces Mozzarella cheese, diced |

Brown beef and green pepper in oil. Remove from heat and stir in diced cheese.

Manicotti:

1 package of 14 manicotti shells

Cook shells in boiling salted water for 10 minutes. Drain and cover with cold water to prevent sticking. Stuff manicotti with meat and cheese mixture. Place ½ the sauce in a casserole. Add stuffed manicotti and cover with remaining sauce. Sprinkle with Parmesan if desired. Bake for 30 minutes at 375 degrees. Serves 6.

Mrs. Rolf R. Schroeder

## TUFOLI

Two 6-ounce packages tufoli

Stuffing:

| | |
|---|---|
| 2 pounds ground meat | Olive oil |
| 2 onions, grated | One 10-ounce package frozen |
| Salt | chopped spinach |
| 4 pods garlic, pressed | 1½ cups grated Romano cheese |
| Red pepper | 1 cups bread crumbs |
| Black pepper | 2 eggs, beaten |
| | 2 tablespoons oregano |

Cook tufoli. Rinse, drain, and let cool. Brown meat, drain, and mix with onions, salt, garlic, red and black pepper. Sauté until done in olive oil. Cook spinach and drain. Add to meat mixture and cool. Add Romano cheese and bread crumbs to hold it together. Add eggs and oregano. Stuff tufoli and place in two 7x11x2-inch casseroles.

Sauce:

| | |
|---|---|
| 3 onions, chopped | Two 16-ounce cans tomato purée |
| 8 pods garlic, finely chopped | 2 teaspoons oregano |
| 5 stalks celery, chopped | Salt |
| 5 tablespoons olive oil | Pepper |

Sauté onions, garlic, and celery in olive oil. Add purée, oregano, salt, and pepper. Simmer until seasonings are done. Pour sauce over stuffed tufoli and sprinkle with Romano cheese. Cover and bake at 350 degrees for 45 minutes. Remove cover, increase heat to 450 degrees and bake 10 minutes longer.

Mrs. Albert J. Kendrick

## MISS MAUDE'S SPAGHETTI CASSEROLE

1 large onion, chopped
1 or 2 cloves garlic, minced
¼ cup chopped bell pepper
2 tablespoons cooking oil
2 pounds ground beef
One 6-ounce can tomato paste
2 cups water

1 tablespoon chili powder
Salt and pepper to taste
One 12-ounce package spaghetti
One 13-ounce can evaporated milk
3 eggs, beaten
¼ pound American or Velveeta
cheese, sliced or grated

Brown onion, garlic, and bell pepper in oil. Add ground beef and cook until red is gone. Add tomato paste and water. Add seasonings and let simmer while preparing spaghetti. Boil spaghetti and drain. In separate bowl, beat milk and eggs together with fork. Grease two 1½-quart casseroles or one 3-quart casserole. Layer spaghetti and meat sauce until all is used. Put cheese on top. Pour milk mixture over all. Bake at 350 degrees for 30 minutes or until cheese is melted and mixture is bubbly. This freezes well and serves 8.

Mrs. Norman Saurage, III

## ITALIAN SUPPER

One 8-ounce package flat
broad noodles
3 medium onions
2 bell peppers
1½ pounds ground round
1½ tablespoons cooking oil
2 tablespoons chili powder
Salt and pepper to taste
One 10-ounce can tomatoes, drained

One 8-ounce can tomato sauce
One 6-ounce can tomato paste
One 4½-ounce can black olives,
pitted and drained
One 7-ounce can niblet corn,
drained
One 4-ounce can whole mushrooms,
drained
½ pound sharp cheese, grated

Cook noodles according to package directions, drain and set aside. In blender, chop onions and peppers, saving the juices. In a Dutch oven brown the meat, onions, and peppers in cooking oil. Add chili powder, salt and pepper, tomatoes, tomato sauce, and tomato paste. Simmer for 15 minutes. Add noodles, olives, corn, and mushrooms. Add the juices only if the mixture is too dry. Pour into a 2-quart casserole. Top with grated cheese and bake for 1 hour at 350 degrees. Serves 8 to 10.

Mrs. Eugene Croxton

## QUICK CHILI

1 tablespoon shortening
½ cup chopped onions
1 pound ground beef
1 green pepper, chopped
One 10½-ounce can tomato soup

1 teaspoon salt
4 teaspoons (or more) chili powder
⅛ teaspoon pepper
Dash ground red pepper
One or two 16-ounce cans red
kidney beans

Melt shortening in a heavy skillet. Add onions, and cook until brown. Add ground beef, and brown. Stir frequently, so that there will be no lumps of meat. Add remaining ingredients. Heat mixture thoroughly, and serve piping hot. Serves 6.

Mrs. Heidel Brown

## MEAT BALLS AND SPAGHETTI

1 pound ground veal
⅓ cup grated Romano cheese
⅔ cup grated American cheese
2½ slices bread, dampened
1 bunch green onions, chopped
3 eggs, beaten
Salt and red pepper to taste
1½ teaspoons sugar

4 tablespoons cooking oil
2 large stalks celery, minced
2 cloves garlic, minced
One 6-ounce can tomato paste
One 8-ounce can tomato sauce
1½ cups water
½ teaspoon sweet basil leaves
3 bay leaves

Mix meat, cheeses, bread, ½ of the green onions, and eggs. Season with salt, red pepper, and ½ teaspoon sugar. Form into balls and fry slowly in oil in iron skillet. Remove meat balls. Add remaining green onions, celery, and garlic; fry until limp. Add tomato paste and tomato sauce; cook down some until red turns to dark orange. Add water to mixture. Season sauce with salt, red pepper, and 1 teaspoon sugar. Put meat balls in gravy; add basil and bay leaves. Allow to simmer very slowly for one hour, covered. Serve over spaghetti. This freezes well and serves 6.

Mrs. Norman Saurage, Jr.

## TACOS

1 pound ground chuck
1 large onion, chopped
2 teaspoons ground cumin seed
1 teaspoon salt
1 teaspoon garlic powder
¼ teaspoon black pepper

Two 8-ounce cans Rotel tomatoes,
 or one 16-ounce can tomatoes,
 with 8 drops red pepper
 seasoning
Taco shells
1½ cups grated Cheddar cheese
1½ cups shredded lettuce

Lightly brown meat and onion in a large saucepan. Add seasonings and tomatoes. Simmer uncovered for 30 minutes, stirring occasionally. Fill taco shells with meat and top with cheese and lettuce. Makes 10 to 12 tacos.

Mrs. Hubert Waguespack

## BLACKEYED PEAS AND SAUSAGE JAMBALAYA

2 pounds chopped white onions
2 bunches green onions, chopped
1 large bell pepper, chopped
5 cloves garlic chopped
1 cup chopped parsley
3 pounds salt meat, boiled once,
 cut in small pieces

3 pounds smoked hot sausage,
 cooked and cut in bite
 size pieces
¾ pound dried blackeyed peas,
 boiled until half done
3 pounds uncooked rice
12 cups water

Sauté onions, pepper, garlic and parsley. Cook until limp. Add salt meat, sausage, blackeyed peas, and rice. Season to taste. Add 12 cups water. Bring to a boil; mix well and cover tightly. Cook on lowest heat for 45 minutes. Do not remove cover during this time. Remove cover for 5 to 10 minutes before serving. Serves 20 to 25.

Mrs. William S. Slack

## DUTCH OVEN DELIGHT

2 pounds lean ground round
3 tablespoons cooking oil
8 ounces elbow spaghetti
1 large onion, chopped
¼ cup finely chopped bell pepper
¼ cup finely chopped celery
   (optional)
¼ cup finely chopped green onion
   (optional)

One 16-ounce can tomato sauce with
   tomato bits
One 16-ounce can stewed tomatoes
1½ to 2 cups water
2 tablespoons Worcestershire sauce
1 teaspoon seasoned salt
8 drops Tabasco sauce
½ teaspoon seasoned pepper
½ teaspoon celery salt
Two 16-ounce cans kidney beans

In large Dutch oven brown meat in cooking oil. Drain and retain liquid. Return 3 tablespoons of liquid to pot and sauté spaghetti, onion, bell pepper, celery, and green onion for about 5 minutes, stirring constantly. Return meat to pot, add tomato sauce, stewed tomatoes, and water. Mix together. Then add the remainder of the ingredients, except for the kidney beans, and mix thoroughly. Cover and simmer for 25 minutes, stirring frequently to prevent sticking. If ingredients appear a bit dry during the cooking, more water may be added. Add kidney beans and simmer for an additional 10 minutes. This freezes well and will serve 8 to 10.

Mrs. Everett L. Wright

## "KIDS LOVE IT" CASSEROLE

1 to 1½ pounds ground beef
1 medium onion, chopped
1 clove garlic, minced
1 tablespoon salad oil
One 10-ounce package frozen chopped
   spinach
Water
One 16-ounce can spaghetti sauce
   with mushrooms
One 8-ounce can tomato sauce

One 6-ounce can tomato paste
½ teaspoon salt
Dash pepper
One 7-ounce package shell
   macaroni, cooked
1 cup shredded sharp American
   cheese
½ cup soft bread crumbs
2 eggs, well beaten
¼ cup salad oil

Brown beef, onion, and garlic in oil. Cook spinach according to package directions. Drain, reserving liquid. Add enough water to make 1 cup liquid. Combine liquid with spaghetti sauce, tomato sauce, tomato paste, salt, and pepper. Stir into meat mixture, and simmer for 10 minutes. Combine spinach with macaroni, cheese, bread crumbs, eggs, and oil. Spread in a 13x9x2-inch baking dish. Top with meat sauce. Bake at 350 degrees for 30 minutes. Before serving, let casserole stand for 10 minutes. This prevents the cheese from being stringy. Serves 8 to 10.

Mrs. Neel Garland

## CHILI CON CARNE

4 tablespoons butter
2 tablespoons salad oil
2 large onions, finely chopped
2 cloves garlic, minced
2 pounds ground beef
2 or 3 tablespoons chili powder
1½ cups beef broth

4 to 5 fresh tomatoes, peeled and
  coarsely chopped (or 3 cups
  canned tomatoes)
Two 15-ounce cans kidney beans,
  drained
1 teaspoon celery seed
1½ teaspoons cumin seed
1 good pinch of oregano
1 good pinch of cayenne pepper
Salt to taste

Heat butter and salad oil in a large, heavy pan. Add the onions and garlic, and cook over moderate heat until onions are soft, but not brown. Add beef and continue to cook until meat has lost its color. Stir in the chili powder (more, if you like it hot), tomatoes, beef broth, kidney beans, and all the seasonings. Continue cooking over very low heat for 1½ to 2 hours. Stir occasionally. If moisture dries out, add more broth. Chili con Carne should be wet, but not soupy. Taste for seasoning. Serve with tortillas, which should be browned on a hot griddle on both sides. Serves 8.

Mrs. E. W. Brousseau

## HOT TAMALE PIE

**Meat Filling:**

1½ pounds ground meat
1 clove garlic, minced
1 large onion, chopped
One 8-ounce can tomato sauce

4 tablespoons chili powder (more
  if desired)
1 cup pimiento stuffed olives,
  sliced
½ cup water

Brown meat with garlic and onions. Add remaining ingredients and cook for 10 to 15 minutes. This mixture should be moist enough to spread.

**Mush:**

3 cups water
1 beef bouillon cube
1 teaspoon salt

Dash garlic salt
1 cup water
1 cup cornmeal
Paprika

Heat 3 cups water in saucepan with bouillon cube, salt and garlic salt. Mix 1 cup cold water with cornmeal. Pour meal and water into boiling water, stirring constantly (this lumps if you do not stir as it is added). Cook until thick. When mush has thickened, pour ½ into casserole. Let it cool enough to become firm, then add meat filling and pour remaining mush over this. Sprinkle top with paprika. Bake in a 2-quart casserole at 350 degrees until very hot (about 30 minutes). This may be made ahead and frozen before it is baked. Serves 6.

Mrs. Robert M. Slowey

## GRILLADES

2½ to 3 pounds veal rounds, sliced
or slivered (sirloin tip or round
steak may be used)
5 tablespoons bacon drippings
3 tablespoons flour
3 medium onions, chopped
6 green onions, chopped
2 medium bell peppers, chopped
2 cloves garlic, chopped
⅓ bunch celery with leaves, chopped

⅓ bunch parsley, chopped
2 cups canned tomatoes
2 cups beef or veal stock (broth)
1 tablespoon or more
Worcestershire sauce
2 teaspoons Kitchen Bouquet
(optional)
1 small bay leaf
½ teaspoon thyme, crushed
Salt and pepper to taste
Burgundy (optional)

Brown meat in bacon drippings. Remove to a platter. Add flour to drippings and stir until a rich brown. Add vegetables (except tomatoes) and sauté until transparent. Add meat and all remaining ingredients. Cover and simmer for 3 hours, adding water as necessary. (You may add burgundy instead of water). Remove bay leaf before serving. Serve over hot grits, garlic grits, rice, or potatoes. Serves 10 to 12.

Mrs. Dean M. Mosely

## VEAL SCALLOPINI

One 2-pound veal steak, ⅜ inch
thick, cut in strips for
scallopini
Flour
3 tablespoons butter
3 tablespoons olive oil
1 cup sliced mushrooms

½ cup finely chopped green
onion tops
1 cup beef bouillon or consommé
3 to 4 teaspoons Italian seasoning
Dash celery salt
½ cup Marsala wine (cream sherry
can be substituted)
¾ cup olives, sliced

Dredge veal in flour and pound. Brown meat in butter and oil. Turn meat. Add mushrooms, onion tops, bouillon, and seasonings. Cover and simmer for about 35 to 40 minutes, stirring occasionally. If mixture gets too thick, add water. Add wine and olives, stir, and simmer for another 10 minutes. (If you wish, this may be fixed in advance and warmed in oven at 350 degrees for 35 to 40 minutes before serving. Add a little more wine before putting in oven). Serves 4.

Mrs. Heidel Brown

## EASY VEAL IN MUSHROOM WINE SAUCE

2 pounds veal
¼ cup oil
Salt
One 10½-ounce can mushroom soup

One 4-ounce can mushrooms,
undrained
½ cup sherry or white wine
Pinch of sage

Cut veal into serving size pieces. Brown in oil. Place in greased casserole. Sprinkle lightly with salt. Make a sauce of soup, undrained mushrooms, sherry, and sage. Pour over veal. Cover and cook 1 hour at 325 degrees. Serve with rice or noodles. Serves 4.

Mrs. Cheney C. Joseph, Jr.

## HOT SAUSAGE AND SHRIMP JAMBALAYA

6 pounds hot link sausage, cut in
½ inch pieces
2 large onions, chopped
1 cup parsley
4 pods garlic, chopped, or
garlic powder
7½ cups water

One 16-ounce can tomatoes
(optional) or equivalent amount
of water
1 teaspoon thyme
Salt to taste
6 cups rice
3 pounds peeled shrimp
(may use frozen)

Put sausage in large, heavy iron skillet and cook. Add onions and let cook with sausage until onions are clear. Add parsley and garlic. Cook for a few minutes until parsley is limp. Add water, tomatoes (mashed with spoon), thyme, and salt. Bring to a boil. (May be prepared in advance|to this point.) If made in advance, bring this mixture to a boil again. Add rice and shrimp. Stir once and put heat on low and cover. Do not stir again. You may check the mixture and lift with fork if it is sticking. If it looks like more liquid is needed, add another ½ cup water. To cook the rice takes approximately 30 minutes or until the grains of rice are tender and separate easily. It can be held until time to serve. Serves 40.

Mrs. Robert L. diBenedetto

## QUICK AND DELICIOUS JAMBALAYA

1 pound ground beef, browned
1½ pounds peeled shrimp
1½ cups raw rice, washed
One 10½-ounce can cream of chicken
soup

One 10½-ounce can onion soup
1 onion, chopped
½ cup chopped bell pepper
1 stalk celery, chopped
Salt and pepper to taste
Tabasco sauce to taste

Mix all ingredients together in a large bowl. Place mixture in a 2-quart casserole. Bake covered in a 350 degree oven for 1½ hours or until done. Serves 6.

Mrs. L. Sonny Fontenot

## SCALLOP OF VEAL IN LEMON BUTTER

6 veal cutlets (pounded to
¼ inch thick)
Salt and pepper to taste
1 egg, slightly beaten

2 cups fresh bread crumbs
3 tablespoons butter
1½ tablespoons oil
2 tablespoons lemon juice
2 tablespoons parsley

Salt and pepper meat; dip in beaten egg, then in the bread crumbs. Sauté in hot butter and oil mixture. (The oil is to prevent the butter from burning). When the meat is browned on both sides, set aside on warm platter. Add lemon juice to the butter in the skillet and stir until slightly thickened. (The butter may have to be replenished.) Add parsley and pour over veal. Serves 6.

Mrs. Charles F. Duchein, Jr.

## MUSHROOM VEAL SAVORY

1½ pounds veal cutlets
2 tablespoons olive oil
1 clove garlic, minced
One 4-ounce can sliced mushrooms,
  undrained

1 bouillon cube
One 8-ounce can small white onions,
  undrained
1 tablespoon cornstarch
2 tablespoons sherry

Pound meat and cut into small pieces. In a deep skillet sauté meat in olive oil. Add garlic, onions, mushrooms, and bouillon cube. Make a paste of the cornstarch and water. Gradually add to the meat. Add the sherry, cover and simmer for 1 hour or until the meat is tender. Serves 4.

Mrs. A. N. Palmer

## VEAL STROGANOFF BAKE

6 slices bacon
2 pounds veal, cut in large bite
  size pieces
2 large yellow onions, chopped

1 pound fresh mushrooms, sliced
2 cups sour cream
1 cup white cooking wine
1 cup white rice, uncooked

Cook bacon and set aside. Brown veal in bacon grease and remove from pan. Brown onions in pan. Combine veal, onions, and mushrooms. Add the sour cream mixed with wine. Cover and cook slowly on very low heat on top of stove for 2 hours. Stir occasionally. Cook rice, and combine with above mixture in layers. Refrigerate. When ready to bake, crumble the cooked bacon on top and bake for 1 hour at 350 degrees or until piping hot. Do not cover. Serves 6 to 8.

Mrs. Charles J. Mittendorf

## SWEET-PUNGENT PORK LOIN

One 4- to 6-pound boneless pork
  loin roast
3 large cloves garlic, crushed
6 tablespoons soy sauce
½ cup catsup
¼ cup lemon juice

½ teaspoon pepper
2 cloves garlic, cut into 6
  slivers each
18 whole cloves
2 cups apricot preserves
Spiced crab apples

The day before serving, combine crushed garlic, soy sauce, catsup, lemon juice, and pepper to use as a marinade. With a sharp knife make 12 small cuts (about ½ inch deep) in the fat surface of roast. Insert slivers of garlic. Stud the remaining fat surface with whole cloves. Place pork roast in a 13x9x2-inch baking dish and cover with the marinade. Cover dish with foil and refrigerate until approximately 3 hours prior to serving. Preheat oven to 325 degrees. Remove roast from marinade and place on rack (fat side up) in a shallow open roasting pan. Cook 1½ hours. Heat apricot preserves until melted. Remove roast from oven and brush on ½ cup heated preserves. Return pork to oven and continue roasting 20 to 30 minutes. Remove from oven. Transfer to large platter. Garnish with spiced crab apples and serve with remaining apricot preserve sauce. Serves 6 generously.

Mrs. Charles Whitehurst

## SAKIR'S SHISH-KABOBS

One 4-pound leg of lamb
2 large onions
2 bay leaves

4 tablespoons olive oil
1 teaspoon garlic salt
1 lemon, thinly sliced

Remove bone, skin and fat from leg of lamb. Cut into 1- or 1½-inch cubes. Grate onions over meat and marinate in bay leaves, olive oil, and garlic salt for 24 to 36 hours. Thread meat on skewers, ½ inch apart, with thin slices of lemon separating each piece of meat. Grill over charcoal for about 15 minutes. Remove from skewers at the table and serve with plain rice or rice pilaf. Sliced green peppers, tomatoes, and onion rings may be served as a garniture, but these must be grilled on separate skewers. If they are included on meat skewers, the meat becomes tough. Serves 6.

Mrs. Egi V. Fasce

## LAMB SHANKS

6 lamb shanks
Bacon grease
One 10½-ounce can cream of
   asparagus soup

2 cups bouillon
2 to 3 pods garlic, minced
1 tablespoon Kitchen Bouquet
1 tablespoon Worcestershire sauce
Salt and pepper to taste

In a large skillet or Dutch oven, brown lamb shanks in hot bacon fat. Remove shanks, and drain fat. Add soup, bouillon, garlic, Kitchen Bouquet, Worcestershire sauce, salt and pepper. Mix well and add meat. Transfer to a large covered pot or a 3-quart casserole and bake at 325 degrees for 1½ to 2 hours (until meat almost falls off bone). Serve over rice. Serves 6 to 8.

Mrs. Robert Bujol

## GERMAN STUFFED PORK FILETS

1 pound pork sausage
2 medium onions, finely chopped
2 small apples, finely chopped
¼ cup apple sauce
½ cup bread crumbs
4½ pounds boneless pork, cut
   into about 30 thin filets

Salt
Pepper
Toothpicks to hold filets
Flour
Small amount margarine
½ of a fifth of sauterne
1 cup water

Crumble sausage in skillet, and sauté with onions over a low heat. Add apples and apple sauce and enough bread crumbs to hold dressing together. When dressing is done, set aside. Season pork filets with salt and pepper. Place 1 tablespoon of dressing on each filet; roll up and hold in place with a toothpick. Roll filets in flour and brown in small amount of margarine over medium fire. Place filets in roasting pan and cover with sauterne and water. Cover pan and cook 2 hours in a 300 degree oven. Add wine or water as needed. Serves 10.

Mrs. W. A. Whitley

## BAKED LAMB CHOPS

| | |
|---|---|
| 2 tablespoons butter | 1 tablespoon water |
| 1 tablespoon or more minced onion | 1½ teaspoons flour |
| ½ cup sliced mushrooms | Salt and pepper |
| 3 tablespoons bottled chili sauce | 4 to 6 lamb chops |

In a 7-inch skillet melt butter. Add onions, mushrooms, and chili sauce. Simmer for 5 minutes. Add flour and water and stir. Salt and pepper chops and place in a 12-inch baking dish. Pour sauce over chops and bake at 400 degrees for 30 to 35 minutes. Serves 4 to 6, depending on size of chops.

Mrs. Dean M. Mosely

## BAKED LAMB CHOPS WITH RICE

| | |
|---|---|
| 4 loin lamb chops, each 2 inches thick | 2 carrots, cut in matchlike strips |
| ½ lemon, sliced wafer thin | 10 small white onions, peeled |
| ¾ cup raw rice, washed | 1 cup dry white wine |
| 1½ cups beef or chicken broth | ¼ teaspoon dried marjoram |
| | Salt and pepper to taste |

Combine chops with lemon slices and refrigerate until ready to cook. Preheat oven to 350 degrees. Combine rice, broth, carrots, onions, and wine in an ovenproof casserole. Add chops, discarding lemon. Bring to a boil on top of stove. Cover and bake for 30 minutes. Season with salt, pepper and marjoram. Stir, cover, and bake 30 minutes longer. Serves 4.

Mrs. Ralph Braun

## PORK CHOPS AND TURNIPS

| | |
|---|---|
| 4 to 6 pork chops | 1 pod garlic, chopped |
| Salt and pepper | 4 young turnips, peeled and cut in large pieces |
| Flour | |
| 2 tablespoons oil | 1½ cups water |
| 1 onion, chopped | 1½ teaspoons Worcestershire sauce |

Salt and pepper chops. Coat with flour. Brown in oil in a Dutch oven. Remove chops. Sauté onion and garlic. Return chops to Dutch oven and add turnips, water and Worcestershire sauce. Cover and simmer for 1 hour. Serve turnip gravy over rice. Serves 4 to 6.

Mrs. E. Kent Caldwell

## CAZAYOUX SMOTHERED PORK CHOPS

| | |
|---|---|
| 6 pork chops | 1 teaspoon chopped parsley |
| Salt and pepper | ½ cup sour cream |
| 1 can cream of mushroom soup | One 3-ounce can French fried onions |
| ½ cup water | |

Brown chops in skillet and sprinkle with salt and pepper. Place chops in casserole. In skillet, heat soup with the water. Add parsley, sour cream, and ½ can of onions. Mix well; pour over pork chops. Cover and bake at 350 degrees for 1 hour. Remove cover and sprinkle remaining onions on top. Return to oven for 5 minutes. Serves 6.

Mrs. Michael J. Rollinger

## PORK CHOPS INDONESIAN

Six 1-inch loin pork chops
Salt and pepper to taste
3 tablespoons shortening or oil
One 16-ounce can sliced peaches
2 tablespoons brown sugar
1 tablespoon grated onion

2 tablespoons soy sauce
1 teaspoon ginger
⅛ teaspoon dry mustard
⅛ teaspoon garlic powder
1 large bell pepper
Cooked rice

Season chops with salt and pepper. Melt shortening in large skillet; brown chops on both sides, and remove from heat. Drain all but 2 tablespoons of fat from skillet. Drain peaches, reserve syrup. Blend syrup, sugar, onion, soy sauce, ginger, mustard, and garlic powder. Pour over chops. Cover and simmer for 30 minutes. Meanwhile, cut bell pepper into slivers. Add with peach slices to chops. Simmer 5 minutes longer. Serve over rice. Serves 6.

Mrs. Dean M. Mosely

## SAUSAGE CASSEROLE

1 pound sausage, hot or mild
1 pound ground chuck
½ cup chopped celery
1 cup minced onion
½ cup chopped bell pepper

Salt and pepper
2 envelopes dry noodle soup
1 cup raw rice
5 cups hot water
½ cup slivered almonds

Brown meat. Add vegetables, salt, and pepper; sauté. Drain. Add soup and rice. Place ingredients in a greased 3-quart shallow pyrex baking dish. Pour in hot water, and stir well. Cover casserole, and bake 45 minutes in a 350 degree oven. Remove cover, add almonds, and bake an additional 15 minutes. Serves 10 to 12.

Mrs. Lloyd Willis

## SAUSAGE, MUSHROOM AND WILD RICE CASSEROLE

1½ pounds bulk sausage
2 cups wild rice, cooked
One 4-ounce can mushrooms, drained

One 10¼-ounce can cream of
mushroom soup
½ cup whole milk
Salt and pepper

Brown sausage. Pour off grease. Crumble. Combine sausage, cooked wild rice, and mushrooms in a 2-quart casserole. Mix soup and milk. Add to casserole. Salt and pepper lightly. Mix well. Bake in a 350 degree oven for 45 minutes. Serves 5 or 6.

Mrs. Dennis Goldston

## SAUSAGE SAUCE PIQUANT

1 pound smoked sausage, sliced
2 tablespoons cooking oil
2 tablespoons flour
1 medium onion, chopped

½ bell pepper, chopped
One 16-ounce can tomatoes
2 cups water
Salt and pepper to taste

Brown sausage, drain well, and set aside. Make a roux by browning oil and flour, stirring constantly. Add onion and bell pepper; sauté. Add sausage, tomatoes, water, salt, and pepper. Cover and simmer at least 1 hour. Serve over rice. Serves 4 to 6.

Mrs. Lloyd T. Leake

## CHICKEN FRIED LIVER

1½ pounds (6 slices) beef
   or calf liver
3 tablespoons lemon juice
¼ cup flour
1 teaspoon salt
¼ teaspoon pepper
Dash basil

⅓ cup milk
¼ cup minced onion
2 eggs, well beaten
1 clove garlic, minced
1½ to 2 cups cracker crumbs
   or Chick-Fri
½ cup cooking oil

Sprinkle liver with lemon juice. Combine flour, salt, pepper, and basil. Dredge liver in flour mixture. Combine milk, onion, eggs, and garlic. Dip floured slices in egg mixture; then dip them in crumbs. Fry quickly on both sides in hot fat. Serves 5 to 6.

Mrs. Douglas Salmon, III

## WIENERS AND HOT SAUCE

¼ cup Worcestershire sauce
½ cup butter
1 cup catsup

1 cup vinegar
Salt and pepper to taste
Red pepper to taste
1 package wieners

Mix above ingredients (except wieners) and place in top of a double boiler. Boil weiners about 5 minutes and place in sauce. Let stand all day or as long as possible. Before serving turn on heat under double boiler and let simmer about an hour. Serve on hot dog buns.

Miss Billie Coates

## COUNTRY SPARERIBS

4 large spare ribs
½ cup soy sauce

1 teaspoon ginger
Garlic salt and pepper to taste
Honey

Parboil ribs for about 20 or 30 minutes, depending on size. Remove from water and pour a mixture of soy sauce, ginger, garlic salt, and pepper over ribs.(Baste with this mixture.) Bake at 300 degrees, uncovered, turning once. When done, cover top side with honey and run under broiler until browned. Serves 2.

Mrs. Charles F. Duchein

## HAM AND RICE CASSEROLE

¾ cup rice
½ cup chopped onions
2 tablespoons cooking oil

2 cups cooked ham
1 cup green beans
One 10¾-ounce can beef broth
½ cup water

Cook rice and onions in oil until lightly browned, stirring frequently. Add ham, beans, broth, and water. Heat to boiling. Turn into 2-quart casserole. Cover and bake at 350 degrees for 45 minutes, or until rice is done. Stir just before serving. Serves 5 to 6.

Mrs. J. Noland Singletary

## HAM AND EGG PIE

| | |
|---|---|
| 4 large eggs, beaten | ½ cup milk |
| ¼ teaspoon pepper | 2 cups cooked ham, cubed |
| ¼ teaspoon baking powder | 1 cup grated Cheddar cheese |
| | One 9-inch pie shell, unbaked |

Beat the eggs slightly. Add remaining ingredients, and mix well. Pour into unbaked shell. Bake at 425 degrees for 35 minutes or until inserted knife comes out clean. *This is an excellent way to use any ham leftovers and is delicious hot or cold.* Serves 6.

Mrs. Stephen Glagola

## HAM SAUCE

| | |
|---|---|
| One 10-ounce jar pineapple preserves | One 10-ounce jar apple jelly |
| 4 teaspoons dry mustard in water to make paste | One 5-ounce jar horseradish (makes sauce very hot; may use mustard with horseradish) |

Heat ingredients in saucepan until well blended. Cool to serve as a dip for ham or ham sandwiches. Keeps for months in refrigerator.

Mrs. John Holland
Jackson, Mississippi

## MUSTARD SAUCE I

| | |
|---|---|
| 4 tablespoons sugar | ½ cup vinegar |
| 4 tablespoons dry mustard | ½ cup cream |
| 3 eggs, beaten | Pinch salt |

Combine ingredients and cook in a double boiler, stirring occasionally, until thick.

Mrs. E. W. Clark

## HOT PINEAPPLE CASSEROLE

| | |
|---|---|
| One 20-ounce can sliced pineapple | Cracker crumbs |
| 1 cup sugar | Butter |

Drain pineapple juice and reserve. Cut pineapple into chunks. Combine sugar and pinapple juice; boil until it makes a light syrup. Place pineapple in a 9-inch casserole and cover with cracker crumbs that have been crumbled by hand. Dot with butter. Pour syrup over this and bake for 1 hour at 300 degrees. *This is particularly good with ham or pork chops.* Serves 4 to 6.

Miss Billie Coates

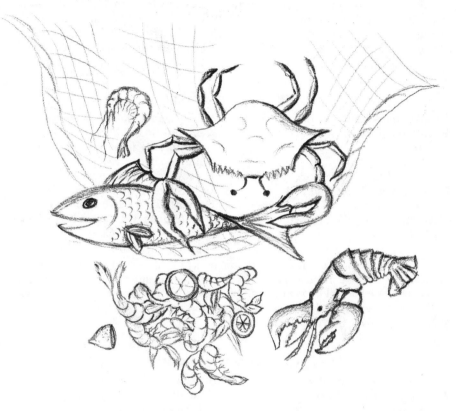

## SEAFOODS

From lakes, rivers, bayous and the gulf, the seafoods of Louisiana are harvested each year to be prepared in dozens of tantalizing ways by Louisiana cooks, many of whom have a special touch with seafood. They use an inspired combination of ingredients, a judicious choice of seasonings, and a flair for making sauces that enhance but don't smother these delicate foods. Many traditional recipes have come to Louisiana from Europe and undergone a subtle change because of local foods and tastes. Other famous Louisiana seafood dishes have been invented right in our own kitchens and also by our great chefs. Some dishes have been born of necessity while others evolved as a result of the sheer joy of experimenting.

## CRABMEAT IN RAMEKINS

1 pound white lump crabmeat
1 cup butter

Tabasco sauce, dash
per ramekin

Handle crabmeat lightly, do not break or pack. In each ramekin, put crabmeat and top with a lump of butter (1 cup butter to 12 ramekins) and a dash of Tabasco sauce. Place ramekins in large pan with a little water on oven shelf in preheated 350 degree oven until butter melts. Serve on luncheon plate with stuffed pepper, stuffed mirliton or stuffed tomato. Serve with bread and butter or cheese sandwiches. Serves 12 in medium ramekins.

Mrs. H. Payne Breazeale, Sr.

## CRABMEAT SUISSE

4 tablespoons butter or margarine
4 tablespoons flour
1¼ cups milk
1 egg yolk, beaten
1½ teaspoons salt
4 tablespoons finely chopped
green onions
4 tablespoons finely chopped
parsley

3 tablespoons butter or margarine
¼ pound Swiss cheese, grated
(preferably imported, as it does
not rope)
½ teaspoon lemon juice
½ teaspoon grated lemon rind
1 pound fresh claw crabmeat
1 tablespoon Worcestershire sauce
Tabasco sauce to taste
Paprika

Make cream sauce with first five ingredients. In skillet, soften onions and parsley in melted butter and add to cream sauce. Blend in three-fourths of the cheese. Add other ingredients. Fill 5 ramekins, sprinkling the remaining cheese on top. Bake at 350 degrees until bubbly and light brown on top. Garnish with parsley, thin lemon slices and paprika. Serves 5.

Mrs. Frank W. Middleton, Jr.

## CRABMEAT MOUSSE

2 envelopes unflavored gelatin
2 tablespoons dry sherry
1 cup boiling chicken broth
2 egg yolks
1 cup heavy cream
3 tablespoons lemon juice
1½ to 2 cups crabmeat,
picked over

5 drops Tabasco sauce
2 small stalks celery, cut up
2 tablespoons scallions, chopped
4 sprigs parsley
¼ teaspoon marjoram
¼ teaspoon thyme
½ cup mayonnaise, preferably
homemade

Place gelatin and sherry in blender and let sit 2 minutes. Add chicken broth and blend at low speed 10 seconds. While continuing at low speed, add egg yolks, cream, lemon juice, Tabasco sauce, crabmeat, celery, scallions, parsley and seasonings. Blend until smooth and well mixed. If size of container allows, add mayonnaise and blend 10 seconds. If not, pour crab mixture into mayonnaise, using wire whisk to mix. Pour into oiled 6-cup mold and chill. Unmold onto platter and garnish with lettuce, olives, or other garnishes. Serves 10 to 12 if used as an appetizer.

Mrs. Ralph F. Braun

## SHERRIED CRABMEAT

½ pound mushrooms
3 tablespoons butter
3 tablespoons flour
1 cup chicken stock or bouillon
½ cup cream
1 pound lump crabmeat

½ cup Parmesan cheese
½ teaspoon salt
¼ teaspoon pepper
¼ teaspoon paprika
2 tablespoons dry sherry
6 patty shells

Sauté mushrooms in a little butter and set aside. Melt butter and stir in flour until well blended. Stir in chicken stock and cream. When sauce is boiling, add crabmeat and mushrooms. When it comes to a second boil, add cheese and seasonings. Remove from fire. Add sherry and serve in patty shells. Serves 6.

Mrs. Dean M. Mosely

## STUFFED CRAB

4 strips bacon
1 medium onion
3 ribs celery
3 slices bread
1¾ cups bread crumbs
1 cup water
1 pound crabmeat
3 green onions and tops

10 sprigs parsley
1 clove garlic
3 eggs, well beaten
1 tablespoon salt
1 scant teaspoon black pepper
½ teaspoon red pepper or
    to taste
Bread crumbs for topping

Grind the bacon, onion and celery. Brown in a large skillet. Add bread and bread crumbs moistened with water. Add crabmeat and cook over a low fire. Grind the green onions, parsley and garlic. Add to the beaten eggs. Add the salt and peppers. Pour this mixture into the crabmeat mixture and mix thoroughly. Spoon into crab shells or ramekins. Sprinkle lightly with bread crumbs and top with a dot of butter. Bake at 350 degrees for 30 minutes or until golden brown. May be baked as a casserole. Serves 8.

Mrs. B. W. Flanagan, Sr.

## BAKED CRAB AND SHRIMP

1 pound lump crabmeat
1 pound peeled medium shrimp, cooked
½ cup chopped green pepper
½ cup chopped green onions
½ cup chopped celery

1 cup mayonnaise
3 tablespoons Worcestershire sauce
1 tablespoon Tabasco sauce
4 tablespoons lemon juice
Buttered bread crumbs

Combine all ingredients in buttered 1½-quart casserole or 6 buttered seafood shells. Top with buttered bread crumbs. Bake at 350 degrees for 25 to 30 minutes or until bubbly hot. This may be made early in the day and cooked at the last minute. Serves 4 to 6.

Mrs. Cheney C. Joseph, Jr.

## SEAFOOD PIE

One 9-inch pie shell
2 tablespoons butter or margarine
¼ cup chopped green pepper
¼ cup chopped green onions
¼ cup chopped celery
One 3-ounce can mushrooms
½ pound lump crabmeat

½ pound shrimp, boiled and peeled
1 cup grated Cheddar cheese
¼ cup grated Parmesan cheese
1 tablespoon lemon juice
⅛ teaspoon Tabasco sauce
1 egg, beaten
¼ cup mayonnaise
¼ cup slivered almonds

Bake pie shell partially at 400 degrees for 5 to 7 minutes. Melt butter in large skillet and sauté green pepper, green onions, celery and mushrooms. Add crabmeat, shrimp, ¾ cup Cheddar cheese, Parmesan cheese, lemon juice, Tabasco sauce, egg and mayonnaise. Stir well to combine. This mixture should be moist but not "runny," so drain off excess liquid. Spoon into pie shell. Bake at 350 degrees for about 20 minutes. Add almonds and remaining ¼ cup Cheddar cheese. Bake 10 minutes longer. Baking time can be shortened slightly by heating combined filling ingredients before spooning into pie shell. If fresh seafood is not available, canned seafood can be effectively substituted. Serves 6.

Mrs. Calvin S. Moore

## SEAFOOD STUFFED EGGPLANT

2 medium eggplants
1 large onion, chopped
4 tablespoons butter or margarine, melted
Two 4½-ounce cans small river shrimp or 1 pound fresh river shrimp
1 pound lump crabmeat
1½ cups seasoned bread crumbs

2 eggs, well beaten
1 teaspoon monosodium glutamate
1 teaspoon crumbled oregano
2 tablespoons chopped parsley
½ teaspoon salt
¼ teaspoon black pepper
3 dashes Tabasco sauce
1 tablespoon butter or margarine
Paprika

Slice eggplants in half and parboil about 10 minutes. Remove from water, drain, cool slightly and scoop centers out of each half of eggplant. Place eggplant pulp in large mixing bowl and set aside. Sauté onion in butter and add to pulp. Add prepared shrimp and crabmeat, 1 cup bread crumbs, beaten eggs, monosodium glutamate, oregano, parsley, salt, pepper and Tabasco sauce. Mix well and fill each eggplant shell. Arrange filled eggplant shells in shallow baking dish filled with ¼ cup water. Top each eggplant with remaining ½ cup bread crumbs; butter and sprinkle with paprika. Bake at 350 degrees for 35 to 45 minutes or until top is brown. Serve with French bread and green salad. Freezes well. Serves 4 to 6.

Mrs. J. Garner Moore

## CRAWFISH ÉTOUFFÉE OR PIE FILLING

1 pound margarine
1 cup flour
3 bell peppers
2 bunches green onions, keep tops separate
1 stalk celery
One 1-pound can tomatoes

3 teaspoons garlic powder
3 tablespoons salt
3 tablespoons Worcestershire sauce
2 to 3 teaspoons cayenne pepper
6 cups water
5 pounds crawfish tails and fat
4 cups uncooked rice, or
four 9-inch unbaked pie crusts

Melt margarine, preferably in iron Dutch oven. Add flour and brown lightly. Finely chop peppers, onion bottoms, celery and tomatoes and add to roux. Add seasonings. Cover and cook slowly for one hour, stirring frequently to prevent sticking. Add water and cook slowly for several hours. If mixture becomes too thick, add more water. Add crawfish tails, fat and onion tops. Cook about 15 minutes or until tender. At this point, mixture may be frozen. If making étouffée, cook rice. When ready to serve, pour crawfish mixture over rice. If making pies, pour filling over bottom crust. Cover with top crust. Cut slits in top. Bake at 350 degrees for about 15 minutes. Reduce heat to 300 degrees and bake for 15 minutes or until golden brown. Bake pies on a cookie sheet to prevent spillage in oven. Serves 12.

Mrs. Wray Edward Robinson

## INDIVIDUAL CRAWFISH PIES

½ cup margarine
3 tablespoons flour
1 medium onion, finely chopped
½ bell pepper, finely chopped
⅓ cup finely chopped celery
2 small pods garlic, finely chopped
1 cup canned chicken broth

2 pounds crawfish meat with fat that clings to them
1¼ teaspoons salt
¼ teaspoon red pepper
Worcestershire sauce to taste
4 green onions, tops and bottoms, finely chopped
Flaky pie crust

Use heavy iron pot with tight fitting lid. Melt margarine over low fire and add flour. Cook and stir over low fire for 10 minutes or longer, but do not brown. Add onion, bell pepper, celery and garlic. Sauté until soft. This takes 30 minutes or so. Add crawfish, hot chicken broth, salt, pepper, Worcestershire sauce and green onions. Cover pot and cook over low, low fire for 30 minutes. Stir often. Check seasonings as it will probably need more salt and pepper. Let crawfish mixture cool. Use as filling for individual pastry-lined pie pans. Cover with top crust. Do not put too much juice. Bake in 425 degree oven for 25 or 30 minutes. Makes 8 individual 3½-inch diameter pies or one 9-inch pie.

Mrs. Dave K. Beer

## CRAWFISH BISQUE

**Stuffing for Heads:**

40 pounds of crawfish tails
12 onions, quartered
12 bell peppers, quartered
2 stalks celery
12 heads garlic
4 large bunches parsley
16 bunches green onions
Fresh oregano

4 tablespoons basil
Fourteen 15-ounce cans bread
   crumbs
13 dozen eggs
Two 10-ounce bottles
   Worcestershire sauce
Salt to taste
Black and red pepper to taste

Prepare onions, bell pepper, celery, garlic, parsley, green onions, oregano and sweet basil for the food grinder. Run through the food grinder alternating with raw crawfish tails. Save all fats and juices during the grinding process; add to the stuffing mixture. Add bread crumbs, eggs (don't bother to beat), Worcestershire sauce, salt and pepper. Mix well with hands to assure proper consistency or "feel." Stuff this mixture into heads. It must not be packed tightly because the eggs and bread must have room for expansion and the gravy must be able to penetrate to assure flavor. Place stuffed heads on a foil-covered baking sheet; brown in a hot oven (400 degrees) 10 to 15 minutes, until sealed and slightly browned. When cool, they may be frozen. On the day of use, add frozen heads to the gravy below and allow to cook slowly for several hours. Freezes well. Yields 1800-2000 heads, depending on size.

**Gravy:**

1 cup bacon drippings
2 cups flour
2 onions, chopped
1 bell pepper, chopped
4 ribs celery, chopped
4 to 5 pods garlic, chopped

Parsley, chopped
One 1-pound 4-ounce can tomato bits
¼ cup Worcestershire sauce
Salt, black and red pepper
   to taste
3 quarts water
Bay leaves

Make a roux with bacon drippings and flour, stirring constantly until a deep brown. Add chopped seasonings, tomato, Worcestershire sauce, salt, pepper and water. Add bay leaves and cook slowly at least 2 hours. Frozen heads may be added and allowed to simmer for hours to enhance the flavor of both the heads and the gravy. This is a sufficient amount of gravy for 100 heads, or about ten people, allowing ten heads per person.

This recipe is designed to be made by four people. The results are then divided. This is the easiest and most economical way to make a bisque. However, if you wish to do it alone the recipe may be divided by four.

Mrs. Naven D. Couvillon
Mrs. Kenneth C. Landry

## CRAWFISH ÉTOUFFÉE

¼ pound butter
2 large onions, chopped
2 stalks celery, chopped
2 cloves garlic, minced
1 medium bell pepper, chopped
Salt to taste
Red and black pepper to taste

Tabasco sauce to taste
1 to 2 pounds crawfish tails and fat
4 tablespoons flour
2 cups water
4 chicken bouillon cubes,
  or equivalent
Green onion tops, chopped (optional)
Parsley, chopped (optional)

Melt the butter in a heavy large skillet. Sauté the vegetables in butter for 30 minutes. Add seasonings to taste and then the crawfish tails and fat. Sauté for a minute and then stir in flour. Continue sautéing for 3 minutes; then add water, chicken bouillon, and optional green onions and parsley. Simmer for 10 to 15 minutes. Serves 4 to 6.

Mrs. H. J. Walker

## CRAWFISH PIE

1 large onion, ground
¼ cup minced green onion
2 cloves garlic, ground
½ bell pepper, ground
2 ribs celery, ground
½ cup butter
One 10¾-ounce can cream of
  celery soup
4 tablespoons tomato sauce

1 pound coarsely ground crawfish
  tails
¼ cup minced parsley
½ cup seasoned bread crumbs
1 teaspoon salt
½ teaspoon red pepper
½ teaspoon black pepper
1 egg, beaten
1 cup milk
Double crust for 10-inch pie

Sauté onions, garlic, pepper and celery in butter until limp. Add soup, tomato sauce, ground crawfish and parsley. Cook slowly for 10 minutes. Turn off heat. Add bread crumbs, salt, pepper, and egg. Add milk and mix well. For 10-inch pie, bake in double crust for 35 to 40 minutes at 350 degrees.

Mrs. William S. Slack

## BAKED FISH WITH TOMATO SAUCE

4 slices bacon
2 cups chopped onion
Two 16-ounce cans tomatoes
1 tablespoon chopped parsley

⅛ teaspoon thyme
2 bay leaves
Salt and pepper to taste
5 pounds red fish or red snapper

Fry bacon in skillet. Remove bacon and wilt onions in bacon fat. Add tomatoes, chopping them up with a spoon. When this is bubbling, add parsley, thyme, bay leaves, chopped bacon, salt and pepper. Cook until most of the water has cooked out and the sauce is thick. Season the fish well inside and out and rub with butter. Cook for 15 minutes in a preheated 400 degree oven. Spread with sauce and finish baking at 350 degrees for approximately 15 minutes or until fish flakes easily. This amount of sauce can be used on a 5 pound fish or on 6 small fish. Serves 6.

Mrs. J. D. Guillory

## TROUT AMANDINE I

**Trout:**

| | |
|---|---|
| 12 trout filets | Cayenne pepper |
| Salt | 1 egg, beaten |
| Black pepper | ¼ cup milk |
| | Fine cracker crumbs |

Season filets generously with salt, black and red pepper. Combine egg and milk. Dip trout in egg mixture and roll in fine cracker crumbs. Fry until golden brown in ½ inch of hot fat.

**Sauce:**

| | |
|---|---|
| ¼ cup butter | ¾ teaspoon cornstarch |
| 3¼-ounce package sliced almonds | 2 tablespoons chopped parsley |
| ¾ cup cold water | 1 teaspoon sugar |
| | Dash cayenne pepper |

Melt butter and fry almonds slowly until brown. Add the cold water with the cornstarch dissolved in it. Add parsley, sugar and cayenne pepper. Spoon over fried trout. Serves 6.

Mrs. Vernon H. Long, Jr.

## TROUT AMANDINE II

| | |
|---|---|
| 8 to 12 trout filets (⅓ pound per person) | 4 drops Tabasco sauce |
| Milk to cover | 1½ cups flour |
| 2 teaspoons salt | 1 teaspoon pepper |
| | ½ cup butter |
| | 2 tablespoons olive oil |

Soak filets in a mixture of milk, 1 teaspoon salt and Tabasco sauce for several hours. Season flour with 1 teaspoon salt and pepper. Remove filets from milk as needed and dip in flour, shaking off excess flour. In an electric skillet at 375 degrees, fry filets until golden brown in the butter and oil. Do a few at a time and, as cooked, place on a warm platter or cookie sheet and keep in a warm oven until ready to serve. These may be kept in a warm oven up to 3 hours.

**Sauce:**

| | |
|---|---|
| 1 cup butter | 2 teaspoons Worcestershire sauce |
| ½ cup sliced almonds | 1 teaspoon salt |
| 2 tablespoons lemon juice | ¼ cup chopped parsley |

Prepare sauce by melting butter and lightly browning almonds in the butter. Add lemon juice, Worcestershire sauce, salt and parsley. Mix and heat well. Just before serving, pour some sauce over trout and serve remaining sauce separately. If the sauce is made ahead of time, add the almonds at the last minute so that they will remain crunchy. Serves 8 to 10.

Mrs. Melvin A. Shortess

## BARBECUED FISH

8 white fish filets (trout,
pompano or others)
Salt and pepper
3 lemons, squeezed
2 garlic cloves, minced

1 cup butter or margarine, melted
⅓ cup Jamaican Choice Tropical
sauce or Pickapeppa sauce
1 tablespoon Tabasco sauce
Fresh parsley, chopped
Lemon slices

Preheat barbecue grill to medium heat. Salt and pepper filets and place in foil-lined pan. Heat lemon, garlic, butter, Jamaican Choice Tropical or Pickapeppa sauce and Tabasco sauce in small pan. Pour over fish. Cook with top down approximately 15 minutes. Baste often. Garnish with freshly chopped parsley and lemon slices. This is very "unfishy" tasting. Serves 6 to 8.

Mrs. Cheney C. Joseph, Jr.

## MUSTARD SAUCE II

4 medium onions
4 medium bell peppers (3 cups)
4 large stalks celery (2½ cups)
1½ cups margarine
4 teaspoons salt

2 teaspoons red pepper
Juice of three lemons
4 tablespoons prepared "hot dog"
mustard
1½ ounces dry white wine

Cut onions, peppers and celery in ½-inch pieces. Sauté in margarine slowly for about 45 minutes. Remove from heat and add salt and pepper to taste (don't skimp). Add lemon juice, mustard and wine. This will make enough sauce for 8 pounds of fish. Less sauce is needed for filets. Pour sauce over cleaned, scored and generously salted and peppered fish. Bake in 350 degree oven at least 1 to 1½ hours for 6- to 8-pound whole red fish. Less cooking time is needed for filets.

Mrs. Weldon L. Smith, Jr.

## FRIED FROG LEGS

Vegetable oil for frying
2 dozen large frog legs
1 teaspoon red pepper
2 teaspoons salt

1 cup yellow corn meal
1 cup flour or fish fry
4 eggs
¼ cup milk
2 lemons, cut into wedges

Preheat oven to warm setting. Line shallow baking dish with paper towels. Place in middle of oven. Pour oil in deep fryer or cast iron Dutch oven to depth of 2 to 3 inches. Heat to 375 degrees. Dry the legs. Season with salt and pepper. Mix cornmeal and flour. Mix eggs and milk in another dish. Roll each leg in flour mixture, then in egg mixture and lightly in flour mixture again. Deep fry 4 or 5 legs at a time turning for even brownness and crispness. As browned, put them in a dish in the oven to keep them warm. Serve heaped on platter with lemon wedges. Serves 4 to 6.

Mrs. Percy Roberts, Jr.

## STUFFED RED SNAPPER

One 5- to 6-pound red snapper
1 large onion, chopped
1 cup chopped celery
Butter or chicken fat
1 cup cooked rice

2 tablespoons minced parsley
8 tablespoons butter, melted
2 tablespoons white wine
Salt and pepper to taste
4 tablespoons water

In cleaning fish, leave head on. Sauté onions and celery in butter or chicken fat. Add to rice. Add parsley, 4 tablespoons butter and wine. Add salt and pepper to taste. Stuff fish with rice dressing pinning fish together with toothpicks. Place fish in baking dish. Pour remaining melted butter over fish. Add 4 tablespoons water. Bake at 350 degrees for 30 minutes. Increase heat to 400 degrees and bake for an additional 30 minutes, basting occasionally. When fish is done, remove from pan and garnish with lemon slices and parsley. Reserve cooking juices.

Sauce:
Juice of ½ lemon
1 egg yolk
Salt and pepper to taste

¼ cup butter, melted
1 tablespoon flour
¾ cup water
Juices obtained from baked fish

Combine first 6 ingredients and stir until a smooth paste is obtained. Add juices that have been drained off stuffed red snapper. Simmer mixture for 5 minutes, stirring constantly. Spoon over fish. Serves 6.

Mrs. Adrian de Montluzin

## KAKEEN'S ROCKEFELLER SAUCE

1 bunch green onions
½ bunch parsley tops
1 rib celery
3 large lettuce leaves
½ cup margarine

2 jars junior baby food spinach
Juice of 1 lemon
Tabasco sauce to taste
Salt, pepper and Beau Monde,
   to taste
¾ cup bread crumbs

Grind onions, parsley, celery and lettuce leaves in grinder or chop in food chopper. (Not as good if puréed in blender, so advise against it). Put in double boiler with margarine and cook slowly 10 or 15 minutes or until wilted. Add spinach, lemon, seasonings and bread crumbs. Top oysters with mixture and broil under broiler. Yield: 2 cups.

Mrs. C. E. Johnson

## OYSTER CASSEROLE

1 cup cracker crumbs
½ cup seasoned bread crumbs
½ cup melted butter
⅔ cup chopped parsley
⅔ cup chopped onions
Tabasco sauce

1 dozen large or 2 dozen small
   oysters
Seasoned salt
Butter
¾ to 1 cup chablis wine
¾ to 1 cup light cream
1 cup American cheese

Mix first three ingredients. In a separate bowl, mix parsley and onions. Put layer of bread crumb mixture, then layer of parsley and onions on bottom of a 2- or 3-quart casserole. Put a layer of oysters. Put 1 drop Tabasco sauce on each oyster. Put a little salt and a dot of butter on each oyster. Repeat procedure. Crumb mixture should be last. When the dish is full, gently pour wine, then cream, over the mixture. Sprinkle cheese over the top. Bake at 400 degrees for 20 minutes. Serves 6-8.

Mrs. Eugene Bahlinger

## OYSTER PIE

¼ cup butter
½ cup all purpose flour
¾ cup milk
1 pint oysters
1 small clove garlic, minced
¼ bell pepper, chopped
¼ cup minced parsley

½ cup chopped green onions, tops and bottoms
2 stalks celery, chopped
Salt, black and red pepper to taste
Hot sauce to taste
8-inch unbaked pie shell, top and bottom

Make a roux with butter and flour, stirring constantly until it reaches hue of a brown paper bag. Add milk. Stir well. Drain juice from oysters and add only oysters to sauce. Cook for 15 minutes or until oysters have thrown off all their juice. If mixture is too thick, add oyster juice. Add chopped ingredients and lastly add salt, peppers and hot sauce to taste. Salt must be added last to keep milk from curdling. Put oyster mixture in unbaked 8-inch pie shell and cover with top crust. Start pie at 450 degrees and cook 15 minutes to prevent inside crust from being soggy. Reduce heat to 350 degrees and continue cooking until nicely browned. Serve while hot. Serves 6 to 8.

Mrs. Charles Garvey

## PUFFED DEVILED OYSTERS

2 cups chopped onions
1 cup chopped celery
3 eggs
4 pints oysters, drained
2 tablespoons chopped parsley (dried kind is fine)

¼ cup soy sauce
15 drops Tabasco sauce, or to taste
8 hamburger rolls (toasted and made into bread crumbs)
Salt to taste
½ cup butter, melted

Put onions, celery and eggs into blender. Mix until you have a finely chopped product. Do not make it completely puréed. (Every blender is a bit different, so you have to work this out. You want to preserve some texture). In a bowl, cut through oysters so they are very coarsely chopped. Add blender mixture, parsley, soy sauce, Tabasco sauce, bread crumbs and salt. Mix well. Put into 3-quart casserole. Pour melted butter over all. Bake for 1 hour at 375 degrees, or until puffed and bubbling. If using individual ramekins, 25 minutes cooking time. This recipe can be halved successfully. The only changes would be to use 2 eggs, cook in 2-quart casserole for 1 hour. Serves 8 to 10. Halved, serves 4.

Mrs. Percy E. Roberts, Jr.

## OYSTERS POULETTE

3 dozen oysters
2 tablespoons butter
2 tablespoons flour
2 shallots, chopped
1 cup oyster liquor
½ teaspoon salt
¼ teaspoon red pepper
1 cup cream
4 egg yolks, beaten
1 tablespoon chopped parsley
2 tablespoons lemon juice
Buttered bread crumbs

Heat oysters to draw out juice. Remove oysters and skim juice. Melt butter, add flour, stir until smooth. Add shallots. Cook a few minutes, add oyster liquor and stir until smooth. Add salt, red pepper and cream to beaten egg yolks; then add to sauce. Add oysters and parsley. Cook 2 minutes. Remove from heat and add lemon juice. Place in 2-quart casserole or shells. Sprinkle with buttered bread crumbs. Heat in 325 to 350 degree oven until bubbling before serving. Serves 4.

Mrs. Anderson Jones


## SEAFOOD MACARONI CASSEROLE

One 7¼-ounce macaroni and cheese dinner
One 10½-ounce can condensed cream of chicken soup
Two 4½-ounce cans shrimp, drained
½ teaspoon Worcestershire sauce
¼ cup chopped bell pepper
Salt and pepper to taste
Crushed crackers
Butter or margarine

Prepare macaroni and cheese according to package directions, except increase total amount of milk to 1½ cups. Stir in soup, shrimp, Worcestershire sauce, bell pepper, salt and pepper. Pour into greased 1½-quart casserole. Sprinkle cracker crumbs on top. Dot with butter. Bake at 350 degrees for 45 minutes. Freezes well. Good for those busy days when you have only a few minutes to prepare a meal. Serves 4.

Mrs. Claude Platte


## SHRIMP REMOULADE

4 tablespoons horseradish mustard
½ cup tarragon vinegar
2 tablespoons catsup
1 tablespoon paprika
½ teaspoon cayenne pepper
1 teaspoon salt
1 whole clove garlic
1 cup salad oil
½ cup finely minced green onions with tops
½ cup finely minced celery

Mix all ingredients together in blender. Pour over cooked shrimp. To really be delicious, the shrimp should marinate for at least 4 or 5 hours. Serve cold on lettuce. Makes 2½ cups of sauce. Serves 8.

Mrs. James F. Fargason
Gulfport, Mississippi

### SEAFOOD CASSEROLE

1 cup white rice
1 cup wild rice
2 onions, finely chopped
2 cups thinly sliced celery
1 green pepper, finely chopped
1 large can mushrooms
Butter

Two 10½-ounce cans mushroom
  soup, undiluted
3 pounds cooked and peeled shrimp
1 cup sharp cheese, grated
½ cup blanched, slivered almonds
1 pimiento, finely chopped
½ cup white wine
Salt and pepper to taste
Paprika
Parsley, chopped

Cook rices separately. Sauté onions, celery, green pepper and mushrooms in butter until onions are transparent. Add soup; stir until smooth. Combine cooked rices, sautéed mixture, shrimp, cheese, almonds, pimiento and wine. Season to taste. Pour into 2½-quart casserole, sprinkle with paprika and parsley. Cover and bake at 325 degrees for 45 minutes. Freezes well. Serves 8.

Mrs. Henry Sabatier

### AVOCADO WITH SHRIMP REMOULADE

¼ cup tarragon vinegar
2 tablespoons horseradish mustard
1 tablespoon catsup
1½ teaspoons paprika
½ teaspoon salt

¼ teaspoon cayenne pepper
½ cup salad oil
¼ cup minced celery
¼ cup minced green onions
2 pounds shrimp, cooked and peeled
4 medium avocados

In small bowl, combine vinegar, mustard, catsup, paprika, salt and pepper. Slowly add oil, beating constantly with electric mixer. Stir in celery and onions. Pour sauce over shrimp. Marinate 4 to 5 hours in refrigerator. Halve and peel avocados. Lift shrimp out of sauce and arrange on each avocado half. Pass sauce. Good served with chilled asparagus, carrot strips, sliced beets and hard-cooked eggs. This is a good luncheon dish and also can be served with toothpicks as an appetizer. Serves 8.

Mrs. Neel Garland

### BROILED SHRIMP

2 pounds shrimp
½ cup margarine
3 tablespoons lemon juice
2 tablespoons Worcestershire sauce

1 tablespoon Jamaican Choice
  Tropical or Pickapeppa sauce
¼ teaspoon red pepper
½ teaspoon salt

Wash, peel and devein shrimp. Melt margarine in saucepan. Add lemon juice, Worcestershire sauce, pepper sauce, red pepper and salt. Let simmer 5 or 10 minutes. Pour over raw shrimp in 9x12x2-inch baking pan. Place on next to lowest rack in oven. Broil 20 minutes, turning shrimp every 5 minutes. Serve shrimp in gravy with plenty of hot French bread for "dunking." Serves 4.

Mrs. Benjamin B. Edwards

## SHRIMP CURRY

⅓ cup butter
½ cup chopped onions
2 cloves garlic, minced
2 cups sour cream
2 teaspoons lemon juice

2 teaspoons curry powder
¾ teaspoon salt
½ teaspoon ginger
Dash pepper
3 cups boiled, peeled shrimp
  (about 2 pounds, whole)

Melt butter. Add onions and garlic. Cook about 3 minutes. Stir in sour cream and other ingredients. Cook over medium heat, stirring until thoroughly heated. Serve over rice accompanied by usual curry condiments: chutney, coconut, almonds, etc. Serves 4 to 6.

Mrs. Bert S. Turner

## SHRIMP AND MUSHROOM CASSEROLE

1 pound shrimp
1½ tablespoons butter or margarine
2 teaspoons chopped onions
2 teaspoons chopped bell pepper
2 tablespoons flour
¾ cup half and half

¼ teaspoon paprika
½ teaspoon salt
One 6-ounce can button mushrooms
½ cup grated Cheddar cheese
Buttered bread crumbs
Parmesan cheese

Boil shrimp in well seasoned water. Melt butter, add onions and green pepper and cook until tender. Add flour and blend. Add all other ingredients, except bread crumbs and Parmesan cheese. (It is not necessary to thicken, but do melt the cheese.) Put in 1½-quart casserole and cover with bread crumbs and Parmesan cheese. Bake at 350 degrees for 20 minutes. Freezes well. Serves 4.

Mrs. C. Lenton Sartain

## SHRIMP MARINIÈRE

½ cup butter or margarine
1 cup finely chopped shallots
3 tablespoons flour
2 cups milk
½ teaspoon salt

¼ teaspoon cayenne pepper
⅓ cup white wine
1½ pounds shrimp, boiled and
  peeled
1 egg yolk, beaten

In a medium skillet, melt butter and sauté shallots until tender. Blend in flour and cook slowly 3 to 5 minutes more, stirring constantly. Stir in milk until smooth. Add salt, pepper and wine. Cook about 10 minutes more. Remove from heat, add shrimp and quickly stir in egg yolk. Return to heat and slowly cook until heated through. Place in ramekins and sprinkle tops with red pepper and heat under broiler until piping hot; or serve over rice or in pastry shells. For cocktail party, recipe should serve 45 to 50 in miniature patty shells or on melba rounds. Recipe may be frozen and reheated, but not over too hot a flame or mixture might separate. Serves 4.

Mrs. Hubert Waguespack

## SHRIMP CREOLE

¼ cup flour
¼ cup bacon grease
1½ cups chopped onions
1 cup chopped green onions
1 cup chopped celery, with leaves
1 cup chopped bell pepper
2 cloves garlic, minced
One 6-ounce can tomato paste
One 16-ounce can chopped tomatoes
 with liquid
One 8-ounce can tomato sauce
1 cup water
5 teaspoons salt
1 teaspoon pepper
½ teaspoon red pepper, optional
Tabasco sauce to taste
2 to 3 bay leaves
1 teaspoon sugar
1 teaspoon Worcestershire sauce
1 tablespoon lemon juice
4 pounds peeled, deveined,
 raw shrimp
½ cup chopped fresh parsley
2 to 3 cups cooked rice

In a large, heavy roaster, make a dark brown roux of flour and bacon grease. Add onions, green onions, celery, bell pepper and garlic. Sauté until soft (20 to 30 minutes). Add tomato paste and mix this well with vegetables. Add tomatoes and tomato sauce, water, salt, pepper, red pepper, Tabasco sauce, bay leaves, sugar, Worcestershire sauce and lemon juice. Simmer very slowly for 1 hour, covered, stirring occasionally. Add shrimp and cook until done, 5 to 15 minutes. This should sit awhile. It is much better made the day before. If made the day before, reheat but do not boil. Simmer. Freezes well. Add parsley just before serving. Serve over rice. Serves 10.

Mrs. Williams D. Wall, IV
Mrs. Clifton Morris, Jr.

## VERSATILE CREAMED SHRIMP

¼ cup butter or margarine
½ cup thinly sliced green onions
Two 3-ounce cans sliced mushrooms,
 drained
3 tablespoons flour
1 cup heavy cream
½ cup milk
¼ cup sherry or Madeira wine
 (optional)
1 teaspoon salt
⅛ teaspoon white pepper
1½ pounds shrimp (cooked,
 shelled, deveined)
2 tablespoons chopped parsley

Heat butter or margarine in heavy skillet. Add onions. Cook, stirring constantly until limp, not brown. Add mushrooms, mixing well with onions. Sprinkle flour evenly over mushrooms and mix. Stir in cream, milk and wine. Cook slowly until thickened, stirring constantly. Season with salt and pepper. Fold in shrimp and heat, stirring often. Serve as an entrée in patty shells, on toast rounds, or over red snapper filets which have been lightly salted and peppered and broiled in butter, or as an appetizer in tiny patty shells or on Melba toast rounds. Sprinkle parsley over each individual serving or over all when serving from chafing dish. This dish may be kept warm for about an hour over hot water but may separate if left much longer or if water is allowed to boil. Serves 6 to 8 in large patty shells; 3 to 4 dozen in small.

Mrs. Jake L. Netterville

## FRENCH FRIED SHRIMP

1 cup flour
1 teaspoon sugar
1 teaspoon salt

1 egg
1 cup ice water
1 tablespoon melted fat
2 pounds large shrimp

Combine all ingredients except shrimp. Beat well. Peel raw shrimp, leaving last section and tail intact. Cut slit through center back and remove vein. Dry shrimp thoroughly and dip in batter. Fry in deep hot fat until golden brown. Drain on paper towels. Serve hot with tartar sauce. Serves 4.

Mrs. Charles J. Mittendorf

## SHRIMP AND ARTICHOKE CASSEROLE

One 14-ounce can artichoke hearts, drained
1½ pounds shrimp (shelled, deveined and boiled)
3 tablespoons butter
1 clove garlic, chopped
1 onion, or 4 green onions, chopped
¼ pound mushrooms, sliced, or 4-ounce can, drained

One 10-ounce can cream of mushroom soup
½ cup mayonnaise
1 tablespoon Worcestershire sauce
2 tablespoons dry sherry
½ cup grated Parmesan cheese
One 10-ounce package frozen, chopped spinach
Salt, pepper and paprika to taste

Place artichokes in buttered 2-quart casserole. Add shrimp. Sauté garlic, onions and mushrooms in butter. Add undiluted soup, mayonnaise, Worcestershire sauce, sherry, cheese, salt and pepper. Add spinach which has been thawed and well drained. Pour this mixture over shrimp. Sprinkle with more cheese and paprika. Bake 20 minutes at 375 degrees or until bubbly. This may be garnished with chopped parsley or bread crumbs. Serves 6.

Mrs. Dean M. Mosely

## SHRIMP QUICHE

One 8-ounce can refrigerated quick crescent dinner rolls
2 eggs, slightly beaten
1 tablespoon grated Parmesan cheese
Salt and pepper to taste

2 cups Italian or Monterey Jack cheese, cut into ½-inch cubes
½ pound shrimp (boiled, peeled, deveined and cut into chunks) or two 4½-ounce cans shrimp, drained
2 tablespoons chopped green onions

Separate triangles of dinner rolls. Place 5 triangles in a 9-inch pie pan, pressing together to form a crust. To make them thin, roll triangles between wax paper. Reserve 3 triangles for top crust. Combine remaining ingredients in large mixing bowl and mix well. Pour into crust. Roll out remaining triangles so longest side is 9 inches. Cut into ½-inch strips. Twist strips and make lattice effect for top crust. Bake at 325 degrees for 50 to 60 minutes. Serves 4 to 6 as entrée.

Mrs. Robert M. Slowey

## SHRIMP RIVIERA

3 tablespoons butter or margarine
1½ cups chopped celery
½ cup sliced onions
1 clove garlic, minced
1 tablespoon flour
2 cups canned tomatoes

One 8-ounce can tomato sauce
2 tablespoons chopped parsley
1 teaspoon oregano
1½ teaspoons salt
2 pounds shrimp (peeled
    and deveined)
½ cup sliced black olives

Melt butter in large skillet and sauté celery, onions, and garlic until tender. Sprinkle in flour and stir until light brown. Add tomatoes, tomato sauce, parsley, oregano and salt; simmer 10 to 15 minutes. Add shrimp and olives. Continue cooking until shrimp are done, about 5 minutes. Serve on fluffy white rice tossed with sliced mushrooms which have been lightly sautéed in butter and drained. Serves 4 to 6.

Mrs. C. B. Berry
Columbia, Mississippi

## SHRIMP LOUISIANNE

½ cup margarine
2 onions, finely chopped
2 stalks celery, finely chopped
2 pounds raw shrimp (peeled)
4 tablespoons flour

1 teaspoon salt
2 teaspoons chili powder
2 cups milk
4 tablespoons catsup
1 tablespoon dried parsley

Melt margarine in heavy skillet. Sauté vegetables. Add raw, peeled shrimp and sauté a few minutes longer. Stir in flour, salt and chili powder. Add milk gradually and cook five minutes over low heat. Add catsup and parsley. Cook, covered, 10 to 15 minutes. Serve over rice with green salad and French bread. Serves 4 to 6.

Mrs. Weldon Smith

## PIMENTS DOUX FARCIS
## (CREOLE STUFFED PEPPERS)

1 egg beaten
2 pounds fresh shrimp (peeled
    and chopped)
Salt and red pepper to taste
¼ cup oil
6 bell peppers, finely chopped

½ large onion, finely chopped
½ to ¾ cup finely chopped celery
1 cup homemade bread crumbs
8 to 10 bell pepper halves
Buttered, seasoned Italian bread
    crumbs

Add egg to chopped shrimp. Salt and pepper well and mix thoroughly. Sauté shrimp mixture in oil until cooked. Add more oil and chopped peppers, onions and celery. Cook until soft and mushy. Add plain bread crumbs and season, if necessary. Scald bell pepper halves and stuff with shrimp mixture. Top with seasoned bread crumbs. Cook in greased pan in a 350 degree oven about 45 minutes. Serves 4 to 6.

Mrs. Hubert Waguespack

## SHRIMP ÉTOUFFÉE

4 pounds shrimp
1 bunch green onions, finely minced
3 medium-sized onions, finely minced
2 cloves garlic, finely minced
¾ cup finely minced parsley

½ cup margarine
1½ tablespoons tomato paste
3½ teaspoons salt
Tabasco sauce to taste
Flour or cornstarch

Peel and devein shrimp. Sauté finely minced onions, garlic and parsley in margarine until soft; do not brown. Add tomato paste, stir well and cook for a few minutes. Add shrimp and seasonings. Cook for about 20 minutes. Thicken slightly with a little flour or cornstarch. Serves 8.

Mrs. Irene S. Liberman

## ARNAUD SAUCE

Two 5¾-ounce jars Zatarain's
  creole mustard
3 tablespoons plus 1 teaspoon
  prepared horseradish
1¾ ounces paprika

¾ cup olive oil
6 drops Tabasco sauce
Salt to taste
Coarse ground pepper to taste
5 pounds shrimp (boiled
  and peeled

Mix first 7 ingredients well. Pour over shrimp and marinate 24 hours, stirring occasionally.

Mrs. Ford S. Lacey

## TUNA CASSEROLE

One 9¼-ounce can tuna, drained
½ cup chopped celery
½ cup chopped onion
⅓ cup chopped green pepper
2 eggs, boiled and chopped

4 ounces sharp Cheddar cheese,
  cut in pieces
One 10½-ounce can mushroom soup
1½ cups cooked rice
Black pepper to taste

Mix all ingredients together in 1½-quart casserole. Bake in 400 degree oven for 20 to 30 minutes or until cheese is melted and casserole is bubbling. This is good as a casserole, or hot dip in chafing dish, or cold as a spread on crackers, but always after being cooked. Can be made a day ahead. Serves 6.

Mrs. Robert A. McLean

## POULTRY AND DRESSINGS

Whether it's for Sunday dinner, a Thanksgiving feast or an *al fresco* picnic in the country, poultry reigns as everyone's favorite. Possibly no other food has the incredible range of recipes that poultry has. It not only features a variety of ingredients and cooking methods, but also a variety of styles: plain or fancy, home-style or gourmet, family fare or banquet menu. In Louisiana, poultry and its various dressings comprise a food category common with all other parts of the country, but with a special Creole touch we think you'll enjoy discovering.

## CHICKEN DOROTHY

4 chicken breast halves
Salt
Pepper
¼ cup margarine

1 cup sour cream
One 10¾-ounce can cream of
mushroom soup
½ cup white wine

Salt and pepper chicken breasts. Brown in margarine. Remove to a 1½-quart casserole. In the same pan in which chicken was browned, combine the sour cream, soup and wine. Pour over chicken. Cover casserole and bake at 350 degrees for 1 hour. This may be prepared ahead and baked when needed. Good served with rice. Serves 4.

Mrs. J. Denson Smith

## HERBED CHICKEN BREASTS

6 chicken breast halves
Salt to taste
Pepper to taste
¼ cup butter
One 10¾-ounce can cream of
chicken soup

¾ cup sauterne
One 5-ounce can water chestnuts,
drained and sliced
One 3-ounce can sliced mushrooms,
drained
2 tablespoons minced bell pepper
¼ teaspoon thyme

Lightly salt and pepper chicken. Brown slowly in butter, using heavy skillet. Remove breasts and arrange skin side up in baking dish. Add soup to skillet drippings and slowly stir in sauterne. When smooth, add remaining ingredients and heat to boiling. Pour sauce over chicken, cover and bake at 350 degrees for 1 hour. Serve with fluffy white rice. Serves 4 to 6.

Mrs. C. B. Berry
Columbia, Mississippi

## CHICKEN BREAST PIQUANTE

6 to 8 chicken breast halves
or 1 whole chicken, cut into
serving pieces
Salt
Pepper
¼ cup sherry
½ cup sauterne
¼ cup soy sauce

¼ cup salad oil
1 tablespoon brown sugar
2 tablespoons water
1 clove garlic, minced
¼ teaspoon ginger
¼ teaspoon oregano
Mushrooms (optional)
Parsley (optional)

Rub chicken lightly with salt and pepper. Combine all other ingredients except mushrooms and parsley in a Dutch oven or greased 13x9x2-inch baking dish (reduce amount of soy sauce if cooking sherry is used). Add salt and pepper if desired. Put chicken in this sauce and marinate in refrigerator for 12 to 24 hours. Bake at 350 degrees for 1 hour. Mushrooms and parsley may be added the last 15 minutes of baking time. Serve over rice. Serves 6.

Mrs. Lloyd T. Leake

## EASY CHICKEN-IN-WINE

6 chicken breast halves
Salt
Pepper
½ cup butter or margarine
1 cup chopped green onions
3 tablespoons Worcestershire sauce

One 4-ounce can sliced mushrooms, undrained
4 tablespoons lemon juice
2 tablespoons chopped fresh parsley
1 cup white wine
Pinch rosemary

Salt and pepper chicken. In a Dutch oven or large casserole, brown chicken in butter. Add all other ingredients. Cover. Bake at 275 degrees for 2 hours.

Mrs. Cheney C. Joseph, Jr.

## CHICKEN BREASTS IN WINE

18 chicken breast halves
Salt to taste
Pepper
Paprika
½ cup butter

Four 10½-ounce cans mushroom soup (undiluted)
1 cup port wine
Two 6-ounce cans mushrooms with liquid

Skin breasts, salt, pepper and put paprika on chicken. Brown lightly in butter and place in baking dish (13x9x2-inch). In same frying pan with butter, add soup, wine, mushrooms and liquid. Stir well and pour over chicken. Cover. Bake 1 hour and 15 minutes at 350 degrees. Serves 10 to 12.

Mrs. Millard Byrd, Jr.

## CHICKEN BREASTS EN PAPILOTTE

4 tablespoons butter
2 tablespoons minced green onions
3 tablespoons flour
¼ cup chicken broth
¼ cup dry vermouth
1 tablespoon lemon juice

⅛ teaspoon thyme
Salt
Pepper
1 cup light cream
⅛ cup butter
6 chicken breasts, boned
18 cleaned mushroom caps

Tear off six 10-inch lengths of 12-inch wide heavy foil. Melt butter and cook green onions, do not brown. Sift in flour and cook for 2 minutes without browning. Remove from heat. Bring chicken broth, vermouth, lemon juice, thyme, salt and pepper to boil. Remove from heat and add cream. Add this liquid to the roux stirring vigorously. Return to heat and stir until sauce simmers. Simmer for 1 minute, stirring constantly. Set aside. Butter the inside of the foil. Place one chicken breast on one side of each piece of foil; put 3 mushroom caps on top of each chicken breast and spoon sauce over all. Fold and seal foil. Bake in 400 degree oven for 45 minutes. May be prepared ahead and baked right before serving. Serves 6.

Mrs. Cooper Harrell

## CHICKEN BREASTS AND SHRIMP

8 boned whole chicken breasts
2 beaten eggs and ¼ cup water
Seasoned salt and pepper
Red pepper (optional)
Parmesan cheese

Bread crumbs
1 pound shrimp
2 small chopped onions
½ cup margarine
½ cup sherry

Dip chicken breasts in egg and water mixture. Season with salt and pepper. Roll in Parmesan cheese and bread crumbs. Jelly roll fashion, stuff breasts with sautéed shrimp and onions. Lay chicken in a pan in which margarine has been melted. Add ½ cup sherry. Bake at 350 degrees for 1½ hours, basting with pan juices. Serves 8.

Mrs. E. D. Bateman, Jr.

## LEMON GARLIC CHICKEN

¼ cup oil
1 broiler or fryer, cut up, or
    chicken pieces
Flour to coat chicken pieces
⅛ teaspoon salt
1 clove garlic, mashed

¼ cup olive oil
½ cup lemon juice
2 tablespoons chopped onion
1 teaspoon black pepper
1 teaspoon thyme
1 teaspoon Tabasco sauce

Pour ¼ cup oil into 9x13x2-inch pyrex baking dish. Flour and salt chicken pieces and place the pieces, skin side down, in a single layer. Bake 30 minutes at 400 degrees. Turn chicken and pour sauce over chicken. To make sauce, use the ¼ cup olive oil and add all other ingredients to it. Bake another 30 minutes. Serves 4 to 6.

Mrs. W. A. Rolston, Jr.

## COQ AU VIN

12 chicken breast halves, deboned
½ cup flour
Salt
Pepper
Nutmeg
Paprika
6 tablespoons butter, divided

6 green onions, chopped
½ clove garlic, crushed
1 bay leaf
Pinch thyme
¼ cup sliced mushrooms
1½ cups Burgundy wine
2 slices bacon, diced

Dredge chicken in flour mixed with salt, pepper, nutmeg and paprika to taste. In a skillet, brown ½ of the chicken breasts in 2 tablespoons of butter. Brown remaining six. Remove chicken to 13x9x2-inch baking dish. Melt the last 2 tablespoons butter in the skillet. Add the next 5 ingredients and simmer for 10 minutes. Add Burgundy and stir. Pour over chicken in casserole. Sprinkle with diced bacon. Cover. Bake at 325 degrees for 1½ hours. This can be prepared a day ahead and baked before serving. Good served with curried wild rice. Serves 8.

Mrs. John Wolff

## CHICKEN IN WINE AND ORANGE SAUCE

| | |
|---|---|
| 1 fryer, cut up | 1 cup sauterne wine |
| Salt | 1 cup orange juice |
| Pepper | One 2-ounce can mushrooms, |
| ½ cup margarine | undrained |

Generously salt and pepper chicken pieces. In electric skillet, melt margarine and brown chicken pieces. Combine wine, orange juice and mushrooms. Pour over chicken. Cover and simmer at low temperature until chicken is tender, about 1 hour. Gravy is good over rice. Serves 4.

Mrs. Weldon Smith

## CHICKEN BREASTS WITH STUFFING

| | |
|---|---|
| One 8-ounce package stuffing mix | 2 cups chicken bouillon |
| 1 cup chopped celery | 6 chicken breasts |
| ½ cup chopped onion | Salt to taste |
| 2 tablespoons pimiento or | Black pepper to taste |
| bell pepper | ½ cup margarine |
| 1 egg | Worcestershire sauce to taste |
| | ½ cup lemon juice |

Mix first six ingredients together. Put mixture in buttered square pyrex casserole. Salt and pepper chicken breasts. Arrange over stuffing mixture. Blend melted margarine, Worcestershire sauce and lemon juice together and baste chicken with this several times during baking. Bake uncovered at 325 degrees for about 1½ hours. Serves 4 to 6.

Mrs. W. A. Rolston, Jr.

## CHICKEN DINNER ELEGANTE

| | |
|---|---|
| One 14-ounce can artichoke hearts | One 6-ounce can mushroom caps |
| 10 small new potatoes, pared | and liquid |
| 6 chicken breast halves | ¼ cup sherry |
| Flour to coat chicken | ½ teaspoon salt |
| ¼ cup butter or margarine | ⅛ teaspoon pepper |
| 2 tablespoons chopped green onion | ½ cup sour cream |
| | 1 tablespoon flour |

Arrange artichoke hearts and potatoes in a 2½-quart casserole. Coat chicken with flour and brown in butter or margarine. When brown on both sides, arrange on top of vegetables. In same skillet, cook green onions until tender. Stir in mushroom caps with their liquid and sherry. Pour this mixture over chicken and vegetables. Sprinkle with salt and pepper. Cover and bake in 350 degree oven for 1½ hours. Place chicken and vegetables on warm serving platter. Pour juices from casserole into small sauce pan. Add 1 tablespoon flour and simmer mixture 2 to 3 minutes stirring constantly. Blend in ½ cup sour cream and heat. Pour sauce over chicken and vegetables and serve. Serves 6.

Mrs. John M. Carnahan

## BAKED CHICKEN

One 3-pound chicken
¼ cup flour
½ teaspoon salt
¼ teaspoon pepper
1 teaspoon paprika

¼ cup butter or margarine
One 10¾-ounce can cream of
chicken soup
One 4-ounce can mushrooms,
undrained
1 tablespoon white wine

Cut chicken in quarters. Combine flour, salt, pepper and paprika in a paper bag. Add chicken and shake to coat. In a 425 degree oven, melt butter in a shallow baking dish which is just large enough to hold chicken. Arrange chicken in the baking dish skin side down. Bake, uncovered, for 30 minutes. Remove dish from oven and turn chicken over. Reduce oven to 375 degrees. Combine soup, mushrooms and wine in a small saucepan. Heat and stir until blended. Pour over chicken. Bake 35 minutes more. Stir in a little water during baking if more gravy is desired. Serves 4.

Mrs. Robert A. Muller

## ORANGE CHICKEN

2 chickens, cut in pieces
Salt
Pepper
1 cup butter or margarine

Two 6-ounce cans frozen
orange juice
1 can slivered almonds
One 11-ounce can mandarin
sections, or 1 bunch seedless
grapes

Salt and pepper chicken. Brown in butter. Arrange in large shallow baking dish. Into remaining butter, pour frozen undiluted orange juice. Mix and pour over chicken. Bake at 300 degrees for 45 minutes or 1 hour. In the last 5 minutes, add mandarin sections, or grapes, and almonds, just to get them warm. Extra gravy can be made with orange juice and butter. Serves 6.

Mrs. J. Theron Brown

## CHICKEN KIEV

8 chicken breast halves, deboned
Eight 1x2-inch slices cooked ham
Eight 1x2-inch pieces
Cheddar cheese
8 strips bacon, partially fried
Salt

Pepper
2 eggs
2 tablespoons half and
half or milk
¾ cup flour
½ cup fine cracker crumbs
Cooking oil

Make a pocket in each breast. Insert a piece of ham and cheese which has been wrapped in a piece of bacon. Fold chicken skin around and secure with a toothpick. Season with salt and pepper to taste. Beat eggs and add milk. Combine flour and cracker crumbs. Dip chicken in egg mixture. Roll in flour and crumbs to coat. Fry at once in oil in a heavy iron skillet. Good served with a rice casserole. Serves 6 to 8.

Mrs. Vernon H. Long, Jr.

## CHICKEN MOZZARELLA

¾ cup butter
One 8-ounce can mushroom stems
  and pieces, drained
Salt and pepper
½ cup chopped parsley
1 cup flour
Red pepper
8 breasts of chicken, boned
4 tablespoons port
  or Madeira wine
⅔ cup dry white wine
1 pound sliced Mozzarella cheese

Do not use black iron skillet. Heat 4 tablespoons of the butter in a heavy skillet. When hot, add the mushrooms and cook 4 or 5 minutes, stirring occasionally, taking care not to allow them to brown. Season lightly with salt and black pepper. Mix in parsley and set aside. In a paper bag, combine flour, salt and red pepper. Add the breasts one at a time and shake to coat with the mixture. Shake off any excess. Heat the remaining butter in a heavy skillet over moderate heat. When butter foams, add the breasts, only as many as the pan will accommodate without crowding. Sauté 3 minutes on one side; then turn and sauté 2 minutes on the second side. Arrange the breasts in a shallow baking pan that just holds them comfortably and can go to the table. Spoon some of the mushrooms and parsley mixture over each of the breasts. Add both wines to the same skillet that you browned the chicken in; heat on high and allow to boil. Remove from stove and pour over breasts. Bake in 300 degree oven for about 20 minutes. During last 3 minutes, place 1 slice of cheese over each breast. Serves 8.

Mrs. Walter R. Bankson

## CHICKEN CORDON BLEU

3 whole chicken breasts, skinned
  and deboned
3 slices boiled ham
3 slices Swiss cheese
½ cup flour
½ teaspoon salt
¼ teaspoon monosodium glutamate
¼ teaspoon pepper
¼ teaspoon paprika
1 egg
2 tablespoons milk
½ cup fine, dry bread crumbs
3 tablespoons butter
½ cup chicken broth or bouillon
½ cup sauterne
2 tablespoons dried
  parsley flakes
One 10¾-ounce can cream of
  chicken soup
½ cup sour cream

Split each chicken breast in half. Put each piece between two sheets of waxed paper. Pound thin to twice the original size using wooden mallet or bottom of bottle. Cut ham and cheese slices in half. Fold chicken piece in half with ham and cheese sandwiched between halves. Seal edges of chicken by pounding together. Mix flour with salt, monosodium glutamate, pepper and paprika. Coat each breast with flour mixture, shaking off excess. Dip in slightly beaten egg which has been mixed with the milk. Then roll in bread crumbs. Brown slowly in butter. Add chicken broth and sauterne. Sprinkle with parsley. Cover and simmer until chicken is tender, about 1 hour. Remove chicken to warm serving plate. Blend undiluted soup into pan drippings. Gradually stir in sour cream, heating gently. Serve chicken and gravy over rice. Using half white rice and half wild rice is especially good. Serves 6.

Mrs. Stephen Glagola

## TURKEY CHEESE RAREBIT

½ cup dry sherry
2 tablespoon chopped onions
½ cup chopped bell pepper
1 cup grated processed
   American cheese

2 tablespoons flour
1 teaspoon salt
1 cup evaporated milk
Left-over turkey, sliced or
   cubed (about 5 cups)
One 6-ounce can mushrooms

Combine all ingredients except mushrooms and turkey in top of double boiler. Add liquid from mushrooms. Stir over hot water until cheese melts and mixture thickens. Add mushrooms. If there is enough turkey to slice, sauce may be served separately. If not, add cubed turkey to sauce. Serve over saffron rice. Serves 6 to 8.

Mrs. John B. Whitley

## NINA'S CHICKEN SPAGHETTI WITHOUT TOMATOES

One 5½-pound hen, or 2 cups
   cooked, cut up chicken
Water
2 onions, sliced
1 bell pepper, quartered
5 ribs celery
Salt
Black pepper
Poultry seasoning
¼ cup margarine
2 onions, chopped
1 cup chopped celery
1 bell pepper, chopped

2 pods garlic, crushed
4 tablespoons flour
One 2-ounce jar stuffed olives,
   sliced and drained
One 4-ounce can mushrooms,
   drained
2 tablespoons chopped parsley
Worcestershire sauce to taste
Tabasco sauce to taste
2 ounces red wine (optional)
Romano cheese, grated
One 2-ounce jar chopped pimiento
   (optional)
¾ pound American cheese, grated*

Simmer chicken approximately 2 hours until tender in enough water to cover the hen or chicken parts, with 2 sliced onions, 1 quartered bell pepper, celery ribs, salt, black pepper and poultry seasoning to taste. Remove chicken; skin, debone and cut up. Strain the broth and save. Sauté for 5 minutes onions, celery, bell pepper and garlic in ¼ cup margarine. Add the flour and sauté for 5 minutes more. Slowly add 2 cups of the chicken broth that you saved. Simmer for 10 minutes. Add chicken, olives, mushrooms, parsley, salt, pepper, Worcestershire sauce and Tabasco sauce. Add wine, if desired, cover and simmer for 2 minutes. Serve over spaghetti which has been cooked in the chicken broth, according to the directions on the package, except do not add salt. Garnish with pimientos, if desired, and provide grated Romano cheese for sprinkling over chicken and spaghetti according to individual taste. Serves 8.

*Instead of serving the chicken sauce over the spaghetti, it may be mixed with the spaghetti, placed in a casserole, topped with grated American cheese and heated in a 250 degree oven until cheese is melted.

Mrs. Thomas B. Pugh II

## CURRIED CHICKEN OR TURKEY

6 tablespoons oil
1 medium onion, chopped
2 tablespoons chopped bell pepper
4 tablespoons flour
1½ cups turkey or chicken broth
1¼ cups sliced mushrooms,
   lightly sautéed, or one
   6-ounce can mushrooms
1½ to 4 teaspoons curry powder

3 cups cooked turkey or
   chicken, cubed
1 tart apple, cored and diced
One 5-ounce can water chestnuts
   (drained and sliced)
3 tablespoons chopped pimiento
1 tablespoon chopped parsley
Salt to taste
Pepper to taste

Heat the oil in a large casserole and sauté the onion and bell pepper until soft. Stir in flour, cook a moment and blend in turkey or chicken broth and the mushrooms, with their liquid if you used canned mushrooms. Simmer the mixture 15 to 20 minutes. Stir in curry powder and check seasoning by tasting. In a large bowl, mix the turkey or chicken pieces, apple, water chestnuts, pimiento, parsley, salt and pepper. Add this mixture to sauce and heat slowly, simmering 10 to 15 minutes over lowest heat. Serve over saffron rice. Place condiments in small bowls on table and let everyone help themselves. This dish can be done ahead and heated before serving (improves the flavor). Serves 6 to 8.

Condiments:
Chopped salted peanuts
Chutney
Chopped green onions

Toasted shredded coconut
India relish
Chopped hard-boiled eggs
Candied or preserved ginger

Mrs. Dean M. Mosely

## CHICKEN OR TURKEY TACO PIE

3 to 4 cups cooked, diced chicken
   or turkey (one 3-pound
   whole chicken)
One 10-ounce can enchilada sauce
One 10¾-ounce can mushroom soup

1 large onion, chopped
½ teaspoon garlic salt
Dash of pepper
One 11-ounce package corn chips
1 cup grated Cheddar cheese
1 cup chicken broth

Combine chicken or turkey, enchilada sauce, mushroom soup, onion, garlic salt and pepper. Grease a 2-quart baking dish and line with corn chips, reserving enough to cover the top. Add chicken or turkey mixture, making an even layer. Sprinkle with cheese and cover with reserved corn chips. Pour chicken broth over all. Bake at 350 degrees for 30 minutes.

Mrs. Charles Garvey

## CHICKEN AND OYSTER PIE

**Chicken:**

| | |
|---|---|
| 3-pound frying chicken | 1 pod garlic, cut in half |
| 1 carrot, quartered | 1 bay leaf |
| 1 onion, cut in half | 1 teaspoon salt |
| 1 stalk celery, with leaves, sliced | 3 peppercorns |

Cut up chicken. Place in heavy kettle. Add next seven ingredients.Cover with water and bring to a boil. Reduce heat and simmer covered for 45 minutes to an hour. Remove chicken from stock; skin, and cut meat from bones. Cut into 1-inch cubes. Strain stock and set aside.

**Filling:**

| | |
|---|---|
| 2 stalks celery, chopped | 4 tablespoons flour |
| 8 green onions chopped, whites and greens separated | Salt and pepper to taste |
| | 2 tablespoons Worcestershire sauce |
| 1 pod garlic, chopped (optional) | 2 to 3 dashes hot sauce (optional) |
| 1 pint oysters, drained and reserved | Chicken from above |
| Chicken stock from above | ½ cup chopped parsley |
| 4 tablespoons shortening | Pastry |

Add chopped celery, chopped white part of the green onions, garlic, and oyster liquid to stock from above. Cook down to 2 cups. Make brown roux with cooking fat and flour. Add stock gradually while stirring. Cook until thick, then add green onions, salt and pepper, Worcestershire sauce and hot sauce to taste. Add meat from above, oysters and chopped parsley. Simmer, stirring often, for about 20 minutes. Cool. Fit bottom crust into 2½-quart casserole; add filling to not more than 1 inch from the top. Adjust top crust pinching edges together. Slash top crust for escape of steam. Bake at 450 degrees for 25 minutes. Serves 6 to 8.

Mrs. James V. Carlisle
Mrs. W. B. Hatcher


## SPIRITED BREAST OF CHICKEN

| | |
|---|---|
| 4 whole chicken breasts | ¼ cup sliced mushrooms |
| Salt | ½ cup dry white wine |
| Pepper | 1 cup canned chicken consommé |
| 2 tablespoons thinly sliced green onion | 2 tablespoons chopped parsley |
| | ½ cup peeled, chopped tomatoes (no seeds) |

Skin the breasts. Salt and pepper them and sauté until light brown in teflon skillet. Remove chicken and add onion and mushrooms. Sauté 1 minute. Add wine and cook 1 minute. Add consommé, parsley and tomatoes. Return chicken to this mixture and simmer until slightly thickened. Cover and place in oven for 15 minutes at 350 degrees. Serves 4.

Mrs. J. W. Lyman

## CHICKEN CASSEROLE

One 10¾-ounce can cream of
  mushroom soup
One 10¾-ounce can cream of
  celery soup

1 cup water
1 cup raw rice
6 to 8 pieces chicken
One 1⅜-ounce package dried
  onion soup

Mix the soups and water together. Put rice in a 2-quart casserole. Pour soup mixture over rice. Arrange chicken on top of rice. Sprinkle onion soup over chicken. Cover. Bake at 325 degrees for 1½ hours. Serves 6.

Mrs. J. A. Todd

## CHICKEN TETRAZZINI

One 4-pound chicken, quartered
1 diced carrot
1 medium onion, chopped
2 stalks celery, coarsely chopped
Salt and pepper
3 tablespoons butter or chicken fat
3 tablespoons flour
2 cups chicken broth

1 cup half and half
½ pound mushrooms, sautéed
  in butter
2 tablespoons sherry
¼ pound grated Parmesan or
  Cheddar cheese
½ cup buttered bread crumbs
½ pound spaghetti

Boil chicken until tender in water to cover, to which has been added diced carrot, onions, celery and salt and pepper to taste. Allow chicken to cool in broth, then remove and cut into bite-sized pieces. Strain broth. Make a medium sauce with the butter or chicken fat, flour, chicken broth, and half and half. Add mushrooms and sherry. Boil spaghetti according to package directions in chicken broth. Combine sauce, mushrooms, chicken and spaghetti in greased baking dish. Sprinkle with grated cheese and bread crumbs and bake in 375 degree oven until heated thoroughly and lightly browned. Serves 8 to 10.

Mrs. W. B. Hatcher

## PAELLA

¼ cup olive oil or salad oil
1 fryer, cut in serving pieces
1 teaspoon monosodium glutamate
1 teaspoon salt
1 cup sliced celery, cut diagonally
½ cup chopped onion
One 4-ounce can mushrooms

2 cups cubed cooked ham
2½ cups water
One 10-ounce package frozen
  green peas
One 6- or 7-ounce package
  yellow rice (saffron)
½ pound cleaned, raw shrimp
  (1½ cups)

Heat oil in electric skillet at 350 degrees. Sprinkle chicken with seasonings. Add chicken to oil in skillet and brown on all sides. Add celery and onions. Cook about 5 minutes. Drain liquid from mushrooms. Add liquid and ham to skillet. Cover tightly and cook over low heat 15 minutes. To skillet mixture, add water, peas and rice. Stir to moisten rice and bring to a boil. Reduce heat. Cover and simmer 20 minutes. Stir in shrimp and mushrooms. Cover and simmer an additional 10 minutes. Serves 6.

Mrs. Wayne Allison

## BUTTERMILK CHICKEN

1 fryer, cut up, or 6 chicken
  breasts
1 tablespoon oil
1 tablespoon butter
⅓ cup chopped onion
1-pound can tomatoes, drained
1 cup buttermilk

½ teaspoon sugar
½ teaspoon salt
⅛ teaspoon white pepper
½ cup chopped chives
½ cup chopped parsley
1½ teaspoon dill weed
Lemon juice (a few drops)
1 cup sour cream

Brown chicken in oil and butter, add onions and sauté. Add tomatoes, buttermilk, sugar, salt and pepper. Cover and simmer 25 to 30 minutes. Add chives, parsley, and dill and cook uncovered 5 minutes. Add lemon juice and sour cream. Heat. Serves 6.

Mrs. Douglas W. McKay
Potomac, Maryland

## CHERRY CHICKEN

3 whole chicken breasts
⅓ cup flour
1½ teaspoons salt
1½ teaspoons garlic salt
1½ teaspoons paprika

¼ cup oil
1-pound can pitted dark
  sweet cherries
1 cup sauterne
4 cups hot cooked rice

Cut breasts in half. Mix flour, salt, garlic salt and paprika. Coat chicken with this mixture. Brown chicken in oil. Add cherries (including liquid) and wine to the chicken. Cover and simmer about 1 hour. Serve over rice. Serves 4 to 6.

Mrs. Whitehead Elmore

## CHICKEN JERUSALEM

8 chicken breast halves
Flour
½ cup margarine
One 14-ounce can artichoke hearts,
  drained
Juice of 1 lemon
One 8-ounce can mushrooms, drained
1 cup sherry
¾ cup water

2 bay leaves
⅓ cup chopped chives or
  green onions
¼ cup parsley
Onion salt
Garlic salt
Pepper
Pinch rosemary
Pinch thyme
½ cup heavy cream

Dust chicken breasts with flour. Brown in margarine. Add artichokes; squeeze the lemon juice over them. Add remaining ingredients except the cream. Cook on low heat in Dutch oven or electric skillet for 2 hours. Just before serving, remove chicken. Stir cream into gravy. Return chicken to gravy. Serve over rice. Serves 8.

Mrs. Carey Guglielmo

## CHICKEN BREASTS AND BROCCOLI

2 whole chicken breasts, or
equivalent dark meat
Water
Onion
Celery
Two 10-ounce packages frozen
broccoli spears
Juice of ½ average lemon, or to taste
Salt
Pepper

Two 10¾-ounce cans cream of
chicken soup
1 cup mayonnaise
(homemade preferred)
1 tablespoon curry powder, or
less to taste
½ cup grated Parmesan cheese
1 cup fresh, buttered, toasted
bread crumbs
Paprika

Boil chicken for 45 minutes in a small amount of water seasoned with onion and celery. Drain. Cut chicken into bite-size pieces. Undercook broccoli in the amount of water specified on package. Arrange broccoli and chicken in a lightly buttered 2- to 3-quart casserole. Squeeze lemon juice over all. Combine soup, mayonnaise, salt, pepper and curry powder. Pour over broccoli and chicken. Top with Parmesan cheese and bread crumbs. Sprinkle with paprika. Bake at 350 degrees for 30 minutes. Serves 4.

Mrs. Charles F. Duchein, Jr.

## BARBECUE SAUCE FOR CHICKEN

½ cup ketchup
⅓ cup vinegar
1½ cups margarine
2 large onions, coarsely cut up
4 cloves garlic, minced
1 large bell pepper, coarsely cut up
1 large rib celery, cut in two
1 lemon, cut in two

1 tablespoon brown sugar
⅓ cup Worcestershire sauce
1 cup chili-flavored barbecue
sauce, Gebhardts brand
if available
1 cup water
3 bay leaves
Tabasco sauce to taste

Combine all ingredients in a 3-quart saucepan. Cook at least 15 minutes. Use to brush on chicken when barbecuing. Makes about 4⅔ cups.

Mrs. Norman Saurage, Jr.

## CHICKEN BARBECUE SAUCE

½ cup butter or margarine, melted
⅓ cup Worcestershire sauce
⅓ cup A-1 sauce
½ cup catsup
Juice of 2 lemons

1 teaspoon salt
½ teaspoon pepper
1 cup water
2 cloves garlic, finely chopped
Dash liquid smoke

Combine all ingredients and bring to a boil. Simmer 20 minutes. Pour generous amount of sauce over chicken before placing on grill. Baste frequently while cooking. Serve remainder of sauce over cooked chicken. Can be stored in refrigerator for future use. Makes enough sauce for 2 chickens.

Mrs. John P. Everett, Jr.

## CHICKEN CASSEROLE WITH SOUR CREAM SAUCE

2 whole chicken breasts, split
Salt
Lemon-pepper marinade (granulated)
¼ cup butter or margarine
¼ cup chopped green onions
1 clove garlic, minced

1 teaspoon paprika
One 10-ounce package frozen
  chopped broccoli
4 canned peach halves
1 cup sour cream
¼ cup mayonnaise
¼ cup grated Parmesan cheese

Season chicken with salt and lemon-pepper marinade. Melt butter in small skillet. Sauté green onions and garlic for a few minutes. Stir in paprika. Turn chicken in the mixture until well coated. Transfer chicken to a shallow broiler-proof baking dish. Cover loosely with foil. Bake at 375 degrees until tender, about 20 to 30 minutes. Meanwhile, cook broccoli. Drain, set aside, and keep warm. Arrange broccoli and peach halves in pan beside chicken. Mix sour cream and mayonnaise together. Spoon over all. Sprinkle with cheese. Broil low in oven until richly flecked with brown, about 5 minutes. Serves 4.

Mrs. John B. Noland

## CORNISH HENS IN ORANGE SAUCE

2 to 6 Cornish hens (depends on how
  many people you want to serve),
  cleaned and split
Melted butter
1 cup orange marmalade
¼ cup brown sugar
3 tablespoons wine vinegar

2 teaspoons Worcestershire sauce
½ teaspoon curry powder
½ teaspoon ground ginger
1 teaspoon monosodium glutamate
Dash of cayenne
Salt
Pepper

Wash and dry hens. Brush with melted butter. Line broiler pan with aluminum foil. Place hen halves, skin side down, in pan. Combine remaining ingredients in saucepan. Heat over medium heat to boiling point. Simmer for 2 minutes, stirring constantly. Remove from heat. Brush surface of hens with sauce. Roast in preheated 350 degree oven for 30 minutes. Turn and roast for 30 minutes on other side, brushing often with sauce. Serves 2 to 6.

Mrs. Dean M. Mosely

## ROCK CORNISH HENS DELUXE

Three 1-pound Rock Cornish hens
Salt
Pepper
3 tablespoons butter or margarine
¼ cup minced onion

One 6-ounce can sliced mushrooms
¾ cup chicken broth
2 tablespoons cornstarch
¼ cup cold water
1 teaspoon Kitchen Bouquet
1 cup sour cream

Cut hens in half, season with salt and pepper. Melt butter or margarine in large skillet using medium heat. Add hens, skin side down and sauté until golden brown. Turn, add onion and brown other side. Drain mushrooms (save liquid) and add the liquid and chicken broth to hens. Simmer, cover, and cook on low heat for 45 minutes. Remove hens and place on warm serving dish. Combine cornstarch, water and Kitchen Bouquet. Stir this mixture into skillet drippings. Cook, stirring constantly, until gravy thickens and is smooth. Switch to low heat and stir in sour cream and mushrooms. Heat but do not boil. Serve sauce in gravy boat or pour over hens. May substitute chicken breasts or thighs for the hens. Serves 6.

Mrs. Wayne T. Davis

### CORNBREAD DRESSING I

1½ cups chopped onion
2 cups chopped celery
½ cup butter, melted
6 cups cornbread (cooked
  and crumbled)
½ cup chopped parsley

1 tablespoon salt
Red pepper
Black pepper
Hot milk
4 eggs (2 raw, 2 cooked)
1 tablespoon baking powder

Sauté onions and celery in butter until soft, not brown. Remove from fire. Add cornbread, parsley, salt, pepper and enough hot milk to moisten. Add beaten raw eggs and chopped cooked eggs. Add baking powder. Mix well. Stuff turkey and place in casserole and heat in oven. This dressing can be made the day before or frozen. Serves 6.

Mrs. Wayne T. Davis

### MOIST CORNBREAD DRESSING

1 cup dry herb stuffing mix
1 cup seasoned croutons, crushed
¾ cup chopped onion
¾ cup chopped celery
⅓ cup chopped bell pepper
2 cups cornbread, crumbled

1 teaspoon poultry seasoning
4 eggs, slightly beaten
6 cups canned chicken broth
2 teaspoons chopped green onions
2 tablespoons chopped parsley
Freshly ground pepper to taste

In an 8x14-inch pan, mix all ingredients together. Bake at 350 degrees for approximately 1 to 1½ hours, or until firm and golden brown. Dressing may be prepared ahead of time. This freezes well. Serves 8.

Mrs. Lloyd T. Leake

### RICE AND CORN DRESSING

2 cups raw rice, washed
½ cup bacon grease
½ cup chopped celery
½ cup chopped bell pepper
½ cup chopped parsley
1 cup chopped onion

One 12-ounce can Mexican corn with
  peppers, undrained
1 cup chopped almonds or pecans
Two 10½-ounce cans chicken broth
Salt
Red pepper

In a 12-inch skillet, lightly brown (don't burn) rice in bacon grease. Add celery, bell pepper, parsley and onion. Cook slowly until wilted. Add corn and nuts. Stir in broth. Add salt and red pepper to taste. Cover and cook on low heat until dry and tender, about 20 to 30 minutes. This is marvelous for a buffet. It may easily be doubled. Makes 8 generous servings.

Mrs. Ronald A. Coco

## LIGHT BREAD DRESSING

| | |
|---|---|
| 1 large onion, chopped | 2 eggs |
| 3 large stalks celery, chopped | Salt to taste |
| ½ cup butter | Pepper to taste |
| 10 slices bread | Two 10½-ounce cans chicken broth |

Sauté onion and celery in butter. In a bowl, break up bread and add eggs, work with fingers to coat bread. Add salt, pepper and sautéed onion and celery. Heat broth and add to mixture (1½ cans may be enough). Stir. Bake at 375 degrees in a greased casserole for 45 minutes. Serves 4 to 6.

Mrs. Matthew W. Hargrove III
LaMarque, Texas

## OYSTER DRESSING

| | |
|---|---|
| ½ cup margarine | Salt |
| 2 large onions, chopped | Pepper |
| ⅓ cup chopped celery | Pinch basil |
| 4 slices bread | Pinch sage |
| Water | Pinch thyme |
| 1 egg, beaten | Pinch marjoram |
| 2 tablespoons chopped parsley | Bread crumbs (optional) |
| 1 pint oysters, drained | Margarine |

Melt margarine in a 10-inch skillet. Sauté onions and celery until transparent. Soak the bread in water. Drain and squeeze water out of bread. Tear into small pieces. Add to onion mixture. Add egg, parsley and oysters. Season with salt, pepper and spices to taste. Simmer until oysters begin to curl. If mixture is soggy, add bread crumbs. It should be very moist, but there should be no excess liquid. Turn into a 2-quart casserole and dot with margarine. Bake at 350 degrees for about 30 minutes. This can be made a day ahead, refrigerated and then baked for 45 minutes. Serves 6.

Mrs. Michael H. Mayer

## CORNBREAD-GRITS DRESSING

| | |
|---|---|
| Chicken giblets (3 gizzards, 3 hearts, 3 necks and 3 livers) | 1½ cups chopped green onions |
| Salt | ½ cup chopped onion |
| 1 small onion, chopped | ¼ cup cooking oil or butter |
| 1 bay leaf | 4 teaspoons salt |
| 2 to 3 stalks of celery | ½ teaspoon black pepper |
| 1½ cups hot water | 2 teaspoons sage |
| 4 cubes chicken bouillon | ½ cup minced parsley |
| 6 slices white bread | 5 cups crumbled cornbread |
| 2 cups chopped celery with tops | ½ cup cooked grits |

Cook giblets in pot with water to cover. Add salt, onion, bay leaf and celery. Cover and cook slowly for 2 hours. Drain, reserve stock, and chop giblets.

Soak bread slices in hot water in which bouillon cubes have been dissolved, save any water that is not absorbed. Saute'celery and onions in cooking oil or butter until tender. Add salt, pepper, sage and parsley (more or less to suit your taste). Combine the crumbled cornbread, bread slices and grits, also any water left from when you soaked the bread slices. Add giblets and if necessary broth from cooking giblets to make dressing moist. Place in casserole and heat in 300 degree oven. This can be made ahead and frozen. Adequate for 14- to 16-pound turkey.

Mrs. Louis C. Christian, Jr.

## CORNBREAD DRESSING II

2 cups chopped celery
1 medium onion, chopped
Chicken or turkey broth as needed to moisten
1 bunch green onions, chopped

6 cups cornbread, crumbled (made without sugar)
5 cups French bread, broken in small bits, toasted
1½ pounds seasoned pork sausage, cooked and crumbled
¼ pound butter (more if desired)

Cook celery and onion until tender in broth. Add green onions. Combine cornbread, French bread bits, seasoning and pork sausage. Toss with melted butter and broth to desired degree of moistness. Adjust for salt and pepper. Use as stuffing in fowl (leaving room for expansion) or bake in greased casserole at 325 degrees for 20 to 30 minutes to serve with fowl.

Mrs. W. B. Hatcher

## SPINACH DRESSING

Two 10-ounce packages frozen, chopped spinach
¼ cup butter
1 onion, chopped
3 green onions, chopped
2 stalks celery, chopped
2 tablespoons chopped parsley
½ pound pork or favorite sausage
1 pound ground beef
1 tablespoon thyme

1 tablespoon Beau Monde seasoning (if unable to find, substitute a mixture of onion salt, celery salt and monosodium glutamate)
Salt to taste
Black and red pepper to taste
2 tablespoons Parmesan cheese
2 eggs
1 cup cooked rice

Cook spinach, set aside to drain. Sauté vegetables in butter. Brown meat. Add seasonings. Mix with spinach. Add cheese, eggs and rice. Stir together until well mixed. Bake in 2-quart casserole for 20 minutes at 350 degrees. Serves 8.

Mrs. S. Pendery Gibbens

## BREAST OF CHICKEN JACQUES

2 chicken breasts, halved
⅓ cup butter
2 tablespoons olive oil
1 garlic clove, minced
½ cup diced red and green sweet
  peppers

12 mushroom caps
½ cup sliced ripe olives
1 cup sour cream
2 tablespoons pâté de foie gras
Salt to taste
Pepper to taste
¼ cup sherry

Sauté chicken breasts and garlic in butter and olive oil until tender, but not brown. Remove to warm platter and keep warm. Sauté the sweet peppers until limp. Add mushroom caps and ripe olives and cook 5 minutes over moderate heat, stirring frequently. Remove mixture and set aside. Stir in sour cream into which pâté de foie gras has been blended. Salt and pepper to taste. Bring to a boil, stirring constantly. Add sherry, chicken breasts and mushroom mixture. Cook over moderate heat for 2 minutes. Serves 4.

Mrs. W. C. Nettles, Jr.

## GAME

    As in many states in which wild game abounds, Louisiana has developed a style of cookery particularly suited to the meats harvested through hunting and trapping. Many of these recipes sprang from the woods themselves. The hunters often prepared the meat with seasonings and utensils at hand. They have been refined for the kitchen and are guaranteed to produce succulent results every time. In Louisiana, the rendering of a delectable game dish is the memorable postscript to the hunt itself.

## WILD DUCK STEW

5 to 6 small ducks
Salt and pepper to taste
Flour
Oil
2 large onions
1 cup celery
½ cup green onions

3 large cloves garlic
½ cup bell pepper
½ cup parsley
One 4-ounce can mushrooms, stems
   and pieces
Tabasco sauce
Worcestershire sauce

Remove skin from ducks; cut ducks in half; wash well and salt and pepper generously. Dredge in flour and sear in 6 to 9 tablespoons of oil. Remove duck and add 6 to 9 tablespoons flour to oil. Make a dark roux. Add chopped seasonings and cook until tender. Return duck to iron pot. Add water to cover duck. Add Worcestershire sauce and Tabasco sauce. Correct seasoning. Cook on low burner for about two hours or until duck is tender. Add mushrooms before serving. Serves 10.

Mrs. May S. Magee

## POT ROASTED DUCKS

3 mallards, pintails or other ducks
Salt and pepper
Oil
2 large onions, chopped
1 large apple, cut into small pieces

½ cup burgundy or other dry
   red wine
3 teaspoons Kitchen Bouquet
1 teaspoon dry mustard
One 6-ounce can mushrooms

Wash ducks thoroughly, especially inside, and dry. Cut off tails which sometimes cause oily flavor. Salt and pepper insides heavily. Put a little cooking oil on a paper towel and rub inside of heavy Dutch oven. Brown ducks in Dutch oven; salt and pepper outside of ducks as you turn and brown them. Add chopped onions. Cover and cook on top of stove for 1 hour. Add cut up apple and wine and cook until fork tender. Add Kitchen Bouquet, dry mustard, mushrooms and additional salt and pepper as needed. Cook 15 minutes. Serve over rice. Serves 6.

Mrs. Freddie Acosta

## DUCK AND SAUSAGE GUMBO

1¾ cups oil
1½ cups flour
3 cups chopped onion
1 bell pepper, chopped
1 cup chopped celery
4 large ducks, cut into
   serving pieces

3 quarts water
1½ tablespoons salt
1 teaspoon black pepper
⅛ teaspoon red pepper
Tabasco sauce to taste
1 pound smoked sausage
1 tablespoon filé
¼ cup chopped green onion tops

In a large black iron pot, make a roux with oil and flour. Cook until dark brown, stirring constantly. Add onion, bell pepper and celery. Cook until wilted. Add duck and stir. Add water and seasonings. Simmer 3 hours. Cut sausage into bite-sized pieces and add to mixture. Cook 1 more hour. Since the ducks were not browned separately, spoon off excess amount of grease that will have cooked out of the duck. If you prefer, you can brown ducks separately. Serve with rice. Serves 10 to 12.

Mrs. Chambliss Mizelle

## DUCK SAUCE PIQUANT

1 cup flour
1 cup oil or shortening
2 large onions, chopped
1 to 2 bunches green onions
7 to 8 stalks celery
One 4-ounce can mushrooms
Two 2-ounce jars pimiento
Parsley

2 small bay leaves
4 to 5 ducks, skinned, seasoned,
   boiled and cut in large pieces,
   reserve stock
3 tablespoons Worcestershire sauce
Salt and pepper (red and black)
   to taste
One 16-ounce can peas, drained,
   optional

Brown flour in oil. Add onions and celery. Cook until well done, about 1 hour. Add mushrooms, pimiento, parsley and bay leaves. Cook 30 minutes. Add ducks, Worcestershire sauce and seasonings. Thin with stock from ducks. Cover and cook until ducks are tender. Right before serving, add green peas. Serve with rice. Turnips are delicious with this. Serves 10 to 12.

Mrs. J. Noland Singletary

## SMOTHERED QUAIL

6 quail
6 tablespoons butter
3 tablespoons flour

2 cups chicken broth
½ cup sherry
Salt and pepper to taste

Dress and season quail. Brown in heavy skillet or Dutch oven in butter. When golden, remove quail to deep baking dish. Add flour to butter in skillet and stir well. Slowly add chicken broth and sherry; blend well. Add salt and pepper to taste. Bring to a boil, then pour over quail. Cover tightly and bake in 350 degree oven for 1 hour. Serves 6.

Mrs. Carlton S. Carpenter, Jr.

## DUTCH OVEN DOVES

8 doves, cleaned and dressed
Salt
Pepper
Flour
3 tablespoons butter
1 teaspoon finely chopped parsley

⅛ teaspoon thyme
⅛ teaspoon rosemary
½ cup finely chopped onion
One 4-ounce can button
   mushrooms, undrained
1 cup white wine

Salt and pepper doves. Dredge in flour and brown in butter in Dutch oven. Sprinkle with parsley, thyme and rosemary. Cover and cook slowly for 15 minutes. Add onions, mushrooms and white wine. Cover and simmer for 1 hour or until tender. Serves 4.

Mrs. John G. Blanche

## VENISON ROAST

| | |
|---|---|
| Venison roast or loin | Garlic |
| 1 cup vinegar | Flour |
| Water | Oil |
| Salt and pepper | 1 envelope dry onion soup mix |

Place roast, frozen or thawed, in a large container with vinegar and enough water to cover it. Marinate for at least three hours in the refrigerator. Wash meat thoroughly under cold water to draw all the blood out of the meat. Pat dry and stuff with garlic. Plug each hole with a little piece of meat. Salt and pepper roast and roll in flour. Heat just enough oil to cover the bottom of the pan and brown roast on all sides. Sprinkle dry onion soup mix over roast and add water to make desired amount of gravy. Baste roast while cooking slowly in a covered pot for about 4 hours or until tender.

Mrs. Thomas Holliday

**HOW MEN COOK**

## COOKING GAME WITH A BROWN GRAVY

The principle of cooking game with a brown gravy is the same whether you cook dove, quail, duck, rabbit or squirrel. Either of two ways is acceptable for making the gravy base. One is to make the roux and the other is to dust the game with flour and fry. When cooking in small quantities, I prefer the dusting with flour and frying method. When cooking for 40 to 50, you should use the roux method. Also use the roux method for cooking ducks, because if you have ever tried dusting them with flour and frying, you will understand why the roux method is preferable. Ducks should be seasoned and browned in the oven before cooking with a gravy.

The base for the gravy is flour and oil, and to this base you add vegetables, salt and spices to season for taste. Onions, celery and bell pepper are the basic vegetables. I use them in the proportion of 3-2-1: three parts onion, two parts celery and one part bell pepper. Little experience is needed to determine the proper amount. In cooking enough for 4 to 6 people, as a general rule, start with two medium-sized onions and by sight make up the other proportions of celery and bell pepper in accordance with the suggested proportions, remembering that the only purpose in adding the vegetables is to make the gravy taste better. In connection with making the gravy taste better, adding mushrooms, bay leaves and garlic, with discretion, may be a very good idea. Some cooks even add prepared gravy mixes to the above, but this only proves that they don't know how to cook.

When using the roux method, you brown the game without flouring. Then, using the same oil, add flour until the oil is saturated and start the browning process. The purpose of the roux is to form the base for the gravy and as a general rule, two heaping tablespoons of flour will make the right amount of gravy for the average meal. To the roux, you add the vegetables, then the water or liquid, and then the game and cook until tender.

Anything young and tender is good, and I prefer young, tender gray squirrels over all other game. I especially like it for a late breakfast or brunch, say around ten or eleven o'clock, after a good morning hunt. The following recipe for squirrels is suggested after an early morning hunt.

## SQUIRRELS

About 5 or 6 young, tender gray squirrels will easily feed four big eaters and six average eaters.

Cut up the squirrels into frying sized pieces. Salt and pepper and dust with flour in a paper bag. Next start browning the squirrels in vegetable oil. Use just enough vegetable oil to cover the bottom of the pot in order to brown properly. Do not float squirrels in oil. As squirrels brown, remove them from the oil and allow to drain on paper towel. Start cutting up vegetables in proportions of 3-2-1: three parts onion, two parts celery and 1 part bell pepper. Use the oil in which you fried the squirrels but pour off excess oil, leaving just enough to sauté vegetables until tender. When vegetables are tender, add the squirrels and fill pot with water into which you have dissolved two bouillon cubes (any kind). Do not cover the squirrels with the water, as your purpose is to steam—not boil. Add 1 or 2 bay leaves, put a lid over the frying pan and turn on low. Let squirrels simmer until tender. If you are lucky and have chicken stock, it is better than water and bouillon cubes. One more hint, if the gravy is not brown enough, a little Kitchen Bouquet will do the trick. Serve with grits and biscuits.

Judge Fred A. Blanche, Jr.

## MILK PUNCH II

½ gallon ice cream 1 quart milk
One fifth bourbon

Let ice cream soften. Add milk and bourbon. Mix well. This should be made the day before serving. Put in freezer. Remove about an hour before serving. It may be poured from a pitcher or put in punch bowl. Sprinkle with nutmeg.

Judge Fred A. Blanche, Jr.

## WILD DUCK

4 ducks, cleaned
Coarse ground salt
Coarse ground pepper
Celery
1 large onion
1 turnip and/or apple
One 10¾-ounce can beef bouillon
4 ounces soy sauce
2 ounces Worcestershire sauce

4 tablespoons Pickapeppa sauce
1½ cups red wine
4 small onions, quartered
Seasoning salt
Marjoram
Garlic salt
Dash of Tabasco sauce
½ cup chopped green onions
4 jiggers Grand Marnier,
Cointreau or Triple Sec

Wash, clean and thoroughly dry ducks. Rub inside and out with coarse ground salt and pepper. Stuff carcass with celery, large onion, turnip and /or apple. Place the ducks in a Dutch oven or baking pan, the more crowded the better. Cover the ducks with hot water until only the upper ⅓ of the ducks are exposed. Add beef bouillon, soy sauce, Worcestershire sauce, Pickapeppa sauce, 1 cup red wine, small onions, salt and Tabasco sauce. Place pan, uncovered, in oven preheated to 550 degrees until sauce is bubbling strongly. Reduce temperature gradually to approximately 400 degrees, but sufficient to maintain the sauce bubbling. Turn ducks over every half hour, baste every half hour in between turnings. When sauce has been reduced to about two inches in depth (approximately 2 hours) add another ½ cup of wine, ½ cup green onions and pour one jigger of Grand Marnier, Cointreau or Triple Sec over each duck. Continue the bubbling until ducks are thoroughly tender. The sauce should then be 1½ inches deep. Remove as much fat as possible with spoon, then remove the rest from the sauce by carefully wiping a paper towel across the sauce. If sauce appears too thin, it can be cooked longer. Ducks should be placed back in the fat-free sauce and warmed thoroughly before serving. Note that there is no fat or grease used at any place in this recipe and by the paper towel method all of the natural fats from the ducks are removed. This is the best gravy you ever tasted. Serves 6.

Mr. Charles F. Duchein

## WILD GAME JAMBALAYA

| | |
|---|---|
| 5 large red onions | 2 ducks |
| 2 bunches green onions | 2 pounds venison |
| 1 pod garlic | 1 cup Italian dressing |
| 2 large bell peppers | Salt to taste |
| 1 bunch parsley | Black pepper, to taste |
| ½ stalk celery | Cayenne pepper, to taste |
| Two 3-ounce cans mushrooms | Monosodium glutamate |
| ¼ cup corn oil | Garlic salt |
| Two 10-ounce cans Rotel tomatoes, | ½ cup corn oil |
|    undrained | 2 pounds hot link sausage |
| 3 squirrels | 4 to 5 cups uncooked long |
| 1 rabbit |    grain rice |

Chop onions, garlic, bell peppers, parsley, celery and mushrooms into small pieces. Sauté in ¼ cup oil. Cook 2 hours. Add tomatoes and simmer 1 hour. Cut wild game in small pieces removing as many bones as possible. Marinate game in Italian dressing and seasonings in a large iron pot for 45 minutes. Add oil and cook over low heat until meat is tender, about 3 hours. Take out game and remove any bones which may be easily taken out. Reserve juice. Cut sausage in ½-inch pieces and fry in skillet. Reserve sausage drippings. Combine sausage drippings, game, juices and seasonings. Simmer for 15 to 20 minutes over low heat. Cook rice as directed on package. Add enough rice to jambalaya mixture to moisten rice thoroughly. Toss gently and serve. Serves 12.

Mr. and Mrs. Eugene Roe, Sr.

## CAPPUCCINO

| | |
|---|---|
| 1 individual package (1 ounce) | 1 ounce cognac |
|    cocoa mix | 6 ounces hot coffee |
| | 1 tablespoon whipped cream |

Add cognac to cocoa mix in large cup. Fill cup with hot coffee. Stir well. Top with whipped cream. Serve hot as after dinner drink. One serving.

Mr. Oran Ritter
Braniff International

## CAFÉ BRÛLOT

| | |
|---|---|
| 1 cup sugar | Peel of 1 orange |
| 1 cup bourbon | Peel of 1 lemon |
| 1 tablespoon whole cloves | 6 cups (36 ounces) hot, brewed dark |
| 2 sticks cinnamon |    roast coffee |

Put all ingredients except coffee in a saucepan and mash together while slowly bringing to the boiling point. When ready to boil, remove from heat and set fire to mixture. After alcohol has burned off, add hot coffee. Can be served immediately, strained, or can be kept hot by placing saucepan in a pan of hot water over burner. Flavor improves after mixture stands for a few minutes. Yield: twelve 4-ounce servings.

Mr. Roland Saurage
Greenwich, Connecticut

## CHERRY TORTE, BLACK FOREST STYLE

| | |
|---|---|
| 1 quart large black cherries | ½ pound butter |
| ½ cup kirsch | 3 egg yolks |
| 1½ pounds (5 cups) | Two 8-inch spongecake layers, |
| confectioners sugar | 1 inch thick |
| 3 tablespoons cornstarch | 1 cup finely shaved |
| | bittersweet chocolate |

Wash cherries; remove stems and seeds. Mix kirsch and 1 cup sugar and pour over fruit in bowl. Let stand at least 2 hours, then heat to boiling. Mix cornstarch with about 2 tablespoons cherry juice and stir into cherries. Cook and stir until slightly thickened. Remove from heat and let cool. This should be consistency of thin jelly. Beat butter and remaining sugar smoothly together. Beat egg yolks into this and continue beating until mixture is light and fluffy. Place layer of cake on plate; make border around edge with butter mixture and spread some butter cream in circle in center of cake. Spread cooled, thickened cherry mixture between butter cream border and center. Place second layer on top; press down just sufficiently to make layers stick together. Cover top and sides of both layers with remaining butter cream. Sprinkle top with chocolate. Serves 6 to 8.

Mr. Charles Brandt
Chalet Brandt Restaurant

## MINT JULEP

There are many recipes for the mint julep, but some are quite tedious and others require post-mix refrigeration. In spite of their excellence, the more sophisticated drinks tend to discourage the host from selecting this noble refreshment for his drop-in guests. The following is not too complicated, but makes a fine toddy.

To a large mixing glass add 1½ teaspoons sugar, 1 teaspoon water, and a dash of Angostura bitters, for each drink. Fill the glass about ⅔ full with washed tender mint leaves. Discard the larger leaves which may be bitter. Lightly bruise the mixture with a blunt instrument. Add about 2¼ ounces (1½ jiggers) of good bourbon per drink with crushed or finely cracked ice. Garnish with pretty clusters of mint leaves and insert straws.

Dr. Richard M. Nunnally

## PÂTÉ

| | |
|---|---|
| 1 pound pork liver | ⅛ teaspoon allspice |
| 1 pound shortening, not melted | ½ package frozen, buttered spinach |
| 1½ large onions | 1½ tablespoons salt |
| 4 cloves garlic | 2 teaspoons black pepper |
| ⅛ teaspoon ground cloves | 2 teaspoons red pepper |

Blend or grind all ingredients together two or three times. Put in iron pot and mix with rotary beater until thoroughly blended. Cover pot and bake in preheated 300 degree oven for 1 hour. Cool for 50 minutes. If grease has settled in center, cut pâté from center to edge at several places. Drain excess fat. Put in small jars or mold and refrigerate. Do not freeze. Serve cold with crackers.

Dr. J. Malcolm Leveque

## ERNEST'S MARINADE FOR CRAB CLAWS

1 cup chopped green onions,          2 cups Spanish olive oil
  tops and bottoms                   2 cups tarragon vinegar
1 cup chopped celery, leaves and stalk   Juice of 6 lemons
4 pods garlic, chopped               2 tablespoons salt
1 cup chopped parsley                1 tablespoon pepper

Chop first four ingredients as fine as possible with French knife. Add remaining ingredients and mix well. Let stand at room temperature for 48 hours. Marinate crab claws for 30 minutes before serving. This marinade is also excellent for boiled shrimp.

Mr. Ernest Palmisano
Ernest's Supper Club and Winner's Club
Shreveport, Louisiana

## COLD AVOCADO SOUP

1½ avocados (average size), diced    1 clove garlic
One 14-ounce can chicken broth or    ½ pint breakfast or whipping cream
  1¾ cup fresh chicken stock         One 8-ounce carton sour cream
Juice of 1 lemon                     Salt, pepper and Tabasco sauce
                                       to taste

Place all ingredients in blender and blend thoroughly. Chill in refrigerator several hours before serving. Surround each bowl with crushed ice and garnish with a dab of sour cream and a sprig of fresh parsley. Serves 6.

Mr. James Carr McAdams

## CREAM OF ONION SOUP

2 medium yellow onions, sliced       2 cups boiling water
½ cup butter                         Salt
2½ tablespoons flour                 Red pepper
2 cubes beef bouillon                Tabasco sauce

In a 1½-quart pot, sauté onions in butter until clear. Do not brown. Stir in flour. Dissolve bouillon in water. Gradually add hot bouillon and bring to a boil. Reduce heat and simmer 20 minutes. Add salt and red pepper to taste. Add a few drops Tabasco sauce to each serving as desired to heighten flavor. This is great on a nippy day when you come in from a hunt. Serves 4.

Mr. C. W. Roberts

## "OLE SOUTH" FRENCH DRESSING

½ cup sugar                          ⅓ cup catsup
¼ cup vinegar                        ½ cup salad oil
1 teaspoon lemon juice               1 teaspoon salt
2 teaspoons onion salt               1 teaspoon red pepper

Put all ingredients in a blender and blend well. Pour in a 1½-cup plastic or glass container and refrigerate at least 24 hours before using to enhance flavor. Serve over a green salad of your choice. Yield: 1½ cups.

Mr. Thomas E. Robinson
Kappa Alpha Fraternity, L.S.U.

## EASY CHEESE BREAD

3¾ cups buttermilk biscuit mix
1½ cups shredded sharp Cheddar
   cheese

1 egg, beaten
1¼ cups milk
½ teaspoon dry mustard
Sesame seeds

Preheat oven to 325 degrees. Grease loaf pan (9x5 inches). In large bowl, mix all ingredients except sesame seeds. Beat by hand 1 minute. Pour into pan and sprinkle top with sesame seeds. Bake for 55 to 60 minutes. Cool slightly before slicing. Spread generously with butter. Serves 6 to 8.

Mr. and Mrs. Lawson Lott

## THE BEST CORN CASSEROLE IN THE WHOLE WIDE WORLD

4 to 5 strips bacon and drippings
2 cups chopped onions
9 ears corn
2 cups grated Cheddar cheese

1 cup half-and-half cream
1 jar chopped pimiento
Salt and pepper
¾ teaspoon powdered ginger

Cook bacon until crisp. Remove and lay aside. In drippings, sauté onions until soft but not brown. Cut corn off the cob and scrape cob to get milk. (Cut only about half-way through kernels, then scrape the rest off.) Add corn and cheese to onions. Cook, stirring about 10 minutes. Add half-and-half cream, pimientos, seasonings and crumbled bacon. Heat in 2-quart casserole until bubbly. Freezes well. Serves 8 to 10.

Mr. J. E. Harper

## EGGPLANT SPINACH CASSEROLE

1 small eggplant
Flour, salt, black and red pepper
Olive oil
One 10-ounce package frozen chopped
   spinach, uncooked and thawed
One 6-ounce package brick cheese,
   sliced

One 6-ounce package Swiss cheese,
   sliced
Grated Parmesan cheese
Grated onion or onion powder
   (optional)
Seasoned bread crumbs
Butter

Peel and slice eggplant. Salt and drain on paper towels about 10 minutes. Dredge in flour that has been mixed with salt and pepper. Fry over medium heat in olive oil until brown. Drain. Grease a deep casserole (a loaf pan is ideal). Line bottom of loaf pan with half of eggplant, half of spinach, a layer of brick and Swiss cheese. Sprinkle with Parmesan cheese and onion (if desired). Repeat layers. Top with bread crumbs and dot with butter. Bake at 325 degrees for 30 minutes or until cheese bubbles. Serves 4.

Mr. James W. Ware

## FETTUCCINE ALL'ALFREDO

| | |
|---|---|
| 1 pound fettuccine noodles | 1 cup heavy cream |
| 2 tablespoons salt (for boiling) | Freshly ground black pepper |
| ½ cup soft butter | ¼ pound Parmesan cheese, grated |

Cook noodles in large pot of salted water for 10 minutes, or until noodles are tender. Drain well. Put noodles immediately into a chafing dish or electric skillet to keep warm. Add butter in several hunks and stir gently until noodles are coated. Add cream and grind in generous amount of black pepper. Continue stirring and tossing the noodles gently until cream thickens and clings to noodles. Add cheese and stir to mix well. Serve immediately. Serves 6.

Mr. Lewis Rieger

## BAKED STUFFED EGGS

Stuffed Egg Mixture:

| | |
|---|---|
| 8 boiled eggs, cooled | 1 tablespoon grated onion |
| ¼ cup butter, melted | ⅓ cup finely chopped ham |
| ½ teaspoon Worcestershire sauce | ½ cup grated Cheddar cheese |
| ¼ teaspoon dry mustard | 1 teaspoon parsley flakes |

Halve eggs lengthwise. Remove yolks and mash with all above ingredients. Stuff eggs and put in a single layer in an oblong dish.

Sauce:

| | |
|---|---|
| 3 tablespoons butter | ¾ cup light cream |
| 3 tablespoon flour | ½ cup grated Cheddar cheese |
| ½ cup hot chicken bouillon | Paprika |

In a saucepan, melt butter. Blend in flour. Add bouillon, cream and cheese. Cook over low heat until thick. Pour over eggs and sprinkle with paprika. Bake 20 minutes at 350 degrees. This can be done the day before, but do not thicken the sauce too much. Keep the sauce separate and cover both sauce and eggs and refrigerate until ready to cook. Serves 4.

Mr. Roland Saurage
Greenwich, Connecticut

## MUFFIN EGGS

| | |
|---|---|
| 1 dozen eggs, beaten | ½ cup milk |
| 1 cup finely chopped ham | Salt to taste |
| 1 cup finely chopped American cheese | Pepper to taste |
| ½ cup finely chopped bell pepper | Tabasco sauce to taste |

Preheat oven to 350 degrees. Mix together eggs, ham, cheese, bell pepper and milk. Add salt, pepper and Tabasco sauce to taste. Pour mixture into a well-greased, 12-mold muffin tin, filling only ¾ full. Bake 15 to 20 minutes or until mixture rises and is firm. Do not allow to brown. Serve at once. Serves 12.

Mr. Fred I. Heroman, Jr.

### PAGE'S RIB EYE ROAST

1 cup soy sauce
2 large pods fresh garlic, crushed

5 slices fresh ginger root (about ⅛x1-inch), minced
One 5-pound rib eye roast

Mix the soy sauce, garlic, and ginger root. Let this mixture stand for about 45 minutes before putting it on meat. Apply mixture to entire surface of roast with pastry brush. Pour any remaining over roast and cover the pan with foil to retain flavor. Let stand for about an hour, turning roast several times. Remove from mixture, and remove all pieces of ginger or garlic that remain on meat. Place roast on rotisserie and cook covered over charcoal, basting occasionally with remaining soy sauce.

Dr. Page Acree

### SAUERBRATEN

1 cup dry red wine
1 cup vinegar
2 cups water
4 onions, sliced
1 stalk celery, chopped
1 carrot, chopped
2 bay leaves
8 peppercorns, crushed

8 whole cloves
¼ teaspoon mustard seed
One 4-pound boneless beef roast
1 teaspoon salt
¼ teaspoon pepper
4 tablespoons flour
½ cup seedless raisins
½ cup sour cream

Combine red wine, vinegar, water, onions, carrot, bay leaves, peppercorns, cloves, and mustard seed in saucepan. Bring to a boil, cool. Place meat in large bowl. Pour marinade over meat. Place in refrigerator; marinate 2 to 3 days, turning several times. Remove meat from marinade; dry well. Sprinkle meat with salt and pepper. Brown meat very well on all sides. Add 2 cups of marinade; cover and simmer 2 to 3 hours or until meat is very tender. Remove meat, keep warm. Strain sauce; skim off fat; add water or marinade to make 2 cups. Stir in flour. Return to pan. Cook over low heat, stirring and scraping browned bits, until thickened. Stir in raisins and sour cream; blend well. Serve with meat. Serves 6 to 8.

Mr. Hubert Conrad
Manager, Baton Rouge Country Club

### BAKED PORK TENDERLOIN

2 small pork tenderloins
Salt and pepper
Flour
2 tablespoons oil

1 celery stalk, sliced
1 small onion, sliced
1 envelope mushroom soup mix
1½ cups water

Season tenderloins with salt and pepper and roll in flour. Brown on all sides in oil. Remove to shallow baking dish. Lightly brown celery and onion in drippings. Pour over meat. Combine soup mix and water; pour over meat. Cover and let stand in refrigerator overnight. Bake in moderate oven (350 degrees) for 2 hours. Serves 6 to 8.

Mr. Jim Regan

## CHILI À LA BYNUM

4 pounds freshly ground boneless stew or ground round (have butcher coarse grind)
Wesson oil (no substitute)
3 large onions, chopped
2 cloves garlic, chopped
Two 16-ounce cans peeled tomatoes

Six 8-ounce cans Ashley's chili purée
Salt
Black java pepper
Red pepper, crushed
Sugar
Four 15-ounce cans B&M pork & beans

Put meat in just enough oil to keep from sticking and sauté until all redness disappears; don't brown. Add onions and garlic, and continue to sauté until onions are transparent. Add tomatoes and chili purée. Remember that you want the chili thick at the end. The point is to keep it from sticking. *Burned chili is horrible!* Cook mixture as slowly as you can until the tomatoes disintegrate and the meat is tender. Add salt, peppers, and sugar to taste. Be sure you taste for sugar after pepper is added and thoroughly mixed. After mixture is done, add beans and cook just long enough to heat and mix well. This makes 5 quarts.

Mr. Bynum Turner


## CRAWFISH AND WINE SAUCE

**Wine Sauce:**

6 tablespoons butter
⅓ cup flour
One 14½-ounce can evaporated milk

3 egg yolks, beaten
½ cup heavy cream
Salt and white pepper to taste
½ cup white wine

Blend in top of double boiler or heavy saucepan the butter, flour and evaporated milk to make cream sauce. Strain sauce if necessary and fold in egg yolks and heavy cream. Add salt and white pepper to taste. Add wine. Reheat, but *do not boil*.

**Crawfish:**

6 tablespoons butter
2 stalks celery, cut in 1-inch pieces
2 green onions, cut in 1-inch pieces
1 cup white wine

2 pounds crawfish tails and fat
1 cup mushrooms, sliced and drained
¼ cup parsley, finely chopped
Salt and white pepper to taste
Bread crumbs

Sauté in butter the celery and green onions until soft but not brown. Add half of the wine. Reduce to one-half volume. Discard celery and green onions. Add crawfish tails and crawfish fat. Fold in mushrooms. Heat and add remaining wine. Add parsley and salt and white or red pepper to taste. Fold wine sauce and crawfish mixture together thoroughly. Place in ramekins and cover with bread crumbs. Bake at 350 degrees until contents bubble and bread crumbs brown, about 20 minutes. Serves 8 to 10.

Mr. Fred A. Blanche, Sr.

## CRAWFISH IN ASPIC BELLERIVE

1½ pints mayonnaise
3 tablespoons gelatin
½ cup cold water
2 chicken bouillon cubes
5 ounces catsup
8 pitted and finely chopped olives
2 boiled eggs, finely chopped
1 tablespoon chopped chives

4 tablespoons finely chopped
  sweet pickles
4 whole pimientos, finely chopped
1 pound boiled, peeled crawfish
  tails
Dash Worcestershire sauce
Dash Tabasco sauce
Salt to taste

Put mayonnaise in bowl. Dissolve gelatin in water. Bring gelatin mixture and bouillon cubes to boil on low fire. Add to mayonnaise with remaining ingredients. Mix well and put in oiled molds. Let stand in refrigerator overnight. Serve on chopped lettuce. Decorate with mayonnaise and tomato wedges and the dressing of your choice. Serves 8 to 10.

Mr. George Ruppeiner
Chef, Baton Rouge Country Club

## CRAWFISH CLAW STEW

1 pound crawfish claws, cooked
1 quart milk
1 teaspoon salt
¼ teaspoon crushed red pepper

¼ teaspoon monosodium glutamate
8 salted soda crackers, crumbled
  with a rolling pin
1 tablespoon finely minced parsley
8 extra cooked claws

Crush or crack all the claws with a pair of pliers. If they are frozen, they won't splatter. Put the crushed claws in a stew pan and add the milk; bring slowly to a boil. Remove from fire and let stand about an hour. Drain all the milk from the claws into another saucepan. Add all the other ingredients, except the parsley and extra claws, to the milk. Heat slowly, while stirring, until hot. Ladle out into 4 bowls. Sprinkle on the parsley and put two claws into each bowl for looks. What a wonderful flavor and beautiful color! Serves 4.

Mr. Fonville Winans

## HAM AND OYSTER CASSEROLE

4 tablespoons butter
3 tablespoons flour
1 cup hot chicken stock or bouillon
1 cup hot cream

¼ cup dry sherry
1 cup cooked ham, cut into ½-inch
  cubes
1 pint oysters, with juice
White pepper and salt to taste

Melt 3 tablespoons butter. Add flour and stir over low heat without permitting flour to brown (about 5 minutes). Add chicken stock and cream gradually. Continue to cook, stirring constantly, until sauce is thick and smooth. Put into a pan over hot water and add sherry and ham. In another skillet, melt 1 tablespoon butter and add oysters and juice. Cook until edges curl. Add oysters to sauce and heat thoroughly without boiling. Salt and pepper to taste. Serve in pastry shells or on toast. Serves 6.

Mr. John G. Blanche

## BROILED FILET OF FISH

| | |
|---|---|
| Fish | Salt and coarse ground pepper |
| Margarine | Seasoned salt |
| Soy sauce, 1 ounce per pound of fish | Marjoram |
| Worcestershire sauce | Green onions, chopped |
| Pickapeppa sauce | Capers |
| Garlic powder | Mushrooms |

Filet the fish, removing all bones. Wash the filet thoroughly and dry with a paper towel. Place in foil-lined pan which has been generously rubbed with margarine. Filets should fill entire bottom of pan. Soak generously with a good soy sauce, approximately 1 ounce per pound. Sprinkle with Worcestershire sauce and Pickapeppa sauce. Sprinkle to taste with garlic powder, salt, coarse ground pepper. seasoned salt and a pinch of marjoram. Cover filets with small slices of margarine, approximately an inch apart, over the entire surface of fish. Sprinkle generously with chopped green onions. Run pan under broiler with temperature set at 350 degrees. If your broiler does not operate with a temperature control, cook in top of oven and run under broiler at the last minute. Filets should slowly simmer for a period of about 45 minutes. Baste occasionally. During the last 15 minutes of cooking, sprinkle on additional chopped green onions and a few capers and mushrooms. If fish had roe, place whole sections of roe between filets.

Mr. Charles F. Duchein

## SHRIMP ITALIAN

| | |
|---|---|
| Olive oil | Salt and pepper |
| 5 pounds shrimp in shells | Cayenne pepper |
| 1 cup chopped onion | Rosemary |
| 1 cup chopped celery | Oregano |
| 1 cup chopped bell pepper | Bay leaves |
| 1 lemon, in small pieces | Garlic powder |
| ½ cup chopped shallots | 4 ounces sherry |

Cover bottom of pot with oil. Add shrimp in shells and cook until pink. Add measured ingredients and season to taste with remaining ingredients. Cover and cook on low fire for about 30 minutes. Stir occasionally. Serves 6.

Mr. Gordon D. Ellis

## DR. LEVEQUE'S CATFISH LOAF

| | |
|---|---|
| 2 pounds filet of catfish | Margarine |
| Salt to taste | 1 teaspoon Tabasco sauce |
| Pepper to taste | Juice of ½ lemon |
| Red pepper to taste | 2 tablespoons Worcestershire sauce |
| Cornmeal | 2 cups tomato catsup |
| Shortening | 1 Bermuda onion, sliced |
| 1 loaf unsliced bread | 6 small sour pickles, sliced |
| | 1 small jar olives |

Cut the catfish in small pieces, about 1½-inch cubes. Season well with salt, black pepper and red pepper. Roll in cornmeal and fry in deep fat until brown. When cooked, drain on paper toweling and keep in a warm place. Prepare the bread by cutting off the top and scooping out the inside. Butter the inside of the bread and the inside of the top. Toast in 350 degree oven. Make a sauce by mixing the Tabasco sauce, lemon juice, Worcestershire sauce and catsup. Coat the inside of the buttered loaf and top crust with this sauce. Then arrange layers of the fish, sliced onion, sauce, pickles and olives in the loaf and replace the top crust. Wrap the loaf in parchment paper or aluminum foil and bake at 300 degrees for 10 minutes. Remove from paper and serve hot. Serves 6.

Dr. Malcolm J. Leveque

## POACHED RED SNAPPER

2 small onions, quartered
2 stalks celery, cut into several
  pieces
1 lemon, quartered
1 teaspoon red pepper
4 or more tablespoons salt

One 4-pound red snapper
Finely minced fresh parsley
Tart homemade mayonnaise (be
  reckless with mustard and salt)
Paprika
Lemon wedges

Put onions, celery, lemon and seasonings in water and boil away for at least 15 minutes. For poaching, preferably use long, narrow aluminum fish poacher with enclosed tray to raise fish when cooked. Otherwise, use cheesecloth. Water should barely cover fish. Do not overcook. If fish is at room temperature, cook around 20 minutes on medium heat and then taste small wedge. A look is not enough. It may need 5 more minutes cooking. Then raise fish on tray and transfer to board or flat dish and cool. Remove skin, and with spatula arrange on individual salad plates or flat bottomed shells in two- or three-inch pieces. Sprinkle with parsley, then place heaping tablespoon of mayonnaise on top. Dust with paprika and serve cold as a first coarse at a dinner party. Serve with homemade Melba toast, using French bread and creamery butter, and chilled white wine. Do not use Sauterne, which is too sweet. A wedge of lemon on the plate completes the picture. This dish, typically French, serves eight if not used as a main course. If using as a main course, allow more fish.

Mr. Ernest Gueymard

## CHICKEN BREAST ROMANO

2 whole chicken breasts, boned
  and skinned
Lemon juice
2 tablespoons butter
One 6-ounce bottle marinated artichoke
  hearts

½ pound sliced fresh mushrooms
2 green onions, chopped
½ cup dry white wine
Salt and pepper to taste
1 tablespoon Pesto à la Genovese
  (green basil sauce)

Wash chicken in fresh lemon juice. Drain chicken. Heat butter in skillet over high flame. Brown chicken on both sides. Pour marinade from artichoke hearts over chicken. Place sliced mushrooms and chopped green onions in skillet with chicken and let fry down. Lower flame to medium. Pour wine over all and let simmer. Salt and pepper to taste. Place artichoke hearts in skillet and let heat through. Blend Pesto into wine sauce. When sauce has cooked down, serve on bed of rice or plain. Serves 2.

Mr. Vern Lanegrasse
The Hollywood Chef

## CHICKEN ROYALE

3-pound fryer
1 cup water
1 stalk celery with top
1 teaspoon salt
¼ teaspoon garlic powder
¼ teaspoon pepper
¼ teaspoon cayenne pepper or
   Tabasco sauce
¼ cup chopped parsley

2 tablespoons olive oil
One 4-ounce can mushrooms
   with juice
¼ teaspoon crushed red pepper
½ teaspoon crushed oregano
1 teaspoon Worcestershire sauce
   or soy sauce
1 tablespoon flour
2 or 3 tablespoons white wine

Place fryer in a covered pot with water, celery, salt, garlic powder, black pepper and cayenne or Tabasco sauce. Boil slowly until chicken is tender. Bone the chicken and save broth. In a large skillet or Dutch oven, sauté parsley in olive oil until soft but not brown. Add chicken broth and bring to a simmer. Add mushrooms and juice, red pepper, oregano and Worcestershire sauce, or soy sauce. Make a paste of flour and some of the hot broth. Slowly add paste to above mixture stirring constantly. Cook until thickened. Add boned chicken and let simmer about 5 minutes. Add wine as you remove from heat. Serves 4.

Mr. V. L. Roy, Jr.

## CHICKEN CRÊPES

Chicken:

4 to 5 chicken breasts or 1 fryer
Water to cover

¼ teaspoon ground oregano
5 dashes Tabasco sauce

Filling:

1 medium chopped onion
2 tablespoons oil
8 fresh mushrooms or 1 small can
5 green onions, chopped
1 small bunch parsley, chopped
1½ tablespoons flour
2 cups half-and-half
1 teaspoon Worcestershire sauce

10 dashes Tabasco sauce
2 teaspoons salt
1 teaspoon pepper
Juice of 1 lemon
1 ounce grated Romano cheese
3 ounces grated Mozzarella cheese
1 to 2 tablespoons dry white wine
Mornay sauce
Sliced mushrooms

Boil chicken in water, oregano and Tabasco sauce until tender. Remove and debone. In a large pot, sauté onions in butter until clear. Add mushrooms, green onions and parsley. Cook until vegetables are wilted. Add flour and brown slightly. Add cream. Stir constantly until it thickens. Add Worcestershire sauce, Tabasco sauce, salt, pepper and lemon juice. Add grated cheese slowly, over low heat, stirring constantly until smooth. Add chicken and wine to taste. Cook for 30 minutes on medium heat stirring often. May need to season to taste, but wait about 20 minutes. Fill each crêpe with a tablespoon of chicken filling roll. Dot crêpes with butter and cook at 400 degrees for 15 minutes. Garnish with mornay sauce and sliced mushrooms. This makes enough filling for 8 to 10 crêpes.

Crêpe Recipe:

| | |
|---|---|
| 1 cup milk | 1½ tablespoons melted butter |
| 2 eggs beaten | 1 pinch salt |
| 1 cup sifted flour | 1 teaspoon oil for pan |

Mix milk with eggs. Slowly add flour and constantly stir with wire whip. The mixture should be smooth and similar to cream. Add melted butter and salt and stir until blended. Place oil in pan, move it around the pan, then pour off excess oil. The heat should be on medium high. Cover the surface of the pan with batter and return excess to bowl. When crêpe begins to brown on edges flip it onto the other side. Always try to make the crêpes as thin as possible. Remove first crêpe from pan and throw in garbage can. Repeat the cooking process, only this time leave out oil used for seasoning the pan and save this crêpe. Place the cooked crêpes on a dish and cover the stack with damp towel. When freezing, place waxed paper between each crêpe. This should make about 20 crêpes.

Mr. Thomas Edward Robinson


## CHICKEN SAUSAGE JAMBALAYA

| | |
|---|---|
| 3 pounds onions, finely chopped | Garlic powder |
| Salt and pepper | 4 pounds sausage |
| 6 bunches green onions, chopped | Cooking oil |
| ½ bunch parsley, chopped | 20 cups of water |
| ½ pod garlic, chopped | Kitchen Bouquet |
| 4 chickens, cut up | 6 chicken bouillon cubes |
| Red pepper | 10 cups rice |

First, you must have a heavy pot such as cast iron, and all is cooked in the same pot. Finely chop onions and place in a bowl and salt and pepper the top of them. Chop green onions and place in a separate bowl. Salt and pepper them. Chop parsley and garlic and put in a separate bowl and salt and pepper them. Cut up chicken and salt and pepper both sides. Sprinkle chicken lightly with red pepper and garlic powder. Cut smoked sausage into one-inch pieces. Brown the chicken in deep hot oil. Do not cook long or chicken will fall apart later. After all the chicken is browned, take out some of the oil and brown the sausage. After browning the sausage, take nearly all of the oil out. Now you are ready to cook the seasonings. It takes very little oil as the onions will make juice. Sauté the onions until tender. Add green onions, parsley and garlic. Cook until green onions are wilted. Now add water to seasonings. Add Kitchen Bouquet to water to give dark brown color. Add 6 chicken bouillon cubes. Put meat back into pot piece by piece. This way you will keep unnecessary oil out. Bring water to a boil fairly rapidly. While waiting for water to boil, add salt until the juice tastes a little too salty. Add black and red pepper to taste. Once water boils a few minutes, cut fire very low and add raw rice. Mix rice in the juice and meat. Cover and keep fire low. Stir only twice. If rice appears too wet, remove top near the end of cooking. Cook until rice is done. Serves 20.

Mr. Joe Nicolosi

## SENATOR ELLENDER'S CREOLE PRALINES

2 cups granulated sugar
1 cup dark or light brown sugar
½ cup butter

1 cup milk
2 tablespoons corn syrup
4 cups pecan halves (If large halves, cut in small pieces)

Put all ingredients except the pecans in a 3-quart saucepan and cook for about 20 minutes, after boiling starts, stirring occasionally. Add the pecans and cook the mixture until liquid forms a soft ball when a little is dropped into cold water. Stir well and then drop by spoonsful on waxed paper. Place a few sheets of newspaper beneath the waxed paper. I find it convenient to place a small table near the stove, over which I put a few sheets of newspaper first, and put the waxed paper over that.

Sen. Allen J. Ellender

## BARBECUED VENISON

Venison roast or loin
1 cup vinegar
Water

Salt and pepper
Garlic
1 bottle Italian salad dressing

Place frozen or thawed roast in a large container and pour vinegar over the roast and then water. If water and vinegar do not cover the meat, turn several times while marinating for at least 3 hours. After marinating, wash meat thoroughly under cold water. This is important because it draws all the blood out of the meat. Pat dry and stuff with garlic. Use as much as you like and plug each hole with a little piece of meat to hold the garlic in while cooking. Salt and pepper the roast and place on grill over very low burning coals. The pit should have a cover. Baste meat with Italian salad dressing throughout cooking. Cook at least 4 hours or until tender.

Mr. Thomas Holliday

## DESSERTS

Louisiana cuisine has always maintained a special love for desserts, from elegant custards and cakes to delicate dishes of fresh fruit with, perhaps, a touch of liqueur or a dusting of sugar. As every good cook knows, the choice of a dessert relies primarily on what has gone before it. Some of these recipes provide just a taste of something sweet after a heavy meal and others are rich and filling enough to round out a light supper or complement a strong, dark cup of Louisiana coffee. Included in this section also are delectable cookies and candies you can be proud to serve or bestow as gifts.

## VANILLA CUSTARD ICE CREAM

| Four Quarts: | Six Quarts: |
|---|---|
| 2 quarts milk | 3 quarts milk |
| 2½ cups sugar | 3¾ cups sugar |
| 2 tablespoons flour | 3 tablespoons flour |
| ¼ teaspoon salt | ⅓ teaspoon salt |
| 8 eggs | 12 eggs |
| One 13-ounce can evaporated milk | One and a half 13-ounce cans |
| 1 tablespoon vanilla | evaporated milk |
| | 1½ tablespoons vanilla |

Scald the milk. In a mixing bowl, mix sugar, flour and salt. Add hot milk to sugar and flour mixture. Cook 3 minutes. Beat eggs well in another mixing bowl. Then slowly add milk mixture to eggs, a little at a time so it will not curdle. Cook over low heat until the mixture coats a spoon (about 15 minutes), stirring constantly. Take off fire and add evaporated milk and vanilla. Let cool completely before you freeze in ice cream freezer. This custard may be made a day ahead and put in refrigerator and then into ice cream freezer.

Mrs. Williams D. Wall, IV
Mrs. Wilmer Leake
Woodville, Mississippi


## VANILLA ICE CREAM

| Two 15-ounce cans condensed milk | 3 half-pints whipping cream |
|---|---|
| Two 13-ounce cans evaporated milk | Milk to fill line on freezer |
| 2¼ cups sugar (approximately) | 2 teaspoons vanilla |

Put all ingredients into freezer bucket (6-quart size) and freeze in hand or electric freezer.

Variation: Add 1 quart of well-crushed fruit before adding milk to the container.

Mrs. Robert Bujol


## APRICOT ICE CREAM

| One 1-pound 13-ounce can unpeeled | 2 cups sugar |
|---|---|
| apricots | One 13-ounce can evaporated milk |
| Juice of 4 lemons | 1 pint whipping cream |
| | Whole milk |

Force apricots through a sieve or purée in an electric blender. Combine with lemon juice and sugar and let stand for 30 minutes. Add evaporated milk and cream. Add enough whole milk to fill ice cream freezer to freezer level. Use 6-quart freezer. Makes 1 gallon.

Mrs. R. E. Tyrone
Mrs. John B. Whitley

### FIG ICE CREAM

One 15-ounce can condensed milk
Two 13-ounce cans evaporated milk
Juice of ½ lemon

3 pints peeled, fresh figs, mashed
2 cups sugar
Whole milk

Put all ingredients in freezer container. If the figs are very ripe, you may not need as much sugar as called for. Add whole milk to level that the freezer calls for, for proper freezing. Then freeze in 6-quart freezer according to directions. Serves 20.

Mrs. W. A. Rolston, Jr.

### MILK SHERBERT

1 quart whole milk
2 cups sugar
½ cup lemon juice
½ cup orange juice

One 13¼-ounce can crushed
pineapple
½ pint whipping cream, whipped
2 egg whites

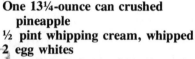

Mix milk, sugar, juices and pineapple. Fold in whipped cream. Beat egg whites until stiff. Fold in. Pour into a pan or flat casserole about 14x9 inches in size. Place in freezer. Stir well every 30 minutes until very firmly frozen. Serves 12 to 16.

Mrs. Eugene Owen

### BLEU CHEESE SALAD SHERBERT

1½ cups sugar
¾ cup lemon juice
1 cup light cream

One 4-ounce package Bleu cheese,
crumbled
2½ cups milk

Combine sugar and lemon juice. Blend cheese, milk and cream. Add to sugar mixture. Pour into 2 ice cube trays. Freeze until firm. Break into chunks and beat with mixer until smooth. Return to trays and freeze until firm. Serve sherbert in small scoops with fresh fruit. Serves 6 to 8.

Mrs. Pat Bonanno

### CRÈME de MENTHE DESSERT

Two 4-ounce bottles green
cherries, drained
¾ cup crème de menthe

½ gallon vanilla ice cream
20 macaroons, crumbled
½ cup toasted pecans, chopped

Soak the cherries in the crème de menthe overnight. Allow ice cream to soften a little. Beat ice cream in electric mixer to further soften it. Add crème de menthe to the ice cream. Fold in cherries, macaroons and pecans. Pour into icebox tray or similar freezer container. Freeze overnight. Serve in sherbert glasses. Serves 8 to 12.

Mrs. Millard Byrd, Jr.

### CHRISTMAS FREEZE

1 quart vanilla ice cream
2 bananas, very ripe, mashed
1 cup dates, cut up

2 tablespoons lemon juice
½ cup chopped cherries
½ cup pecans, toasted in butter

Allow ice cream to soften slightly. Mix in fruits and nuts and freeze.

Mrs. William H. Dodson, Jr.

## ICE CREAM HOT FUDGE SAUCE

¼ cup butter or margarine
2 squares unsweetened chocolate
¾ cup sugar

¼ cup cocoa
½ cup evaporated milk
1 teaspoon vanilla
Salt

Melt butter and chocolate in top of double boiler. Remove from heat and stir in sugar and cocoa. Blend in milk, vanilla and a pinch of salt. Cook over hot water, stirring constantly until thickened, about 3 to 4 minutes. Serve hot. May be stored in heat-proof jar and reheated in jar in pan of boiling water. Serves 10 to 20.

Mrs. Lenton Sartain

## CHERRIES JUBILEE

One 1-pound can (2 cups) pitted,
   dark, sweet cherries
¼ cup sugar

2 tablespoons cornstarch
¼ cup brandy, kirsch, or cherry
   brandy
Vanilla ice cream

Drain cherries, reserving syrup. In saucepan, blend sugar and cornstarch. Gradually stir in cherry syrup, mixing well. Cook and stir over medium heat until mixture thickens and bubbles. Remove from heat and stir in cherries. Turn into heat-proof bowl or top pan of chafing dish. Be sure bottom pan of chafing dish is filled with hot water, or keep hot over flame. Heat brandy or kirsch in small metal pan with long handle. If desired, pour heated brandy into large ladle. Carefully ignite heated brandy and pour over cherry mixture. Stir to blend into sauce and serve immediately over ice cream. Makes 2½ cups sauce. For a most dramatic effect, dim lights just before lighting brandy. Serves 4 to 6.

Mrs. E. W. Brousseau

## LEMON BAKED ALASKA

1 box lemon cake mix
1 ounce brandy

2 tablespoons sugar
1 or 2 quarts lemon ice cream, or
   ice milk

Meringue:

4 eggs whites

¾ cup powdered sugar

Cook cake mix as directed in layers, but this recipe uses only 1 layer. Place the layer on an oven-proof plate. The day before, or early in the day, poke holes in the cake and pour brandy over the cake and sprinkle with sugar. Just before serving, beat egg whites until very stiff and add sugar gradually and continue to beat until it stands in peaks. Place mounds of ice cream (shape in half balls) on top of layer and cover completely with meringue. Place in a preheated hot oven until it browns (about 10 minutes). At the table, add 2 ounces brandy to the tray and light. Serves 8 to 10.

Mrs. Don McAdams

## MILE-HIGH MOCHA ALASKA

**Alaska:**

| | |
|---|---|
| 2 pints chocolate ice cream | 1 recipe brownie layer |
| 1 to 2 pints coffee ice cream | 1 recipe meringue |

Line a deep 1½-quart bowl with aluminum foil allowing an inch extra to extend over edge of bowl. Soften chocolate ice cream slightly. Spread a layer about 1 inch thick over bottom and sides of foil using back of spoon. Put in freezer. Soften coffee ice cream slightly. Pack into center of mold. Cover with foil. Smooth top with hands. Freeze firm.

**Brownie Layer:**

| | |
|---|---|
| ½ cup shortening | ½ teaspoon salt |
| Two 1-ounce squares unsweetened | 2 eggs |
|   chocolate | 1 cup sugar |
| ½ teaspoon baking powder | 1 teaspoon vanilla |
| ¾ cup sifted flour | 1 cup chopped pecans |

Melt shortening and chocolate in pan over hot water. Cool. Sift together baking powder, flour and salt. Beat eggs until light. Stir in sugar. Blend in chocolate mixture. Stir in flour mixture, vanilla and pecans. Bake in a greased 8-inch round pan at 350 degrees for 30 or 35 minutes. Cool. Remove from pan.

**Meringue:**

| | |
|---|---|
| 5 egg whites | ⅔ cup sugar |

Beat egg whites until soft peaks form. Gradually add sugar, beating to stiff peaks.

**To Assemble:**

Place cooled brownie layer on a cookie sheet or wooden cutting board. Remove foil from top of mold and invert onto brownie layer. Lift off bowl and remove foil. Quickly cover ice cream with meringue. Return to freezer. When ready to serve, place on lowest rack in oven and bake about 3 minutes at 500 degrees. Let stand a few minutes before serving. For easier cutting, let stand 20 or 30 minutes. This gives you time to clear the table and serve the coffee before serving the Alaska. If in a hurry, use a brownie mix.

Mrs. John S. Campbell, Jr.

## HEATH MERINGUE DESSERT

| | |
|---|---|
| 7 egg whites | 9 Heath bars |
| 1¾ cups sugar | 1 pint whipping cream |
| | Vanilla |

Beat egg whites and sugar together making the meringue. Place in two well greased pans lined with brown paper. Use 9-inch round cake pans. Bake 1 hour at 300 degrees. Grind Heath bars. Whip cream and flavor with vanilla and a little sugar. Place one meringue on a cake plate. Ice with whipped cream and sprinkle half of Heath bars on the cream. Place other meringue on this and ice with whipped cream and remainder of the Heath bars. Refrigerate 10 hours before serving. Serves 6 to 8.

Mrs. Robert Witcher
Manhasset, New York

## CARAMEL ANGEL WHIP

1 cup brown sugar

3 cups whipping cream
1 angel food cake

Mix brown sugar and whipping cream in large bowl. Stir well and chill for at least ½ hour. Cut the angel food cake in 3 layers. When the sugar and cream mixture is thoroughly chilled, beat with mixer until whipped. Spoon this very generously over the 3 layers of cake, being sure to cover sides. Refrigerate at least 12 hours; 24 hours is better. Serves 12 to 14.

Mrs. W. Warren Munson

## MANDARIN DREAM

One 6-ounce can frozen orange juice
1 package gelatin
½ cup sugar
2 tablespoons flour
2 egg yolks
Pinch salt

1 cup milk
2 egg whites, stiffly beaten
1 loaf angel food cake
¼ pint whipping cream
One 11-ounce can mandarin orange
   sections

Thaw orange juice concentrate. Sprinkle gelatin on top and set aside. Combine sugar and flour. Mix thoroughly and set aside. Beat egg yolks until thick with pinch of salt and set aside. Heat milk to scalding in double boiler. Pour a small amount of milk into flour mixture, stirring vigorously. Return to double boiler. Cook 2 to 3 minutes stirring constantly. Pour some of this hot mixture into eggs, stirring constantly. Return to double boiler. Cook until thickened and mixture coats spoon. Combine with gelatin and orange juice while hot. Stir until gelatin dissolves. Cool. Beat egg whites and add to mixture. Slightly oil large loaf pan. Break up angel food cake in small pieces and add to custard. Place in pan and let refrigerate for several hours or overnight. Unmold and ice with whipped cream that has been whipped and sweetened to taste. Garnish with mandarin oranges and replace in refrigerator. Serves 7 to 8.

Mrs. James E. Toups

## FLOATING ISLAND

3 eggs, separated
4½ tablespoons sugar
1½ tablespoons flour

¼ teaspoon salt
3 cups milk
1 teaspoon vanilla
6 tablespoons sugar

Cream egg yolks, sugar, flour and salt. Add milk. Cook in a double boiler or in a 2-quart saucepan, using medium heat. Stir as this mixture cooks until it thickens slightly (coats the spoon). Stir in vanilla. Pour in a 2-quart casserole. Make meringue of egg whites and sugar. Drop by spoonsful on cooked custard. Brown meringue slightly under broiler. Refrigerate. Serves 6.

Mrs. Wayne T. Davis

## STRAWBERRY CHARLOTTE

Two ¼-ounce envelopes unflavored
    gelatin
¾ cup sugar, divided
¼ teaspoon salt
4 eggs, separated
½ cup water

Two 10-ounce packages frozen,
    sliced strawberries
2 tablespoons lemon juice
2 teaspoons grated lemon rind
One 3-ounce package unfilled lady
    fingers
1 cup whipping cream

Mix gelatin, ¼ cup sugar and salt thoroughly in the top of a double boiler. Beat egg yolks and water together. Add to the gelatin mixture. Add 1 package of the strawberries. Cook over boiling water, stirring constantly, until gelatin is dissolved and strawberries thawed, about 8 minutes. Remove from heat and add remaining package of strawberries, lemon juice and rind. Stir until berries have thawed. Chill in refrigerator, stirring occasionally, until the mixture mounds when dropped from spoon. Split lady fingers in half and stand around edge of 8-inch spring form pan. Beat egg whites until stiff. Beat in remaining ½ cup sugar, fold in gelatin mixture. Whip cream and fold into mixture. Turn into pan and chill until firm. When ready to serve, remove sides of pan and slice between lady fingers. Serves 10.

Mrs. Lewis S. Doherty, III

## CREOLE COFFEE SOUFFLÉ

2 envelopes unflavored gelatin
½ cup sugar
3 cups freshly brewed hot coffee,
    any roast, pure coffee

2 egg whites
¼ cup sugar
2 cups heavy cream, whipped, or
    4 cups whipped topping
1 square unsweetened chocolate

Stir gelatin and sugar together well. Pour coffee over and stir to dissolve. Chill until slightly thickened. Meanwhile, beat egg whites until foamy, then continue beating and add sugar gradually until they form stiff peaks. Whip cream, or use the prepared topping. Reserve ½ cup for decoration. Fold the egg whites and remaining whipped cream into the thickened gelatin mixture and pour into soufflé dish. Chill until firm, at least 3 hours. Spoon reserved whipped cream on top to decorate and shave chocolate over, if desired. Yield: 1½ quarts and will serve 8 to 10.

Mrs. Norman Saurage III

## FUDGE MUFFINS

4 squares semisweet or unsweetened
    chocolate
1 cup  butter or margarine
1 cup flour

1¾ cups sugar
4 eggs
2 cups pecans, or less
1 teaspoon vanilla

Melt chocolate with butter. Combine flour and sugar. Add eggs and melted chocolate mixture to flour mixture. Stir well. Add pecans and vanilla. Pour in paper muffin cups in muffin tins. Bake at 300 degrees for 40 to 45 minutes. Makes 24 muffins.

Mrs. William Bizzell
Cleveland, Mississippi

## CHOCOLATE MOUSSE

One 6-ounce package chocolate bits
2 eggs
3 tablespoons strong hot coffee

2 tablespoons rum, or orange-
    flavored liqueur
¾ cup milk, scalded

In blender, combine above ingredients. Blend at high speed 2 minutes. Pour into 4 dessert cups or demitasse cups and chill.

Mrs. Ralph G. Braun

## WORLD'S FASTEST STRAWBERRY MOUSSE

One 10-ounce package frozen,
    sweetened strawberries

½ pint sour cream
½ cup sugar
1 tablespoon vanilla

Mix all ingredients in blender and freeze. Serve in sherbert glasses. Serves 4 to 6.

Mrs. T. O. Perry, Jr.

## FROZEN LEMON MOUSSE

4 eggs, separated
1½ cups sugar
Grated rind of 2 lemons

Juice of 3 lemons
Two 6-ounce cans evaporated milk
Box of graham cracker crumbs

Cook egg yolks, sugar, grated lemon rind and lemon juice for three minutes, stirring constantly. Cool. Fold in evaporated milk, that has been chilled and whipped, and the stiffly beaten egg whites. Place ¼ inch of graham cracker crumbs in bottom of 8-inch square dish. Pour in mousse. Place another ¼-inch layer of crumbs on top. Cover with plastic wrap and place in freezer, preferably overnight. Do not remove until ready to serve. Serves 8.

Mrs. James E. Toups

## CHOCOLATE MARSHMALLOW BARS

Bars:

1 cup margarine
⅓ cup cocoa
4 eggs, beaten
2 cups sugar

1½ cups all purpose flour
1½ cups chopped pecans
One 10-ounce bag miniature
    marshmallows

Melt margarine. Add cocoa. Pour into bowl containing beaten eggs. Add sugar, flour and nuts. Mix well. Bake at 350 degrees for 30 minutes in an ungreased 13x9x2-inch pan. Turn off oven. Spread marshmallows on top. Put back into oven to melt. Do not brown.

Icing:

4 tablespoons margarine
⅓ cup cocoa

One 1-pound box powdered sugar
⅓ cup milk
1 teaspoon vanilla

Melt margarine. Add cocoa. Beat in sifted powdered sugar. Add milk and vanilla. Makes 2 dozen squares.

Mrs. David S. Bell

## CARAMEL CUSTARD

½ cup sugar
3 eggs
¼ cup sugar

½ teaspoon vanilla
Dash salt
2 cups milk

In a small skillet, cook ½ cup sugar over moderate heat until it forms a light caramel-colored syrup. Pour the syrup into 6 custard cups or into a 6- to 7-inch ring mold. In a bowl, beat 3 eggs lightly and stir in ¼ cup sugar, vanilla and salt. Gradually beat in the milk that has been scalded. Pour the mixture into prepared cups or mold and set in a baking pan. Pour hot water around the mold to reach ¾ of the way up the sides. Bake the custard in a 350 degree oven for about 45 minutes. Remove from water and let cool on a wire rack. Refrigerate and invert when ready to serve. Makes 6 servings.

Mrs. Hudson Ford Bell, III

## CHOCOLATE CUSTARD DESSERT

**Graham Cracker Crust:**

2 cups graham cracker crumbs          ¼ cup butter, melted

Line an 8x8-inch pan with cracker crumbs mixed with butter. Press down firmly.

**Chocolate Filling:**

2 cups powdered sugar
½ cup butter
2 squares unsweetened chocolate

1 teaspoon vanilla
3 egg yolks
3 egg whites

Cream the powdered sugar with the butter. Add the melted chocolate, vanilla and egg yolks. Fold in egg whites that have been stiffy beaten. Spread on crumb crust and chill.

**Topping:**

1 quart vanilla ice cream          ½ cup chopped nuts

When filling is firm, spread softened ice cream over it. Sprinkle nuts on top. Freeze. About 10 minutes before serving, remove from freezer for easier cutting. Makes 12 servings.

Mrs. Frank Kean, III

## ORANGE CAKE CUPS

2 eggs, separated
½ cup sugar
4 tablespoons margarine
½ teaspoon vanilla

¼ cup frozen orange juice
concentrate, thawed
2 tablespoons flour
¼ teaspoon salt
1 cup milk

Beat egg whites until stiff. Add 2 tablespoons sugar, one at a time. Cream margarine with remaining sugar until fluffy. Beat in egg yolks, orange juice and vanilla. Stir in flour and salt. Slowly stir in milk. Gently fold in egg whites until fluffy smooth. Spoon into 6 buttered 6-ounce cups. Set in shallow pan of boiling water. Bake at 325 degrees for 30 minutes. Remove from water and cool. Invert into serving dishes. Serves 6.

Mrs. John B. Heroman, Jr.

## CHOCOLATE DELIGHT

Two 4-ounce bars German sweet
  chocolate
4 tablespoons water
4 tablespoons powdered sugar
4 eggs, separated

1 teaspoon vanilla
18 ladyfingers
1 cup pecans, coarsely chopped
½ pint whipping cream, whipped
  and sweetened

Melt chocolate with water in double boiler. Add sugar and beat over hot water until smooth. Beat egg yolks until very creamy. Add to chocolate mixture, then remove from stove. Beat egg whites until very stiff. Fold into chocolate mixture. Add vanilla. Line 7½x12-inch pyrex dish with halved ladyfingers. Pour ½ chocolate mixture over ladyfingers. Sprinkle with ½ cup pecans. Cover with remaining halved ladyfingers, rest of chocolate mixture, and the remaining pecans. Cover and refrigerate overnight. When ready to serve, spread sweetened whipped cream over top. Cut into squares and serve. This dish keeps well in the refrigerator for 2 to 3 days if covered tightly. Serves 12.

Mrs. Carlton L. Carpenter, Jr.

## BREAD PUDDING

Pudding:

4 cups toasted bread cubes
½ cup raisins
1 quart milk
4 egg yolks, beaten

1 cup sugar
½ teaspoon vanilla
3 tablespoons melted butter
¼ teaspoon salt

Place bread cubes and raisins in buttered 3-quart casserole. Scald milk. In separate bowl, combine remaining ingredients. Add scalded milk to this mixture, mix well, and pour over bread cubes and raisins. Set casserole in pan and pour hot water in pan to a depth of about 1 inch. Bake at 325 degrees until knife inserted in center comes out clean.

Topping:

4 egg whites                    4 tablespoons sugar

Beat egg whites with the sugar for the meringue topping and brown in oven. This will serve 10 people.

Mrs. Edwin W. Edwards

## BREAD PUDDING WITH WHISKEY SAUCE

Pudding:

2 cups stale bread cubes
  (French bread is best)
4 cups milk, scalded
¾ cup sugar
1 tablespoon butter

¼ teaspoon salt
4 eggs, slightly beaten
1 teaspoon vanilla
½ to 1 cup coarsely chopped pecans
  (optional)

Soak bread in milk 5 minutes. Add sugar, butter, salt, eggs, and vanilla. Mix well. Stir in pecans. Pour into 1½-quart baking dish. Bake in pan of hot water for one hour at 350 degrees.

**Whiskey sauce:**

½ cup sugar                          2 tablespoons butter
¼ cup water                          1 or 2 jiggers bourbon whiskey

Cook first three ingredients until dissolved. Remove from heat and add whiskey. Serve over bread pudding. Best served warm.

Mrs. James Marks
New Orleans, Louisiana


## MOCHA PUDDING

**Chocolate Batter:**

¾ cup sugar                          ¼ cup cocoa
1 cup flour, sifted                  ½ cup butter
2 teaspoons baking powder            ½ cup milk
¼ teaspoon salt                      1 teaspoon vanilla

Sift first 5 ingredients together in a bowl. Melt butter and mix into dry ingredients along with milk and vanilla. Beat until smooth. Pour into 9-inch square pan.

**Topping:**

½ cup sugar                          ¼ cup cocoa
¼ cup brown sugar                    1 cup strong coffee, hot
                                     Whipped cream (optional)

Mix dry ingredients together and sprinkle over batter. Pour hot coffee over top. Bake in 350 degree oven 40 minutes.

Good hot or cold with or without whipped cream. Serves 8.

Mrs. Dean M. Mosely


## LEMON SQUARES

**Crust:**

1 cup butter, melted                 ½ cup powdered sugar
2 cups sifted flour                  ¼ teaspoon salt

Mix above ingredients and pat into bottom of 13x9-inch baking pan. Bake at 350 degrees for 20 minutes.

**Topping:**

4 eggs, beaten                       4 tablespoons sifted flour
2 cups granulated sugar              5 tablespoons lemon juice
                                     1½ tablespoons grated lemon rind

Mix above ingredients and pour on top of baked crust. Put back into 350 degree oven for 25 to 30 minutes. When cool, sprinkle with powdered sugar and cut into squares. Makes 24 small squares.

Mrs. David B. Wood

## DATE BARS

| | |
|---|---|
| 1 egg | ¼ cup pecans, chopped |
| ½ cup sugar | ½ cup flour |
| ½ cup melted shortening, or | ½ teaspoon baking powder |
|    salad oil | ¼ teaspoon salt |
| 1 cup dates, chopped | Powdered sugar |

Beat egg; add sugar. Mix well. Add shortening. Add dates and nuts. Sift flour, baking powder and salt together. Add and mix well. Spread in greased and floured pan 8x8x2 inches. Bake at 325 degrees for 30 minutes. Do not over-bake. Cool for about 10 minutes. Cut into bars and roll in powdered sugar. Yields about 24 bars.

Mrs. William H. Dodson, Jr.

## PEARS HELÈNE

**Pears:**

| | |
|---|---|
| 4 eating pears | 3 cups water |
| | 1 cup sugar |

Select sweet, but not over-ripe pears. Peel them with potato peeler, leaving stems on, but scooping out bottom. Poach the pears in the water and sugar over medium heat for 20 minutes. Drain and set aside.

**Custard Sauce:**

| | |
|---|---|
| 1 cup milk | 4 egg yolks |
| 1 cup whipping cream | ½ cup sugar |
| 1 teaspoon vanilla | ½ teaspoon flour |

Scald milk and cream. Add vanilla. Mix egg yolks, sugar and flour well. Pour hot milk mixture into yolks slowly, while beating, using double boiler. Cook until custard coats the back of a metal spoon. The sauce will keep a few weeks in refrigerator.

**Topping:**

3 squares semisweet chocloate

Melt chocolate in double boiler for 10 minutes. Pour several spoons of custard sauce over each pear. Then top each with a spoonful of chocolate. Serves 4.

Mrs. Francis X. Guglielmo

## BANANA FLAMBÉE

| | |
|---|---|
| 3 tablespoons butter | One 10-ounce package frozen |
| 1 tablespoon brown sugar |    raspberries, partially thawed |
| 4 ripe bananas, peeled and cut | 2 tablespoons Grand Marnier |
|    in half lengthwise | 2 tablespoons sugar |

Melt the butter in a copper or other heavy skillet and add the brown sugar. When the sugar has dissolved, add the bananas to it. Sauté them on each side for about three minutes. Put raspberries, Grand Marnier and sugar in blender and blend until smooth. Strain through a fine sieve and add to bananas and reheat. Pour a little more Grand Marnier over the banana mixture and ignite with a match. Serve while it is still burning. Serves 4.

Mrs. Dean M. Mosely

## PECAN SLICE TORTE

**Crust:**

| | |
|---|---|
| **1 cup flour** | **½ cup butter** |

Mix to a paste the flour and butter. Press on bottom of buttered 9x9-inch square pan. Bake 15 minutes at 350 degrees, until a very light brown.

**Filling:**

| | |
|---|---|
| **2 eggs, slightly beaten** | **2 tablespoons flour** |
| **1½ cups brown sugar** | **¼ teaspoon baking powder** |
| **¾ cup coconut** | **½ teaspoon salt** |
| **1 cup chopped nuts** | **1 teaspoon vanilla** |

While crust is baking, mix filling ingredients in order given above. Pour this filling on the baked crust and again bake at 350 degrees for 20 minutes. Remove from oven and cool. When cool, spread the icing.

**Icing:**

| | |
|---|---|
| **2 tablespoons butter** | **3 tablespoons orange juice** |
| **1½ cups powdered sugar** | **1 tablespoon lemon juice** |
| | **½ cup finely chopped nuts** |

Mix icing ingredients. Spread on torte. Sprinkle top with nuts. Let this cool in the pan you bake it in. Cut in small squares to serve, as it is very rich and delicious. Makes 16 or more servings.

Mrs. Gene Fleming

## TEA TIME TASSIES

**Crust:**

| | |
|---|---|
| **½ cup butter or margarine less** | **One 3-ounce package cream cheese** |
| **1 tablespoon** | **1 cup all purpose flour** |

Reserve 1 tablespoon butter for filling. Let butter and cream cheese soften to room temperature. Mix with flour. Make small balls of crust about the size of a marble. Chill. Press into well greased small muffin tins to form tart shells.

**Filling:**

| | |
|---|---|
| **¾ cup granulated or brown sugar** | **Dash salt** |
| **¾ cup chopped pecans** | **1 teaspoon vanilla** |
| **1 egg** | **1 tablespoon butter** |

Mix all ingredients together and put in crust about ¾ full. Bake 20 to 30 minutes in 350 degree oven. Makes about 2½ dozen.

Mrs. Millard Byrd, Jr.
Mrs. Weldon L. Smith, Jr.
Mrs. St. Clair J. Bergeron

## PEAR MINCEMEAT

8 pounds pears, ground
3 pounds brown sugar
1 cup vinegar
1 tablespoon nutmeg
1 tablespoon cloves
1 tablespoon cinnamon

1 box raisins
One 16-ounce can crushed
    pineapple
3 oranges, peeled
3 apples, or more, peeled and
    finely chopped

Combine all ingredients in a large pot and cook until thick. Seal in sterilized jars. Serve in individual pastry shells topped with whipped cream.

Mrs. John B. Whitley


## PERFECT APPLE DUMPLINGS

2 cups sugar
2 cups water
¼ teaspoon cinnamon
¼ teaspoon nutmeg
¼ cup butter
2 cups flour

1 teaspoon salt
2 teaspoons baking powder
¾ cup shortening
½ cup milk
6 to 8 apples, smallest possible
Additional sugar, cinnamon, and
    nutmeg

**Sauce:**

Combine sugar, water, cinnamon and nutmeg. Cook 5 minutes. Add butter.

**Dumplings:**

Pare and core apples. Sift flour, salt and baking powder. Cut in shortening. Add milk all at once and stir just until flour is moistened. Roll the dough to ¼-inch thickness. Cut in 5-inch squares and place one apple on each square. Sprinkle generously with additional sugar and spices (cinnamon and nutmeg). Dot with butter. Fold corners and pinch all edges together. Place one inch apart in greased baking dish. Pour on sauce. Bake at 375 degrees for 35 minutes. Serve with hot cream. Serves 6 to 8.

Mrs. William Bizzell
Cleveland, Mississippi


## CHAMPION COBBLER AT RUSTON PEACH FESTIVAL

**Filling:**

8 or 9 peaches, peeled and sliced
½ cup water
1½ cups sugar

2 tablespoons flour
Pinch salt
½ cup margarine or butter, melted

Cook peaches in water until tender. Mix flour, salt and sugar. Add to peaches. Mix. Add melted margarine or butter.

**Pastry for Cobbler:**

1 cup flour
½ teaspoon salt

⅓ cup shortening
4 tablespoons sweet milk, or
    enough for stiff dough

Blend flour, salt and shortening to coarse meal texture. Add milk. Chill. Roll on floured board. Cut enough dumplings to cover first layer of peaches. Pour half of peaches in pan. Put on dumplings. Pour rest of peaches. Cover with lattice strip top. Use 9x13-inch pan to make a shallow pie. Bake at 350 degrees 40 to 45 minutes or until top is brown.

Submitted by
Mrs. Frank Duke

# CAKES AND ICINGS

## HARVEY WALLBANGER CAKE

**Cake:**

1 package orange cake mix
One 3¾-ounce package instant
  vanilla pudding
½ cup oil

4 eggs
¼ cup Galliano liqueur
¼ cup vodka
¾ cup orange juice

Blend all ingredients, then mix 5 minutes on medium speed. Pour into greased (use unsalted shortening) bundt pan or tube pan. Bake at 325 degrees for one hour, or until done. Drizzle the frosting over cake while hot.

**Frosting:**

1 cup powdered sugar
1 tablespoon orange juice

1 tablespoon Galliano liqueur
1 tablespoon vodka

Sift powdered sugar, and blend the liquid in thoroughly. Cake remains moist for days.

Mrs. H. P. Breazeale, Jr.

## RUM CAKE

**Cake:**

½ cup chopped pecans
One 18½-ounce package yellow
  cake mix
½ cup cooking oil

One 3¾-ounce package vanilla
  pudding (instant or non-instant)
½ cup rum
½ cup water
4 eggs

Grease and flour tube or bundt cake pan. Sprinkle nuts into bottom of pan. Mix other ingredients with electric mixer for 2 to 3 minutes. Bake at 325 degrees for 40 to 60 minutes. Pour hot rum glaze over cake while hot. Cool glazed cake in pan 30 minutes and turn out. May be frozen.

**Glaze:**

1 cup sugar
½ cup butter

¼ cup rum
¼ cup water

Place ingredients in small saucepan and boil 2 to 3 minutes. Variation: Rum Pound Cake—omit water in both cake and glaze. Use ½ cup rum in glaze.

Betty Burnett
Mrs. J. H. Benton
Mrs. E. M. Clark
Mrs. W. F. Williamson, Jr.

## WINE CAKE

**Cake:**

| | |
|---|---|
| 4 eggs | 1 box yellow cake mix |
| ¾ cup salad oil | One 3¾-ounce box instant |
| ¾ cup sangria or sherry | vanilla pudding |
| | 1 teaspoon nutmeg, optional |

Beat eggs with fork until foamy. Add oil and sangria or sherry. Add dry ingredients and mix on low speed. Pour into greased and floured tube or bundt pan. Bake at 350 degrees for 40 minutes until done. Cool 5 minutes and remove from pan. Glaze while still hot.

**Glaze:**

2 tablespoons butter, melted      ¾ cup sifted powdered sugar
                                  3 tablespoons sangria or sherry

Beat butter and sugar. Slowly add sangria or sherry to mixture while beating.

Mrs. Don R. McAdams


## EGGNOG CAKE

| | |
|---|---|
| 1 cup butter | 1 cup chopped nuts |
| One 1-pound package powdered sugar | Three 3-ounce packages plain lady |
| 5 eggs | fingers |
| 5 tablespoons bourbon | ½ pint whipping cream |
| | 2 teaspoons sugar |

Cream butter and sugar. Separate eggs. Add bourbon to yolks and beat well. Add egg mixture to creamed butter and sugar. Add pecans. Beat egg whites and gently fold into above mixture. Line bottom and sides of spring mold pan (9'' with hole) with lady finger halves. Pour in mixture. Cover top with halves of lady fingers. Refrigerate 24 hours. Prior to serving, remove from pan and ice with whipped cream that has been whipped with the 2 teaspoons of sugar. Serve thinly sliced. Serves 20.

Mrs. A. Hays Town, Jr.


## BANANA CAKE

| | |
|---|---|
| 1 cup ripe bananas (3 medium sized) | 5 eggs |
| ¾ cup oil | 1 teaspoon vanilla |
| ½ cup sugar | 3 tablespoons brown sugar |
| One 18½-ounce box yellow cake | ½ cup chopped pecans |
| mix | 1 teaspoon cinnamon |

Put bananas and oil in blender and liquefy. Add this mixture and sugar to cake mix. Beat thoroughly in electric mixer. Add eggs one at a time, beating well after each addition. Add vanilla. Combine brown sugar, pecans and cinnamon. Pour half of batter into greased and floured bundt pan. Sprinkle sugar, nuts and cinnamon mixture over batter. Pour remaining batter into pan. Bake at 350 degrees for about 1 hour.

Mrs. Rolfe H. McCollister

## "BEST EVER" COCONUT FRUIT CAKE

½ pound candied pineapple, red and green
½ pound candied cherries, red and green
1 quart pecans, coarsely chopped
1 pound dates, coarsely chopped
1 cup sugar
1 fresh coconut, finely grated (save milk)
4 eggs
1 teaspoon vanilla
1 cup all purpose flour
½ teaspoon salt
1 teaspoon baking powder
½ cup apricot brandy

Save 4 pieces of pineapple, 6 red and 6 green cherries and 1 dozen pecan halves to garnish top. Chop rest of fruit and pecans. Grate coconut and add dates. Add the coconut milk to the fruit. Refrigerate overnight. Next day put fruit in large pan and mix well. Add sugar, well beaten eggs and vanilla. Sift flour, salt and baking powder and combine thoroughly with fruit mixture. Grease tube pan with shortening and line with 2 layers of brown paper cut to fit bottom of pan. Grease paper lining and flour lightly. Poor mixture into pan; garnish and bake at 300 degrees for 15 minutes, then at 325 degrees for 1 hour or longer. Test with straw for doneness. Let cool 20 minutes, then peel off paper and place on wire rack until completely cooled. Pour ½ cup of apricot brandy over cake and wrap well in foil. Ever so often pour ½ cup brandy over the cake and keep in airtight container in cool place until ripened. *Bake last of November in order for it to be ripe at Christmas.*

Mrs. Evangeline Callens Artigue
Krotz Springs, Louisiana

## APPLESAUCE OATMEAL CAKE

**Cake:**

1¼ cups applesauce
⅓ cup water
½ cup butter
1 teaspoon cinnamon
½ teaspoon nutmeg
¼ teaspoon cloves, ground
1 cup raisins
1 cup quick oats
⅓ cup granulated sugar
1 cup light brown sugar
2 eggs
1⅓ cups self-rising flour

Heat first 7 ingredients to boiling and pour over oats. Let stand 20 minutes. Stir in remaining ingredients. Pour into greased 2-quart rectangular dish (10x6x2 inches). Bake at 350 degrees for 35 to 40 minutes. Pour topping over cake in pan while cake is hot. (Note: You can use 1½ cups sifted all purpose flour, 1 teaspoon soda and ¾ teaspoon salt in place of the self-rising flour.)

**Topping:**

¾ cup sugar
⅓ cup butter
½ cup milk
1 teaspoon vanilla

Bring to boil the sugar, butter and milk. Add vanilla and pour over cake after cake is cooked. Allow to sit long enough for sauce to be absorbed—approximately 15 minutes.

Mrs. Dean M. Mosely

## SPICY PRUNE CAKE

**Cake:**

| | |
|---|---|
| 1½ cups sugar | ½ teaspoon salt |
| 1 cup oil | 1 teaspoon each: nutmeg, allspice, |
| 3 eggs | and cinnamon |
| 2 cups flour | 1 cup mashed, cooked prunes |
| ½ teaspoon soda | 1 cup finely chopped nuts |
| ½ cup buttermilk | 1 teaspoon vanilla extract |

Cream sugar, oil and eggs. Combine flour and soda and add alternately with buttermilk. Add salt and spices. Fold in prunes, nuts and vanilla. Bake in a greased tube pan at 350 degrees for 1 hour.

**Glaze:**

| | |
|---|---|
| ½ cup butter or margarine | 1 cup sugar |
| | ½ cup buttermilk |

While cake is baking, combine the margarine, sugar and buttermilk in a saucepan. Boil for about 3 minutes. Pour over warm cake in pan. Loosen sides of cake with knife. This lets the edges soak up sauce. Repeat several times. When cool, turn onto cake plate. May be frozen. Serves 15 to 20.

Mrs. D. J. Daly

## PLUM CAKE or
## APRICOT-APPLESAUCE CAKE

**Cake:**

| | |
|---|---|
| Two 4¾-ounce jars baby food, plums with tapioca or apricot-applesauce | 2 cups self-rising flour |
| | 3 eggs |
| | 1 or ½ teaspoon cinnamon |
| 2 cups sugar | 1 or ½ teaspoon nutmeg or |
| 1 cup salad oil | ground cloves |
| | 1 cup chopped pecans |

Mix all ingredients well, either by hand or at low speed with an electric mixer. Grease tube or bundt pan and sprinkle with flour before pouring in batter. Bake in 325 degree oven for 1 hour and 15 minutes.

**Topping:**

| | |
|---|---|
| 1 to 2 cups powdered sugar | Juice of 1 lemon or 2 tablespoons orange juice |

Combine 1 cup of the sugar with the lemon or orange juice. Add more sugar until topping is very stiff and will absorb no more sugar. Put topping on cake while cake is still warm.

Mrs. Bodo Claus
Mrs. Gerald A. Byars
Mrs. Vernon P. Middleton

## GRANDMOTHER BESS' APPLESAUCE CAKE

3½ cups cake flour
2 teaspoons soda
½ teaspoon salt
3 teaspoons cinnamon
2 teaspoons allspice
2 teaspoons nutmeg

½ teaspoon cloves
1 cup black walnut pieces
½ to ¾ cup chopped raisins
1 cup shortening
2 cups sugar
2 eggs, beaten
2 cups applesauce

Sift together twice flour, soda, salt and spices. Stir ¼ cup of this flour mixture with nuts and raisins; set aside. In a large bowl cream shortening. Add sugar gradually and cream well. Add beaten eggs; mix well. Add flour alternately with applesauce. Stir in nuts and raisins. Pour into greased and floured angel food cake pan. Bake at 350 degrees about 1 hour 15 minutes. Cool completely before removing from pan.

Mrs. Eugene H. Owen

## BANANA SPLIT CAKE
### (no-bake layered cake)

2 cups graham cracker crumbs
1½ cups margarine
2 cups powdered sugar
2 eggs
5 bananas, sliced

One 16-ounce can crushed
 pineapple, drained
1 large container whipped topping
One 4-ounce jar cherries, chopped
1 cup chopped pecans

Mix cracker crumbs with ½ cup of melted margarine. Put in a 14x9x2-inch pan. Cream 1 cup of margarine and gradually add sugar. Add eggs, one at a time, beating well after each addition. Spread margarine mixture over cracker crust and cover with sliced bananas. Sprinkle with drained pineapple. Spread whipped topping over pineapple. Garnish top with chopped cherries and nuts. Chill thoroughly. Better if made the day before serving. Serves 20.

Mrs. Chambliss Mizelle
Lafayette, Louisiana

## PEACH ICE BOX CAKE

1 pound vanilla wafers, crushed
½ cup margarine
1½ cups powdered sugar

2 large eggs
1 quart peaches or strawberries
1 cup whipping cream, whipped

Crush vanilla wafers and put most in an 8x12x2-inch pan. Save some for sprinkling over top. Cream butter and sugar very well. Add eggs, one at a time. Mix well and pour over vanilla wafers. Slice peaches or strawberries and spread on top. Whip the cream and spread over top of fruit, being sure to spread to the edges. Sprinkle crumbs on top and let stand overnight in refrigerator. *Try to always use fresh fruit instead of canned.* Serves 8 to 10.

Mrs. Joseph D. Guillory

## ORANGE SLICE CAKE

**Cake:**

| | |
|---|---|
| 1 cup margarine | 3½ cups unsifted flour |
| 2 cups sugar | ½ pound dates, chopped |
| 3 eggs | 2 cups chopped pecans |
| 1 teaspoon soda | 2 cups grated coconut |
| 1 cup buttermilk | 1 pound candied orange slices, chopped |

Cream margarine and sugar. Add eggs one at a time, beating well. Dissolve soda in buttermilk. Add 2½ cups flour alternately with buttermilk to creamed mixture. Use the remaining flour to coat dates and pecans. Fold dates, pecans, coconut and orange slices into batter. Bake in greased and floured tube pan at 300 degrees for 1½ hours or until done. Let cake cool 10 minutes in pan then remove cake from pan and glaze.

**Orange Glaze:**

| | |
|---|---|
| 2 cups powdered sugar | ¼ cup orange juice |

Heat above ingredients in saucepan to boiling and pour over cake. This cake is similar to a fruitcake and is very pretty. May be frozen. Yields 16 slices.

Mrs. Norman Saurage III

## RED VELVET CAKE

**Cake:**

| | |
|---|---|
| 2 ounces red food coloring | 1 cup buttermilk |
| 2 teaspoons cocoa, heaping | 2½ cups flour |
| ½ cup shortening | 1 teaspoon salt |
| 1½ cups sugar | 1 teaspoon vanilla |
| 2 eggs | 1 teaspoon soda |
| | 1 tablespoon vinegar |

Make a paste of red food coloring and cocoa. Cream shortening and sugar thoroughly. Add eggs and mix well, then add the paste. Add buttermilk alternately with the flour and salt. Beat well after each addition and then add vanilla. Put soda into the vinegar and fold into the batter. Pour batter into 2 greased 9-inch cake pans and bake in a 350 degree oven for 25 to 30 minutes. Cool and split each layer in half, making 4 layers. Frost layers with icing.

**Icing:**

| | |
|---|---|
| 3 tablespoons flour | 1 cup margarine |
| 1 cup milk | 1 cup sugar |
| | 1 teaspoon vanilla |

Cook flour and milk until thick. Then cool. *Be sure it is cool.* Cream together margarine and sugar. Add vanilla. Beat the two mixtures together until the consistency is that of whipped cream.

Mrs. St. Clair Bergeron, Jr.

## HERSHEY CAKE

Eight 1.26-ounce plain Hershey bars
1 cup margarine or butter
2 cups sugar
4 eggs
2½ cups flour
¼ teaspoon salt

½ teaspoon soda
1 cup buttermilk
One 5½-ounce can Hershey
    Chocolate Syrup
2 teaspoons vanilla
2½ cups chopped nuts

Melt Hershey bars in double boiler. Cream margarine and sugar. Add melted Hershey bars. Add eggs one at a time, beating well after each addition. Sift together flour, salt and soda and add alternately with buttermilk. Add chocolate syrup, vanilla and nuts. Bake in a greased and floured tube pan at 325 degrees for 1½ hours.

Mrs. Frank Duke

## CHOCOLATE BRANDY CAKE

Cake:

1 box devil's food cake mix
4 eggs
1 cup water

½ cup oil
One 3-ounce box instant
    chocolate pudding
3 tablespoons brandy

Thoroughly mix all ingredients together. Pour into bundt pan. Bake for 45 to 55 minutes at 350 degrees. Remove from pan and glaze while hot.

Chocolate glaze:

2 tablespoons cocoa
5 teaspoons water

1 tablespoon margarine or butter
1 tablespoon white corn syrup
1 cup powdered sugar

Place all ingredients in a pan on a low fire. Stir until butter melts. Do not overcook. Pour over cake.

Mrs. Don R. McAdams

## CHOCOLATE APRICOT NECTAR CAKE

Cake:

One 18½-ounce package chocolate
    cake mix
½ cup sugar

4 eggs
1 cup apricot nectar
¾ cup oil

Blend all ingredients except oil and beat 1 minute. Continue beating and *slowly* add the oil. Beat 1 more minute. Pour into greased and floured bundt pan. Bake at 350 degrees for 45 minutes. Cool before turning cake out on plate.

Glaze:

1 cup powdered sugar, sifted

1 tablespoon apricot nectar
1 tablespoon lemon juice

Mix well and spoon over cake.

Mrs. Robert R. Snellgrove

## STRAWBERRY REFRIGERATOR CAKE

One 3-ounce package strawberry jello
1 cup boiling water
½ cup cold water

Two 10-ounce packages frozen
strawberries, drained
(save juice)
1 pint whipping cream, whipped
One 10-inch angel food cake

Dissolve jello in 1 cup boiling water. Add ½ cup cold water. When "syrupy" beat to a froth and add berries that have been well drained, reserving juice. Fold in the whipped cream and the cake that has been broken into small pieces. Place in refrigerator and congeal in tube pan.

**Glaze:**

1 cup reserved strawberry juice
1 tablespoon cornstarch

1 teaspoon butter
Drop of red food coloring (optional)

To juice from the berries, add cornstarch and cook about 3 minutes until it clears. Add 1 teaspoon butter and food coloring. Drizzle glaze over cake. Return to refrigerator. This may be garnished with whipped cream and fresh strawberries if desired. Makes 12 servings.

Mrs. E. D. Bateman, Jr.

## CARROT CAKE

**Cake:**

1¾ cups sugar
1¼ cups oil
4 eggs
2 cups cake flour
2 teaspoons baking powder

1 teaspoon salt
2 teaspoons soda
2 teaspoons cinnamon
3 cups finely grated carrots
¼ cup chopped nuts

Cream sugar and oil. Add eggs, one at a time. Sift flour, baking powder, salt, soda and cinnamon together and add to the first mixture. Fold in carrots and nuts. Bake in three 9-inch greased and floured cake pans at 350 degrees for 20 to 25 minutes. Cool layers before icing.

**Icing:**

One 8-ounce package cream cheese
¼ cup butter
2 teaspoons vanilla

One 1-pound box powdered sugar
1 cup crushed pineapple,
well drained

Cream together cream cheese and butter. Mix in vanilla, sugar and pineapple. Spread between layers and on top of cake. This cake may be frozen.

Miss Kathleen Flanagan

**Cake:**                          CHEESECAKE

24 ounces cream cheese
1 cup sugar

5 eggs
¼ teaspoon salt
¾ teaspoon almond extract

Beat cream cheese until soft. Add sugar and beat well. Add eggs one at a time, beating well after each addition. Add salt and almond extract. Beat until thick and lemon colored. Bake at 325 degrees for 45 minutes in a spring form pan. Let cool for 20 minutes.

**Glaze:**

| | |
|---|---|
| **2 tablespoons sugar** | **1½ cups sour cream**<br>**½ teaspoon vanilla** |

Mix sugar, sour cream, vanilla and pour over cooled cheese cake. Bake 10 minutes at 325 degrees. Cool and refrigerate. Serves 12.

Note: This may be baked in a graham cracker crust if desired. When using crust increase amounts of glaze to 3 tablespoons sugar, 2 cups sour cream and ¾ teaspoon vanilla.

Mrs. Fred Gowdy

## ICE BOX CHEESECAKE

**Crust:**

| | |
|---|---|
| **1 small box graham crackers,**<br>  **crushed (about 30 crackers)** | **½ cup sugar**<br>**½ cup butter or margarine,**<br>  **melted** |

Combine ingredients and pat into a spring form pan or a 15x9-inch baking dish forming a crust.

**Filling:**

| | |
|---|---|
| **One 3-ounce package lemon jello** | **½ cup sugar** |
| **1 cup boiling water** | **One 13-ounce can evaporated milk,** |
| **One 8-ounce package cream cheese** | **chilled** |
| | **2 teaspoons vanilla** |

Dissolve jello in boiling water. Cool. Cream together cream cheese and sugar. In a large bowl whip *chilled* evaporated milk until stiff. Add cheese mixture, vanilla and lemon jello. Pour into crust and top with a few reserved crumbs. Refrigerate 24 hours.

## COCONUT POUND CAKE

| | |
|---|---|
| **6 eggs** | **½ teaspoon almond extract** |
| **1 cup shortening** | **½ teaspoon coconut extract** |
| **½ cup margarine** | **3 cups sifted cake flour** |
| **3 cups sugar** | **1 cup milk** |
| | **2 cups flaked coconut** |

Separate eggs and allow them to reach room temperature. Cream egg yolks, shortening and margarine at high speed, and gradually add sugar. Add extracts. On low speed, beat in flour and milk alternately, beginning and ending with flour. Add coconut. Beat egg whites until stiff peaks form and gently fold into cake batter. Bake in a greased 10-inch tube or bundt pan at 300 degrees for 2 hours or until done. Cool 15 minutes and remove from pan.

Mrs. John S. Campbell

## APPLE CIDER POUND CAKE

**Cake:**

1 cup margarine
½ cup shortening
3 cups sugar
6 large eggs
3 cups flour
½ teaspoon salt

½ teaspoon baking powder
½ teaspoon allspice
¾ teaspoon cinnamon
½ teaspoon nutmeg
¼ teaspoon cloves, ground
1 cup apple cider
1 teaspoon vanilla

Soften margarine and shortening. Add sugar. Beat 10 minutes with mixer at medium speed. Add eggs one at a time. Add other ingredients. Beat well. Bake in a large tube pan at 325 degrees for 90 minutes.

**Caramel Glaze:**

½ cup sugar
½ teaspoon baking soda
¼ cup margarine

¼ cup buttermilk
¼ cup dark corn syrup
1 teaspoon vanilla

Combine all ingredients and boil for 10 minutes. Drizzle over cake while cake is still warm. Note: If well covered, cake will stay moist for many days. This is a large cake. It makes a little too much batter for a bundt pan.

A winner at the Texas State Fair
Submitted by: Mrs. J. B. Maguire, Jr.
Pampa, Texas

## SOUR CREAM SOMERSAULT CAKE

Margarine
½ cup sugar
2 tablespoons cinnamon
1 cup pecans, finely chopped
One 18½-ounce box yellow cake mix
4 eggs

One 3¾-ounce package instant
 vanilla pudding mix
¾ cup water
1 cup sour cream
1 teaspoon vanilla extract
¼ cup cooking oil

Grease bundt cake pan heavily with margarine. Mix sugar, cinnamon and pecans. Use part of this mixture to coat all sides of pan well. Save the rest to use between layers. Blend remainder of ingredients with electric mixer in large mixing bowl for time indicated on cake mix box. Alternate layers of batter with sugar, cinnamon and pecan mixture. Bake at 350 degrees for 1 hour. Cool completely before removing from pan. If desired you can wrap it in foil and let stand for 2 to 3 days. Stays fresh for 2 weeks. Freezes very well.

Mrs. Joel Safer

## SOUR CREAM POUND CAKE

**Cake:**

| | |
|---|---|
| 1 cup margarine | 3 cups flour |
| 3 cups sugar | ¼ teaspoon soda |
| 6 eggs, separated | 1½ cups sour cream |
| | 1 teaspoon lemon extract |

Cream margarine and sugar. Add egg yolks one at a time. Sift together flour and soda. Add this alternately to mixture with sour cream; first flour, then sour cream, ending with flour. Add lemon extract. Beat egg whites until stiff. Fold in with rubber scraper. Grease and flour bundt or tube pan (if Teflon, just grease). Bake at 300 degrees for 1½ hours. Remove from oven and let stand 10 minutes and invert pan on cake plate. Let cake cool completely before icing.

**Icing:**

| | |
|---|---|
| 2 cups sifted powdered sugar | ½ of a 6-ounce can of frozen concentrated orange juice, thawed |

Mix together and ice cake.

Mrs. Norman Saurage Jr.

## CHOCOLATE CAKE, HUNGARIAN STYLE

**Chocolate Batter:**

| | |
|---|---|
| 5 large eggs, separated | ¼ cup sifted unsweetened cocoa |
| ¼ teaspoon salt | 1 teaspoon vanilla |
| 1 cup sifted powdered sugar | Toasted sliced almonds |

Separate the eggs and beat whites with salt until stiff but not dry. Beat in sugar, 1 tablespoon at a time. Fold in cocoa. Beat yolks until thick and lemon colored, and fold into cocoa mixture. Add vanilla. Spread in 15x10x1-inch pan lined with waxed paper and greased. Bake at 350 degrees for 20 minutes. (While baking, make whipped cream filling and refrigerate). Turn cake out on towel and very gently peel off waxed paper. Sprinkle with powdered sugar. Cool. (While cooling, make chocolate glaze). Cut cake in quarters. Put layers together with whipped cream. Spread with glaze. Decorate with almonds. Chill and slice.

**Whipped Cream Filling:**

| | |
|---|---|
| 1 cup heavy cream | 1 tablespoon powdered sugar |
| | ½ teaspoon vanilla |

Whip cream and add sugar and vanilla.

**Chocolate Glaze:**

| | |
|---|---|
| 1 tablespoon butter or margarine | 2 tablespoons boiling water |
| 1 square unsweetened chocolate | Dash of salt |
| ½ cup sifted powdered sugar | ½ teaspoon vanilla |

Melt butter and chocolate. Remove from heat and add sugar, water, salt, and vanilla. Beat until smooth and glossy. *Delicious and pretty.* Serves 8.

Mrs. Michael J. Coerver

## CHOCOLATE SHEET CAKE

**Cake:**

| | |
|---|---|
| 2 cups flour | ½ cup shortening or oil |
| 2 cups sugar | 1 teaspoon soda |
| ½ cup margarine | ½ cup buttermilk |
| ¼ cup cocoa | 2 eggs |
| 1 cup water | 1 teaspoon vanilla |

Combine flour and sugar in large mixing bowl. In saucepan heat to boiling point the margarine, cocoa, water and shortening or oil. Pour this over the dry ingredients and mix with a spoon or on low speed of mixer. Dissolve soda in buttermilk and vanilla. Add to mixture. Add eggs one at a time, increasing mixer speed to medium. Mix until thoroughly combined. Pour into a greased 11x15x1-inch pan. Bake 20 minutes at 400 degrees.

**Icing:**

| | |
|---|---|
| ½ cup margarine | One 1-pound box powdered sugar, |
| ¼ cup cocoa | sifted |
| 6 tablespoons milk | 1 teaspoon vanilla |
| | ½ cup chopped nuts |

Melt margarine in saucepan. Add cocoa and milk. Bring to a boil and remove from heat. Mix in powdered sugar. Add vanilla and chopped nuts. Pour icing on hot cake as soon as you take it from the oven. Cut into squares. Serve hot or cold. Stays moist for a week. Freezes beautifully. Yields 35 squares.

Mrs. George Deer
Mrs. Williams D. Wall IV
Mrs. Dennis Goldston

## ALMOND POUND CAKE

| | |
|---|---|
| 4 eggs | 1 teaspoon baking powder |
| Milk | ¼ teaspoon salt |
| 2 cups flour | 1 cup vegetable shortening |
| 2 cups sugar | 1½ teaspoons almond flavoring |
| | ¾ cup milk |

Break eggs into a measuring cup; then fill to the 1 cup mark with milk. In a mixing bowl, combine the egg-milk mixture, flour, sugar, baking powder, salt, vegetable shortening and almond flavoring. Beat at medium speed with electric mixer for 3 minutes using rubber scraper to stir batter away from sides of bowl. Add additional ¾ cup milk and beat a minute or so more. Pour into a greased and floured tube cake pan. Bake at 325 degrees for about an hour, or until toothpick comes out clean. Cool on rack about 30 minutes before removing from baking pan. May be frozen. Serves 12 to 16.

Mrs. John Day Powers

## BUTTERMILK POUND CAKE

3 cups sifted all purpose flour
¼ teaspoon soda
1 cup butter or margarine
2¾ cups sugar

4 eggs
1 tablespoon grated lemon rind
or 1 teaspoon vanilla or both
1 cup buttermilk

Sift flour and soda together. Cream butter or margarine and sugar until well blended. Add eggs, one at a time, beating well on high speed of the mixer after each addition until light and fluffy. Using low speed of mixer, mix in lemon rind or add vanilla to buttermilk. Add dry ingredients alternately with milk to creamed mixture. Mix only until flour is moistened. Pour into greased 10-inch tube pan or greased bundt pan. Bake at 350 degrees for 1 hour and 10 minutes. May be frozen. Serves 16 to 20.

Mrs. Hubert F. Brennan

## DUMP CAKE

1 22-ounce can cherries or
blueberry pie filling
1 white cake mix, regular size,
used dry

¾ cup pecans (halves or smaller)
¾ cup margarine, melted
Ice cream or whipped cream,
(optional)

Grease with "Pam" or vegetable oil a 9x12-inch pyrex baking dish. Pour pie filling in bottom, followed by cake mix. Sprinkle nuts on top. Add melted margarine or butter. Bake 30 minutes at 350 degrees. Cool before serving. Serve in individual dessert bowls, topped with ice cream or whipped cream, if desired. Serves 12.

Mrs. Dennis L. Judice

## COLA CAKE

Cake:

1 cup margarine
3 tablespoons cocoa
1 cup cola
2 cups sugar
2 cups flour

1 teaspoon baking soda
2 eggs, beaten
½ cup buttermilk
1 teaspoon vanilla
1½ cups miniature marshmallows

Heat margarine, cocoa, and cola and bring to a boil. Combine sugar, flour and soda. Pour cola mixture into sugar-flour mixture. Add eggs, buttermilk, vanilla and marshmallows. Mix well. Bake in a 11x15-inch greased and floured cake pan at 350 degrees for 30 to 35 minutes.

Icing:

One 1-pound box powdered sugar
½ cup nuts

½ cup margarine
3 tablespoons cocoa
6 tablespoons cola

Combine sugar and nuts. Heat margarine, cocoa and cola and bring to a boil. Add to sugar-nut mixture. Ice cake while hot. This cake stays moist for weeks. May be frozen. Serves 12.

Mrs. Wendell Harris

## PRIZE WHITE LAYER CAKE

**Cake:**

| | |
|---|---|
| 1¾ cups sugar | 3 teaspoons baking powder |
| ⅔ cup butter | 1 cup milk |
| ½ teaspoon salt | 1½ teaspoons vanilla extract |
| 3 cups sifted cake flour | 1 teaspoon almond extract |
| | 5 egg whites |

Reserve 2 or 3 tablespoons of the sugar for meringue. Cream butter, sugar, and salt until light and fluffy. Sift flour with baking powder 3 times. Add flour alternately with milk and extracts, a small amount at a time. Beat after each addition until smooth. Beat egg whites, gradually adding the 2 or 3 tablespoons of sugar until meringue forms stiff peaks. Fold into batter very lightly. Do not beat. Pour batter into two 9-inch cake pans that have been greased, floured and lined with waxed paper. Bake at 350 degrees for 30 to 45 minutes.

**Marshmallow and Pecan Seven Minute Frosting:**

| | |
|---|---|
| 2 egg whites | 1½ cups sugar |
| 6 marshmallows, chopped | ½ cup cold water |
| 1½ teaspoons light corn syrup | 1½ cups broken pecans (a few |
| (or ¼ teaspoon cream | whole ones for decoration) |
| of tartar) | 1 teaspoon vanilla extract |

Place all ingredients except vanilla extract and pecans in double boiler. Beat 1 minute. Then cook over boiling water, beating constantly with beater until mixture forms peaks (about 7 minutes). Remove from heat, add vanilla extract. Beat until a spreading consistency is reached. Add pecans. Frost cake and decorate with whole pecans.

Mrs. Huey P. Long

## CHESS CAKE

| | |
|---|---|
| 1 cup margarine | 2 teaspoons baking powder |
| One 1-pound box brown sugar | ¼ teaspoon salt |
| 1 cup granulated sugar | 1 cup chopped nuts |
| 4 egg yolks | 1½ teaspoons vanilla |
| 2 cups flour | 4 egg whites |
| | Powdered sugar |

Melt margarine and add both sugars. Blend well. Add egg yolks. Beat well. Sift flour, baking powder and salt together and add to mixture. Fold in nuts and vanilla. Beat egg whites until stiff. Fold into mixture. Spread batter in greased and floured 9x12-inch pan. Bake at 350 degrees for 30 to 45 minutes. When done, sprinkle with powdered sugar and cut into squares. Keeps very moist and chewy in a covered tin.

Mrs. Harry McPeake
Carthage, Tennessee

## ITALIAN CREAM CAKE

**Cake:**

2 cups sugar
½ cup shortening
½ cup oil
5 eggs, separated
1 teaspoon soda

1 cup buttermilk
2 cups flour
1 cup angel flake coconut
½ teaspoon butter flavoring
½ teaspoon vanilla

Cream sugar, shortening, and oil. Add egg yolks one at a time, beating after each addition. Stir soda into buttermilk. Add buttermilk alternately with flour to batter. Fold in coconut. Beat egg whites and fold into mixture. Add flavorings. Pour into 3 greased and floured 9-inch pans. Bake in 350 degree oven for 25 minutes. Cool cake layers before icing.

**Icing:**

One 8-ounce package cream cheese
½ cup margarine
One 1-pound box confectioners sugar

1½ cups chopped pecans
½ teaspoon butter flavoring
½ teaspoon vanilla

Cream cheese and margarine. Beat in sugar gradually. Add pecans and flavorings. This makes lots of icing for each layer top and sides. Serves 16.

Mrs. A. Dennis Landry
Lafayette, Louisiana
Mrs. Robert E. Wiemer
Mrs. Joe W. Abbott

## SOUR CREAM CINNAMON COFFEE CAKE

**Cake:**

½ cup butter
1 cup sugar
2 eggs, well beaten

½ pint sour cream
1 teaspoon soda
1½ cups cake flour
1½ teaspoons baking powder

**Topping:**

¼ cup sugar

1 tablespoon cinnamon
2 tablespoons nuts (optional)

Preheat oven to 350 degrees. Grease a bundt pan or angel food cake pan very well. Cream butter and sugar. Add eggs. Combine sour cream and soda and add it to the mixture. Sift flour and baking powder together. Add to the creamed mixture. Pour ½ of batter into the cake pan. Sprinkle ⅔ of topping; add other half of batter, then rest of topping. Marbelize. Bake about 30 to 40 minutes. Let cool 10 minutes and then turn out of pan. *Very tasty and pretty.* May be frozen. Serves 12 to 15.

Mrs. Charles E. Shea

## COFFEE ALMOND CAKE

⅔ cup slivered almonds
One 11¼-ounce frozen pound cake
¾ cup margarine
1½ cups powdered sugar

3 egg yolks
1½ teaspoons instant
  coffee powder
3 tablespoons Kirsch or light rum
1 teaspoon vanilla

Toast almonds in 350 degree oven. Watch carefully so they don't get too brown. Cut frozen pound cake into 5 layers, and set aside. (It is easier to cut when still frozen.) Cream margarine until soft, and gradually add powdered sugar. Beat in egg yolks, one at a time, and add instant coffee powder, Kirsch (or rum) and vanilla. Stir in most of the almonds, saving some to decorate the top. (Be sure they are cool before you add them to the butter mixture.) Ice cake layers, sides and top. Decorate the top with the remaining almonds. Chill. Can be served after chilling a few hours, but better if allowed to mellow in refrigerator overnight. May be frozen. Serves 10 to 12.

Mrs. J. D. Guillory

## CRAZY COFFEE CAKE

Cake:

One 18½-ounce package yellow
  cake mix
4 eggs

One 4-ounce package instant
  butterscotch pudding
⅔ cup oil
¾ cup water

Pour above ingredients into bowl and beat with electric mixer for 10 minutes. Set aside.

Sugar Mixture:

½ cup sugar
1 tablespoon cocoa

1 teaspoon cinnamon
½ cup chopped pecans

Mix above ingredients. Pour ½ cake batter into greased bundt or tube pan. Sprinkle sugar mixture over batter. Pour remaining batter into pan, swirl with a knife to obtain marble effect. *Caution*—when swirling with knife, be careful not to touch bottom or sides of pan. Bake at 350 degrees for 1 hour. Cool. Sprinkle with powdered sugar. Freezes well.

Mrs. R. Wendel Foushee

## SPICED CUPCAKES

1 cup oil
1½ cups brown sugar
2 eggs
1 cup buttermilk
2 cups flour
1 teaspoon soda

1½ teaspoons salt
2 teaspoons cinnamon
1 teaspoon cloves, ground
½ teaspoon nutmeg
1 cup raisins (optional)
1 cup nuts (optional)

Mix ingredients in order given. Add raisins and/or nuts. Bake in cupcake paper cups in muffin tins at 400 degrees for 20 minutes. Note: For coffees, bake in tiny muffin tins. Yields 2½ dozen regular size cupcakes.

Mrs. Ned Clark

## MILE-A-MINUTE CUPCAKES

½ cup butter
1 cup sugar
1 egg, beaten
1⅓ cups flour
¼ teaspoon salt

1 teaspoon baking powder
½ cup cocoa
½ teaspoon soda
½ cup milk
1 teaspoon vanilla
½ cup hot coffee

Thoroughly cream butter and sugar. Add egg and beat well. Sift flour with salt, baking powder, cocoa and soda. Add dry ingredients alternately with milk and vanilla. Add hot coffee. Place paper baking cups in muffin pans and fill ½ full. Bake in a moderate oven at 375 degrees for 20 minutes. Ice and decorate according to occasion. These may be frozen. Yields 24 cupcakes.

Mrs. Douglas Salmon III

## CREAMY BLENDER CHOCOLATE FROSTING

6 blocks (6 ounces) unsweetened
  baking chocolate
1½ cups sugar

1 cup evaporated milk
1 teaspoon vanilla
6 tablespoons margarine

Cut chocolate into small pieces. Put all of the ingredients in a blender. Cover. At *low* speed, blend until larger pieces are chopped. Stop motor and stir. Blend at *high* speed until frosting becomes thick and creamy. *This frosting is absolutely scrumptious.* Makes 3 cups frosting.

Mrs. Norman Saurage III

## RAISIN-NUT FILLING

2 cups pecans
1 cup raisins
Dates (optional)
1 cup sugar

¾ cup milk
2 tablespoons plus 2 teaspoons
  butter
2 yellow cake layers
White or marshmallow frosting

Grind pecans, raisins and dates. Add sugar and milk. Cook over low heat, stirring continually until sugar is melted. Add butter. Spread between layers of yellow cake. Take two regular layers and slice through the center of each to make four thin layers. Outside of cake should be frosted with white or marshmallow icing.

Mrs. Charles Garvey

## KARO ICING

2 egg whites
Pinch salt

1¼ cups white Karo syrup
1 teaspoon vanilla

Beat egg whites until they form peaks. Add salt. Heat Karo to boiling point and slowly add to egg whites while still beating. Keep beating at high speed 2 or 3 minutes or until fluffy and stiff. Add vanilla. Yields enough icing to ice a three-layer cake.

Mrs. Clarke Spring, Jr.

# COOKIES

### POTATO CHIP COOKIES

2 cups butter
  (best with butter, but margarine
  and butter flavoring may be used)
1 cup sugar

3 cups flour
2 teaspoons vanilla
1½ cups crushed potato chips
Powdered sugar

Beat butter until light and fluffy—a long time! Add sugar and beat well. Add vanilla and flour gradually. Crush potato chips with your hand and add them last. Drop from teaspoon onto cookie sheets. Bake in a 350 degree oven until slightly brown. Sprinkle with powdered sugar. These keep well in a tightly closed tin—actually taste better the second or third day. Makes 9 to 10 dozen.

Mrs. J. D. Guillory

### BREAKFAST COOKIES

1 cup unsifted all purpose flour
¾ cup sugar
¼ teaspoon soda
1 egg

½ cup well drained crisp bacon
  (8 to 10 slices) broken into bits
½ cup soft margarine
2 cups raisin bran
½ teaspoon vanilla

Measure flour, sugar and soda in bowl. Mix well. Add bacon pieces, egg and margarine. Mix until all ingredients are well blended. Then add raisin bran and vanilla. Drop by spoon on ungreased baking sheet. Bake at 375 degrees, 13 to 15 minutes or until cookies are lightly browned, but still soft. Cool slightly before removing from pan. Makes 2½ to 3 dozen.

Mrs. J. W. C. Wright, Jr.

### BUTTER COOKIES

1 cup butter, softened
2 cups sugar
1 egg
4 cups flour, unsifted
1 teaspoon baking soda

½ teaspoon nutmeg or mace
  (optional)
4 tablespoons milk
2 teaspoons vanilla
Granulated sugar

Cream butter and sugar. Add egg. Beat well. Sift flour together with baking soda and nutmeg or mace. Add to creamed mixture alternately with milk. Add vanilla. Mix until blended. Refrigerate dough in a covered bowl overnight. The next day roll dough as thinly as possible on a lightly floured board. Cut dough into desired cookie shapes. Sprinkle lightly with granulated sugar. Place on an ungreased cookie sheet. Bake at 350 degrees until lightly browned, about 10 to 15 minutes. Makes 6 dozen.

Mrs. Everett Oertel

## GEORGIA'S SUGAR COOKIES

¾ cup margarine, softened
1¾ cups granulated sugar
2 eggs
4 cups flour

1 teaspoon baking powder
Dash salt
¼ cup margarine, melted
¼ cup granulated sugar

Cream margarine. Add 1¾ cups sugar gradually, creaming well. Add eggs. Blend well. Sift flour together with baking powder and salt. Add to creamed mixture. Blend thoroughly. Roll dough into a thin sheet on a board which has been sprinkled lightly with a mixture of 2 parts flour and 1 part sugar. Cut into desired shapes using cookie cutters or pastry wheel. Place on ungreased cookie sheet. Brush top with melted margarine. Sprinkle lightly with the ¼ cup sugar. Bake at 400 degrees until edges just begin to lightly brown, about 7 to 8 minutes. Cookies may be stored in tins for 2 to 3 weeks. Makes 6 to 8 dozen.

Mrs. Eugene H. Owen

## ALMOND CRESCENTS

½ cup powdered sugar
1 cup *real* butter
1 egg yolk

2½ cups all purpose flour
½ pound sliced, then broken,
   almonds
½ (scant) teaspoon almond extract

Sift sugar. Beat butter until soft. Add the sugar gradually. Blend these ingredients until very light and creamy. Beat in egg and sift and stir in flour. Add almonds and extract. Chill the dough. Preheat oven to 350 degrees. Pinch off about 1 tablespoon dough at a time, and roll between hands, forming into crescent shape. Place on greased cookie sheet. Bake for 10 to 15 minutes, until dry and crumbly, but do not let them brown. When cool, roll in powdered sugar. Makes 4 dozen.

Mrs. James Toups

## PECAN SQUARES

1 cup flour
½ cup margarine
2 beaten eggs
1½ cups brown sugar
½ cup chopped pecans

¼ cup flour
½ teaspoon salt
½ teaspoon baking powder
1 teaspoon vanilla
2 cups powdered sugar
lemon juice (and sherry, optional)

Combine flour and margarine. Spread in a 9x12-inch pan. Bake in a preheated 300 degree oven for 12 minutes. Mix other ingredients, except powdered sugar, lemon juice and sherry. Spread mixture on top of baked crust. Bake at 350 degrees for 25 minutes. While warm, spread with the confectioners sugar thinned with lemon juice. (Some sherry may be combined with lemon juice). Cut into small squares while warm. Makes about 4 dozen.

Mrs. Neel Garland

## CONGO SQUARES

One 1-pound box light brown sugar
3 eggs
⅔ cup oil
2¾ cups flour
2½ teaspoons baking powder
½ teaspoon salt
1 cup broken nuts
(pecans, walnuts)
One 6-ounce package chocolate chips

Combine sugar, eggs and oil in mixing bowl. Mix until thoroughly blended. Sift together flour, baking powder and salt. Add to mixture in bowl and mix until well blended. Mixture will be very thick and sticky. Stir in chips and nuts. Pour into greased and floured 9x13-inch pan and spread evenly over bottom. It will rise to about an inch in height when baked. Cook in 350 degree oven for 25 to 30 minutes. Do not overcook. Let cool in pan and cut into squares. Do not store in air tight container. Makes forty 1½-inch squares.

Mrs. Norman Saurage III

## COCONUT SQUARES

**Crust:**

½ cup margarine, softened
½ cup light brown sugar, packed
1 cup sifted flour

Combine margarine and sugar. Beat with mixer until light and fluffy. Add flour, mixing well. Pat into greased 13x9x2-inch pan. Bake at 375 degrees for 12 minutes.

**Filling:**

2 eggs, slightly beaten
½ teaspoon salt
1 teaspoon vanilla extract
One 3½-ounce can flaked coconut
1 cup chopped nuts
¼ cup sifted flour
1 cup light brown sugar, packed

Beat eggs. Add remaining ingredients. Mix well. Spread evenly over the crust. Bake again at 375 degrees until lightly browned, 15 to 20 minutes. Cool. Cut into squares. These freeze well. Makes 24 or more squares.

Mrs. Rodney Chastain

## CARAMEL SQUARES

½ cup butter
2 cups light brown sugar
2 eggs
¾ cup flour
1 teaspoon baking powder
1 teaspoon vanilla
¼ teaspoon salt
1 cup chopped nuts

Cream butter and sugar. Add eggs, flour, and remaining ingredients. Spread in 8x10-inch pan. Bake at 325 degrees for 30 minutes. Cut into squares.

Mrs. Ned Clark

## BUTTERSCOTCH CRISPS

Two 6-ounce packages butterscotch chips

One 3-ounce can chow mein noodles
One 5½-ounce can slivered almonds

Heat butterscotch chips in double boiler until just melted. Add the noodles and almonds. Mix well. Using a teaspoon, drop the desired amount of the mixture onto waxed paper. Let cool and harden. Remove and serve. These may be frozen. Makes 3 to 4 dozen.

Mrs. Michael T. Delahaye

## LEMON BARS

1 cup soft butter
2¼ cups flour
½ cup powdered sugar

2 cups granulated sugar
1 teaspoon baking powder
4 eggs, beaten
4 tablespoons lemon juice

Mix butter, 2 cups flour, and powdered sugar. Pat in bottom of 8½x13½-inch pyrex pan. Bake at 325 degrees for 15 minutes. Sift granulated sugar, remaining flour and baking powder. Combine dry ingredients with eggs and lemon juice. Spread over crust. Bake 25 minutes longer. Frost with a powdered sugar and lemon juice frosting. Cut into small squares. This freezes well.

Mrs. John B. Whitley

## ORANGE BALLS

One 12-ounce package vanilla wafers
½ cup margarine, softened
1 cup finely chopped nuts
One 1-pound box powdered sugar

One 6-ounce can concentrated frozen orange juice, thawed and undiluted
Flaked coconut or crushed pecans (optional)

Crush vanilla wafers to make fine crumbs. Add next four ingredients and mix well with hands. Form into small balls. Balls may be left plain, rolled in crushed pecans or flaked coconut. May be refrigerated or frozen.

Mrs. John B. Whitley

## CHOCOLATE ORANGE COOKIES

2 cups sifted flour
1 teaspoon baking soda
½ teaspoon salt
½ cup butter or margarine
1 cup sugar

1 egg
½ cup cornflake crumbs
1¼ teaspoon grated orange rind
¼ cup orange juice
One 6-ounce package (or 1 cup) semi-sweet chocolate pieces

On wax paper, sift together the flour, soda and salt. In a medium mixing bowl cream the butter and sugar. Thoroughly beat in egg. Stir in flour mixture and cornflake crumbs alternately with orange rind and orange juice. Mix well. Stir in chocolate. Drop by level tablespoons, a few inches apart, onto greased cookie sheet. Bake in 350 degree preheated oven until lightly browned, about 15 minutes. Makes 4 dozen.

Mrs. Dean M. Mosely

## PEANUT BUTTER COOKIES (KISSES)

1 cup sugar
3 egg whites

1 cup crunchy peanut butter
Pinch of salt

Beat egg whites until stiff. Add sugar. Fold in peanut butter and mix well. Drop by demi-tasse spoonsful on greased cookie sheet. Bake at 325 to 350 degrees for 12 minutes. Makes about 6 dozen cookies.

Mrs. John B. Whitley

## PEANUT BLOSSOMS

½ cup shortening or margarine
½ cup brown sugar
½ cup granulated sugar
½ cup smooth peanut butter
1 egg
2 tablespoons milk

1 teaspoon vanilla
1¾ cups flour
1 teaspoon soda
½ teaspoon salt
Granulated sugar
Chocolate kisses

Cream together the shortening or margarine, sugars, peanut butter, egg, milk, and vanilla. Sift flour, soda, and salt together. Add to creamed mixture. Make heaping teaspoons of dough into balls. Roll in granulated sugar. Put on ungreased cookie sheet. Bake at 350 degrees until lightly browned, about 10 to 15 minutes. As cookies come out of oven, stick a chocolate kiss in center. They will crack a little. Makes 5 dozen.

Mrs. John F. Davis, Jr.

## PEANUT BUTTER STICKS

1 loaf sandwich bread

1 cup peanut butter
1 cup salad oil

Cut crust off loaf of bread. Cut each slice of bread into five fingers. Electric knife makes this easier and neater. Put fingers and crusts on cookie sheets in 200 degree oven for one hour. Crush crust into crumbs. Dip bread fingers into mixture of oil and peanut butter. Roll in crushed crumbs. Place on wax paper to dry. Store in a tight container. They will stay crisp for a long time. Makes 90 to 100 sticks.

Mrs. Barry Bailey

## CHOCOLATE PEANUT PILLOWS

One 6-ounce package chocolate pieces
1 tablespoon margarine
½ cup peanut butter

2 tablespoons powdered sugar
3 cups spoon-size shredded wheat
    biscuits
½ cup finely chopped peanuts

Melt chocolate pieces and margarine over heat. Remove from heat and stir in peanut butter and powdered sugar. Dip shredded wheat biscuits in chocolate mixture, coating all sides. Gently shake off excess. Roll in chopped peanuts. Cool on rack. Store in refrigerator or very cool place. Makes 140 pillows.

Mrs. Ira Woodfin

## WAGON WHEELS

4 eggs
2 cups sugar
2 teaspoons vanilla
½ cup shortening, melted
Four 1-ounce squares unsweetened
  chocolate, melted

2 cups sifted flour
2 teaspoons baking powder
½ teaspoon salt
½ cup chopped nuts
Powdered sugar

Beat eggs. Add sugar and vanilla. Blend in shortening and chocolate. Sift flour together with baking powder and salt. Add to chocolate mixture. Stir in nuts. Refrigerate dough until easy to handle or overnight. Roll into balls. Sprinkle with powdered sugar. Bake on cookie sheet at 350 degrees for about 10 minutes.

Mrs. James Lea
Murfreesboro, Tennessee

## CREAM CHEESE DAINTIES

½ cup butter or margarine
One 3-ounce package cream cheese,
  softened
½ cup sugar
¼ teaspoon almond extract

1 cup sifted flour
2 teaspoons baking powder
¼ teaspoon salt
1½ cups crisp rice cereal,
  coarsely crushed
Red and green candied cherries

Cream butter, cheese, sugar and almond flavoring until light. Sift flour, baking powder and salt. Stir into butter mixture just until combined. Chill 1 to 2 hours. Shape into balls, roll in cereal and place on ungreased cookie sheet. Top each with a cherry. Bake at 350 degrees 12 to 15 minutes. Cool on racks. Makes 4 dozen.

Mrs. Charles Wynn

## CHEESECAKE SQUARES

**Crust:**

1 cup all purpose flour, unsifted
½ cup butter, softened

⅓ cup brown sugar, packed
½ cup chopped pecans

In a large bowl combine flour, butter, and brown sugar. Blend with mixer until particles are fine. Stir in nuts. Press into ungreased 9x13x2-inch pyrex pan. Bake at 350 degrees until lightly browned, about 12 to 15 minutes. Do not overbake.

**Filling:**

Two 8-ounce packages cream cheese,
  softened
½ cup sugar
2 eggs

¼ cup milk
¼ cup lemon juice
1 teaspoon vanilla extract
One 7¾-ounce jar junior apricots

In bowl, combine all ingredients except apricots. Blend well. Pour over partially baked crust. Stir apricots. Swirl them lightly over the filling. Bake at 350 degrees until filling is set, about 25 to 35 minutes. Cool. Cut into squares using a knife dipped in hot water. Refrigerate. These freeze well. Makes about 60 squares.

Mrs. J. P. Tomsula

## WILLIEMEL'S PECAN COOKIES

1 cup brown sugar
1 tablespoon flour
¼ teaspoon salt

1 egg white
½ teaspoon vanilla
2 cups pecan halves

Sift dry ingredients together. Beat egg white until stiff. Fold into dry ingredients. Add vanilla and pecans. Using a teaspoon, drop onto heavily greased cookie sheet. Bake at 275 degrees for 20 minutes. Store in tin box. Makes 2 dozen.

Mrs. Roland B. Howell

## DOLLY COOKIES

½ cup margarine
1 to 1½ cups graham cracker crumbs
½ cup coconut flakes (optional)
One 6-ounce package chocolate
  chips

One 6-ounce package butterscotch
  chips (optional)
1 cup chopped pecans
One 15-ounce can condensed milk

Melt margarine in 9x13-inch pan. Add other ingredients in the order listed. Spread evenly over the melted margarine. Bake 20 to 30 minutes at 350 degrees. Cookies should be golden brown. Cut around edges while warm to avoid sticking. Cool thoroughly before cutting into squares. Prepare a day ahead or early in the day. Makes about 24 small squares.

Mrs. Maurice J. Wilson
Mrs. William H. Lee
Mrs. Ronnie Merrill

## BASIC CAKE MIX COOKIES

One 10-ounce package cake mix
  (any flavor)
½ cup cooking oil
2 eggs, beaten

Vanilla or almond extract (optional)
1 cup of one or more of following for
  decoration: chopped nuts; M & M
  candies, broken and whole; chocolate chips, or caramel chips

Combine first three ingredients and mix until smooth. Add extract if desired. Drop cookie dough on ungreased cookie sheet by half teaspoonsful. Add desired decorations. Bake at 375 degrees for 10 to 12 minutes. Makes 3 to 4 dozen.

Mrs. R. Lewis Rieger

## CRUNCH COOKIES

1 cup butter
1 cup brown sugar
1 cup granulated sugar
2 eggs
½ teaspoon baking powder
½ teaspoon salt

1 teaspoon soda
2 cups flour
1½ cups quick rolled oats
2 cups corn flakes
1 cup coconut
1 teaspoon vanilla
1 cup chopped nuts

Cream butter and sugars. Add eggs, salt, soda, and flour. Slowly add rest of ingredients. Mix well. Drop by spoonfuls on a greased baking sheet. Bake at 375 degrees for 10 minutes.

Mrs. Ned Clark

## COWBOY COOKIES

2 cups flour
½ teaspoon baking powder
½ teaspoon soda
½ teaspoon salt
1 cup margarine or butter
1 cup granulated sugar

1 cup brown sugar (packed)
2 eggs
1 teaspoon vanilla
2 cups quick rolled oats
One 6-ounce package butterscotch
  chips or chocolate chips

Sift the flour, baking powder, soda, and salt together. Cream the butter with the sugars. Add eggs to the creamed mixture. Beat until smooth. Add the flour mixture gradually to the creamed ingredients. Now add the vanilla, rolled oats and the chips. Drop by spoonsful on a greased baking sheet and bake at 350 degrees approximately 15 minutes. Makes 4 dozen.

Mrs. H. Thompson Smith

## OATMEAL COOKIES

¾ cup shortening
1 cup sugar
¼ cup milk
2 eggs
2½ cups quick rolled oats

2 cups flour
¾ teaspoon cloves
1 teaspoon cinnamon
1 teaspoon baking powder
½ cup chopped raisins
1 cup broken pecans

Cream shortening and sugar. Blend in milk and eggs. Add oats. Sift flour together with cloves, cinnamon, and baking powder. Combine with first mixture. Stir in raisins and pecans. Drop by heaping teaspoons onto greased cookie sheet, allowing room for spreading. Bake at 350 degrees until lightly browned, about 18 to 20 minutes. Makes 5 dozen.

Mrs. Norman Saurage, Jr.

## ALMOND OATMEAL COOKIES

1 cup shortening
1 cup brown sugar
1 cup granulated sugar
2 eggs

½ teaspoon almond extract
½ teaspoon vanilla extract
2 cups quick rolled oats
2 cups flour
1 teaspoon baking soda

Cream shortening, sugars, eggs, and extracts. Beat well. Add oats. Stir and let stand while sifting flour and soda together. Add to oat mixture. Mix well. Drop by heaping teaspoons onto greased cookie sheet. Bake at 350 degrees until lightly browned—do not overcook—about 10 to 12 minutes. Makes 6 to 7 dozen.

Mrs. Walter Donalson
Albion, Michigan

## BROWNIES WITH ICING

**Brownies:**

Three 1-ounce squares
  unsweetened chocolate
1 cup butter or margarine

4 eggs
2 cups sugar
1 cup flour
2 cups broken pecans

Melt together chocolate and butter. Beat eggs with sugar. Mix with chocolate and butter. Add 1 cup flour (unsifted) and pecans. Mix. Pour into 10x14-inch pan lined with greased wax paper. Bake at 375 degrees about 30 minutes. Turn out on flat surface. Cool. Ice. Cut into squares.

**Icing:**

½ cup butter or margarine
2 heaping tablespoons cocoa

¼ cup milk
One 1-pound box powdered sugar

Melt butter. Add remaining ingredients and mix with electric mixer.

Mrs. J. Theron Brown

## BROWNIES

**Brownies:**

¾ cup sifted all purpose flour
1 cup sugar
5 tablespoons cocoa
½ teaspoon salt

½ cup shortening
2 eggs
1 teaspoon vanilla
½ cup chopped nuts

Place all ingredients in a large mixing bowl. Beat until well blended. Pour into greased and floured 7- or 8-inch square pan. Bake at 350 degrees for 30 minutes. Cool and frost with the following:

**Chocolate Butter Frosting:**

1½ squares unsweetened chocolate
  (1½ ounces)
2 tablespoons butter or margarine

1½ cups powdered sugar
1 teaspoon vanilla
3 tablespoons milk or cream

Melt chocolate and butter over low heat. Combine chocolate mixture with other ingredients. Beat until thoroughly blended. If not the desired consistency add more milk or sugar. Makes 3 to 4 dozen bite-size pieces.

Mrs. Hudson Ford Bell, III

## PRALINE COOKIES

½ cup dark brown sugar
½ cup light brown sugar (or use
  all light)
2 level tablespoons flour

½ teaspoon salt
1 egg white, beaten stiff but not
  dry
1 teaspoon vanilla
2 cups whole pecans

Sift sugars, flour, and salt. Fold in egg white and vanilla. Fold in nuts carefully. Drop small bits (two large pecans or three small pecans to cookie) on well buttered cookie sheet. Preheat oven to 275 degrees. Bake for 30 to 35 minutes until firm. Makes 5 dozen.

Mrs. Carlos G. Spaht, Sr.

## DATE NUT SQUARES

¼ cup butter, softened
1 cup sugar
2 eggs, separated
½ teaspoon baking powder
½ cup flour

One 8-ounce package dates, cut up
1¼ teaspoons lemon juice
1 cup chopped pecans
Pinch salt
1 teaspoon cinnamon
3 teaspoons sugar

Blend together the butter, 1 cup sugar, and egg yolks. Sift baking powder with flour. Add dates, lemon juice, nuts, and salt. Mix thoroughly. Beat egg whites until stiff. Fold into batter. Line a well greased 9-inch square pan with waxed paper. Pour batter into pan. Bake at 325 degrees for 25 to 30 minutes. Meanwhile, combine cinnamon with the 3 teaspoons sugar. Remove cake from oven. Sprinkle half the cinnamon and sugar on top. Invert pan onto plate. Peel paper off carefully in strips. Sprinkle cake with remaining cinnamon and sugar. Cool and cut into squares or bars. Makes 16 squares or 32 bars.

Mrs. Glenn S. Darsey

## DOUBLE DECKER DATE BARS

**Bottom Layer:**
1¼ cups sifted flour

⅓ cup sugar
½ cup butter or margarine

Combine flour, sugar and butter. Blend to fine crumbs. Pack or press into 9-inch square baking pan. Bake at 350 degrees for 20 minutes until light brown.

**Top Layer:**
½ cup light brown sugar, packed
⅓ cup granulated sugar
2 eggs
1 teaspoon vanilla
2 tablespoons flour
1 teaspoon baking powder

½ teaspoon salt
¼ teaspoon nutmeg
1 cup chopped pecans or walnuts
One 8-ounce package chopped
   pitted dates
Powdered sugar

Combine first four ingredients and beat well. Add flour, baking powder, salt and nutmeg; beat well. Stir in dates and nuts. Spread over baked pastry. Bake at 350 degrees for 25 minutes. Cool and sprinkle with powdered sugar. Cut into 32 bars.

Mrs. Stephen Glagola

## STRAWBERRIES

1 cup pecans
1 cup coconut
½ cup condensed milk

Two 3-ounce or one 6-ounce
   package strawberry gelatin
½ teaspoon vanilla
Red and green sugar crystals

Chop nuts and coconut together in blender. Combine with all other ingredients except colored sugars. Roll into strawberry-shaped pieces. Then roll in red sugar crystals, trying not to get red sugar on "stem" end of strawberries. Dip stem end in green sugar crystals.

Mrs. William H. Gatchell
Memphis, Tenn.

# PIES

## LEMON ANGEL PIE

**Meringue Crust:**
**4 egg whites**                  **¼ teaspoon cream of tartar**
                                  **1 cup sugar**

Preheat oven to 275 degrees. Grease 9-inch pie plate. Beat egg whites and cream of tartar until foamy. Beat in sugar, 1 tablespoon at a time. This should take approximately 25 minutes. Spread meringue over bottom and sides of prepared 9-inch pie plate. Shape with back of spoon so bottom is ¼ inch thick and sides are 1 inch thick. Bake 60 minutes. Turn oven off leaving meringue shell in oven 1 hour to cool. Remove and cool to room temperature on wire rack.

**Filling:**
**4 egg yolks**                   **¼ cup lemon juice**
**½ cup sugar**                   **1 cup heavy cream**
**2 tablespoons grated lemon peel**   **Toasted coconut, if desired**

Beat egg yolks in saucepan until thick and lemon colored. Beat in sugar gradually. Blend in lemon peel and juice. Cook over medium heat, stirring constantly 5 to 8 minutes or until thick. Cool. Whip heavy cream until soft peaks form, saving ¼ of the whipped cream as topping. Fold ¾ of the whipped cream into lemon mixture and spread on cooled meringue shell. Chill at least 12 hours. Before serving, spoon remaining whipped cream into center of pie. Sprinkle with toasted coconut if desired. This pie should be made a day ahead to allow the flavors to blend. Serves 8.

Mrs. Chambliss Mizelle
Lafayette, Louisiana

## OLD FASHIONED LEMON PIE

**Two 8-inch pie shells, unbaked**   **4 whole eggs**
**1 cup sugar**                       **1 cup lemon juice**
**6 tablespoons butter**              **lemon rind, grated**

Bake pie crusts in a 450 degree oven for 4 to 6 minutes. Set aside. Cream sugar and butter together until light and fluffy. Add eggs one at a time, beating well after each addition. Slowly pour in lemon juice while beating constantly. Add rind and mix. Pour into partially baked pie shells and bake at 350 degrees until filling is firm. Serves 12.

Mrs. R. E. Couhig
Asphodel Plantation

## LEMONADE PIE

**1 small carton whipped topping**    **One 6-ounce can frozen pink**
**One 15-ounce can condensed milk**      **lemonade**
**Red food coloring (about 2 drops)**  **One 9-inch baked pie crust**

Mix thoroughly whipped topping, condensed milk, frozen lemonade and food coloring. Put into baked pie shell. Chill in refrigerator. Do not freeze. Serves 8.

Mrs. Neel Garland

## LEMON CHIFFON PIE

6 egg yolks
¾ cup sugar
3 lemons, grated rind and juice
1 envelope unflavored gelatin

⅓ cup water
6 egg whites
¾ cup sugar
½ pint heavy cream, whipped
Two 9-inch baked pie shells

Cook egg yolks, sugar, lemon juice, and grated rind in top of double boiler until thick. Dissolve gelatin in water; add to thickened egg yolk mixture and stir well. Let cool. Beat egg whites with sugar until stiff. Fold egg whites into lemon mixture. Pour into 2 baked 9-inch pie crusts. Refrigerate 2 hours. When serving, put a generous spoonful of whipped cream on top of each piece of pie. Serves 16.

Mrs. Eugene H. Owen

## NESSELRODE CHIFFON PIE

1 envelope unflavored gelatin
⅔ cup sugar, divided
⅛ teaspoon salt
3 eggs, separated
1 cup heavy cream

1¼ cups milk
2 teaspoons rum flavoring or
   3 tablespoons rum or sherry
1 tablespoon chopped cherries
One 9-inch baked pie shell
Shaved chocolate

Mix gelatin, half of sugar, and salt in top of double boiler. Beat egg yolks, cream and milk together. Add to gelatin. Cook over boiling water, stirring constantly until gelatin is dissolved, about 4 minutes. Remove from heat and stir in flavoring. Chill in bowl of ice and water, stirring occasionally, until mixture mounds when dropped from spoon. Beat egg whites until stiff. Beat in remaining sugar. Fold gelatin mixture and cherries into egg whites. Put in pie shell and top with chocolate. Chill in refrigerator until firm. Serves 6 to 8.

Mrs. Neel Garland

## FLAMING PECAN PUMPKIN PIE

Pie:

One 1-pound can pumpkin pie filling
3 tablespoons bourbon
2 eggs, slightly beaten
¾ cup brown sugar
1½ cups light cream

1 teaspoon cinnamon
½ teaspoon ginger
½ teaspoon salt
One 9-inch unbaked pie shell,
   chilled

Combine pumpkin and bourbon. Add eggs, sugar, cream, spices and salt. Pour into shell. Bake at 425 degrees for 10 minutes. Reduce heat to 350 degrees and bake 50 minutes or until knife inserted in center comes out clean. Cool completely.

Topping:

2 tablespoons butter or margarine
¼ cup brown sugar

¼ cup bourbon
1 cup pecan halves

Combine butter and brown sugar in saucepan. Heat, stirring until sugar is completely dissolved. Stir in 2 tablespoons bourbon. Add pecans and stir to glaze. Spoon around edge of pie. At serving time, warm remaining 2 tablespoons bourbon, ignite and pour flaming onto pecan border. Serve when flames subside.

Mrs. Katherine Hattic Long

## INDIVIDUAL PECAN PIES

**Crust:**

One 3-ounce package cream cheese    1 cup, 1 tablespoon sifted all
½ cup butter                        purpose flour

With spoon, combine cream cheese, butter and flour until well mixed. Press mixture with fingers into well buttered 1-inch muffin pans, completely covering sides.

**Filling:**

1 whole egg, beaten                 1 tablespoon melted butter
½ cup dark brown sugar, firmly      1 teaspoon vanilla
  packed                            ¾ cup chopped pecans
¼ cup granulated sugar              ⅛ teaspoon salt

Combine the above ingredients with a spoon. Spoon filling into 1-inch muffin tins, filling them to the top. Bake in 350 degree oven for 25 minutes or until golden brown. Cool 5 minutes. Remove from tins with a pointed knife being careful not to break crust. Makes 24 individual pies.

Mrs. Richard F. Hickman
Huffman, Texas

## BOURBON PECAN PIE

One 9- or 10-inch pie crust         2 tablespoons flour
1¼ cup pecan halves                 1 tablespoon margarine, soft
⅓ cup bourbon                       1 cup dark corn syrup
1 cup brown sugar, packed           3 eggs, beaten
                                    ¼ teaspoon salt

Toss pecans and bourbon until pecans are coated. Let stand 1 hour or until most of the bourbon is absorbed. Heat oven to 325 degrees. Mix brown sugar and flour. Beat in margarine until creamy. Beat in corn syrup, eggs, and salt. Stir in pecans and bourbon. Pour into pie shell. Cover edge with ½-inch aluminum foil strip to prevent excessive browning. Remove foil last 15 minutes. Serves 8.

Mrs. Claude Platte

## RAISIN PECAN PIE

½ cup margarine                     ½ teaspoon ginger
2 cups sugar                        3 tablespoons vinegar
4 eggs                              ¾ cup chopped pecans
4 tablespoons milk                  ½ teaspoon vanilla
½ teaspoon cinnamon                 1 cup raisins
½ teaspoon nutmeg                   Whipped cream (optional)
½ teaspoon allspice                 One 10-inch unbaked pie shell

Cream margarine and sugar. Add eggs, one at a time, beating after each addition. Blend in milk, spices, vinegar, nuts and vanilla. Boil raisins (in water to cover) about 5 minutes, drain and add to pie mixture. Pour into 10-inch pie shell and bake 40 minutes at 350 degrees or until pie is firm. Top with whipped cream if desired. Serves 8.

Mrs. Wayne T. Davis

## LUCY'S PECAN PIE

3 eggs     1 teaspoon vanilla
1 cup light brown sugar     1½ cups pecans (halves)
1 cup white corn syrup     One uncooked 9-inch pie shell

Using fork or wire whisk, beat together eggs and sugar until well mixed. Add corn syrup and vanilla and mix well. Stir in pecans. Pour into prepared, uncooked 9-inch pie shell and bake at 300 degrees for one hour and 45 minutes, or until lightly browned. Let cool slightly before serving. Serves 6 to 8.

Mrs. E. J. Capbern

## CHEESECAKE PIE

1½ cups graham cracker crumbs     ½ teaspoon vanilla
5 tablespoons melted butter     1 pint sour cream
11 ounces cream cheese     ¼ cup sugar
2 eggs     One 1-pound box frozen
½ cup sugar     strawberries, thawed (optional)

Combine graham cracker crumbs with melted butter. Use the mixture to line a 9- or 10-inch pie plate. Preheat oven to 350 degrees. Place the cream cheese in a large mixing bowl and blend slowly with an electric mixer. When cream cheese is fairly smooth, add eggs, one at a time, beating the mixture well after the addition of each. Continue beating the filling on low speed. Gradually add ½ cup sugar and then the vanilla. Pour cream cheese mixture into the prepared graham cracker crust. Bake the pie for 20 minutes at 350 degrees. Meanwhile, blend the sour cream with ¼ cup of sugar. Spread the mixture evenly over the top of pie. Turn off oven heat and return pie to oven for 4 minutes. Cool. Chill in refrigerator until set. Garnish, if desired, with a package of strawberries that has been thawed. Serves 8.

Mrs. Ben Thompson, Jr.

## BRANDY ALEXANDER PIE

One envelope unflavored gelatin     3 eggs, separated
½ cup cold water     ¼ cup cognac
⅔ cup sugar     ¼ cup crème de cocoa
⅛ teaspoon salt     2 cups heavy cream, whipped
    One 9-inch graham cracker crust

Sprinkle gelatin over cold water in saucepan. Add ⅓ cup sugar, salt and egg yolks. Stir to blend. Place over low heat; keep stirring while gelatin dissolves and mixture thickens. Do not boil. Remove from heat and stir in cognac and crème de cocoa. Chill until mixture starts to mound slightly. Beat egg whites until stiff, gradually beating in remaining ⅓ cup sugar and fold into mixture. Fold in 1 cup whipped cream. Pour into crust, and chill several hours. Garnish with remaining cup of whipped cream, sweetened with ¼ cup sugar and bitter chocolate shaved into curls. Serves 6 to 8.

Mrs. Charles D. Baldridge, Jr.

## BUTTERMILK PIE

2 cups sugar
¼ cup flour
1 teaspoon vanilla
3 eggs, slightly beaten

½ cup margarine, melted
¾ cup buttermilk
One 9- or 10-inch unbaked
   pie shell

Mix all ingredients together, beating well, and pour into unbaked pie shell. Bake in a slow oven until set and well browned. Bake about 45 minutes at 325 degrees. Serves 6 to 8.

Mrs. J. Buffington Maguire, Jr.
Pampa, Texas

## CHERRY CHEESE PIE

One 9-inch unbaked pie shell
One 20-ounce can cherry pie filling
One 8-ounce package cream cheese,
   softened

½ cup sugar
2 eggs
½ teaspoon vanilla
1 cup sour cream
Nutmeg

Place cherry pie filling in pie shell and bake at 425 degrees for 15 minutes. Meanwhile, beat cream cheese, sugar, eggs, and vanilla until smooth and creamy. Lower oven temperature to 350 degrees. Gently spoon cheese mixture over cherries. Bake 30 minutes. Cool. Spread sour cream over top of cooled pie, sprinkle with nutmeg and refrigerate until served. Serves 8.

Mrs. Norman Saurage III

## CHESS PIE

½ cup butter or margarine
2½ cups sugar
½ cup processed American cheese,
   finely grated

4 eggs
1 tablespoon flour
1 tablespoon vanilla
One 9-inch unbaked pastry shell

Cream butter with electric mixer. Add sugar, beating until light. Add cheese and cream until uniform in color. Add eggs one at a time, beating well after each addition. Add flour and vanilla and blend. Pour into unbaked pastry shell. Bake at 325 degrees for 55 minutes or one hour. Top crust will be very dark brown. Prick top of pie with toothpick while baking to allow steam to escape. This will cause top brown layer to adhere to filling. Cool thoroughly, about two hours. Serves 8.

Mrs. Charles Wynn

## EASY COCONUT PIE

3 eggs
1⅓ cups sugar
½ cup milk
2 tablespoons melted butter

¼ teaspoon salt
1 teaspoon vanilla
One 3½-ounce can coconut
One 9-inch uncooked pie shell

With fork, beat together eggs and sugar until well blended. Mix in all other ingredients. Pour into pie shell and bake at 350 degrees for 1 hour. Serves 6 to 8.

Mrs. Norman Saurage III

## RUM PIE

| | |
|---|---|
| 1 scant envelope unflavored gelatin | 5 tablespoons rum |
| ⅓ cup sugar | 4 egg whites |
| ⅛ teaspoon salt | ⅓ cup sugar |
| 4 egg yolks | 1 cup whipping cream |
| 1⅔ cups milk | Two 9-inch baked pie shells |

Mix gelatin, sugar, salt, egg yolks and milk in top of double boiler. Cook over hot water stirring until custard coats spoon. Remove from fire and stir in rum. Refrigerate until mixture cools and begins to thicken. Beat egg whites, slowly adding ⅓ cup sugar and fold into rum custard. Whip cream and also fold into mixture. Pour into two 9-inch baked crusts. Baking chocolate may be shaved over pies before serving, or nutmeg may be sprinkled over the finished pies. Refrigerate until served. Serves 16.

Mrs. Vernon L. Shallcross
Mrs. Charles E. Colvin, Jr.

## GRASSHOPPER PIE

| | |
|---|---|
| 14 chocolate Oreo cookies | 4 tablespoons green crème |
| 2 tablespoons margarine, melted | de menthe |
| 24 marshmallows | 2 tablespoons white crème |
| ½ cup milk | de cocoa |
| Dash of salt | ½ pint whipping cream, whipped |
| | Grated bitter chocolate |

Crush cookies. Mix with melted margarine. Press into 8-inch pie plate. Melt marshmallows in milk over very low heat in heavy pot. Add dash of salt. Remove from heat and let cool. Stir in crème de menthe and crème de cocoa. Fold in whipped cream and pour into prepared pie shell. Sprinkle grated bitter chocolate on top. Put in freezer, leave until ready to serve, and serve frozen. This will keep frozen for a long time. Serves 6 to 8.

Mrs. D. H. Garland
Houston, Texas

## BLACK BOTTOM ICE CREAM PIE

**Crust:**

| | |
|---|---|
| 1¼ cups chocolate wafer crumbs | ¼ cup melted butter |

Combine cookie crumbs and melted butter. Mix well. Press mixture evenly on bottom and side of a 9-inch pie plate. Place in freezer.

**Filling:**

| | |
|---|---|
| 2 pints chocolate ice cream | 1 cup heavy whipping cream |
| 2 squares melted semi-sweet | ¼ cup sugar |
| chocolate | 2 tablespoons golden rum |

Let ice cream soften slightly. Beat with electric mixer until smooth. Gradually add melted chocolate, beating constantly. (Chocolate will harden and form fine pieces.) Pour into crust. Return to freezer. When ice cream filling hardens a bit, beat whipping cream until thick. Add sugar and rum and beat until stiff. Spoon on pie. Freeze until very firm, 6 or 8 hours. If desired, garnish with chocolate curls. Serves 8.

Mrs. Rolf Schroeder

## DIXIE PIE

One 9-inch unbaked pie shell
One 6-ounce package semi-sweet
   chocolate pieces
4 tablespoons butter

1 cup sugar
½ cup flour
2 eggs
1 cup pecans, chopped

Spread bottom of pie shell with chocolate pieces. Stir together melted butter, sugar, and flour. Beat in eggs one at a time. Stir in pecans and pour over chocolate pieces. Bake at 350 degrees for one hour. Let cool before serving. Serves 8.

Baton Rouge State-Times

## RIBBON ALASKA PIE

Fudge Sauce:

2 tablespoons margarine
Two 1-ounce squares unsweetened
   chocolate
1 cup sugar

One 6-ounce can evaporated milk
1 teaspoon vanilla
2 pints vanilla ice cream
One 9-inch baked pie shell

Mix margarine, chocolate, sugar and milk in saucepan. Cook and stir over low heat until thick. Remove from heat. Add vanilla. Cool. Spread 1 pint ice cream in pastry shell. Cover with half the fudge sauce. Repeat layers. Freeze until firm.

Meringue:

3 eggs whites
¼ teaspoon salt

6 tablespoons sugar
¼ cup crushed peppermint candy

Beat egg whites with salt until soft peaks form. Gradually add sugar beating until stiff peaks form and all sugar is dissolved. Reserve 2 teaspoons candy and fold rest into meringue. Spread over pie, sealing edges. Top with candy. Bake at 475 degrees, about 4 minutes, or until lightly browned. Serve at once or freeze. Serves 8.

Mrs. John S. Campbell, Jr.

## STRAWBERRY CREAM PIE

1 cup sugar
6 tablespoons flour
Dash of salt
2½ cups milk
2 egg yolks, slightly beaten
2 tablespoons butter

1 teaspoon vanilla
2 pints fresh strawberries
1 cup whipping cream
2 tablespoons sugar
1 teaspoon vanilla
One 9- or 10-inch baked pie shell

Sift sugar, flour and salt together. Scald milk in top of double boiler and then place over boiling water. Gradually add dry ingredients, mixing with egg beater or portable mixer. After all dry ingredients have been added, cook 10 minutes stirring occasionally. Take a couple of teaspoons of hot mixture and add to beaten egg yolks and add all back to custard mixture and stir well. Cook 3 minutes. Mixture will be thick. Remove from heat; add butter and vanilla and stir until melted. Let cool slightly. Put a layer of sliced berries on bottom of crust and pour custard over them. Refrigerate until cool and add another layer of berries and top with sweetened whipped cream flavored with vanilla.

Mrs. James R. Ourso

## CHAMBLISS'S CHOCOLATE PIE

**Crust:**

1⅓ cups all purpose flour
½ cup shortening

3 tablespoons cold water
¼ teaspoon salt

Mix salt with 1 cup flour in a mixing bowl. Cut shortening into flour. Add 3 tablespoons cold water into ⅓ cup flour stirring into a paste with a fork. Add to flour and shortening, stirring with a fork to form a ball. Roll on floured board. Place in 9-inch pie pan. Turn under a half inch of crust on edges and flute edge with fingers. Prick well all over. Bake until golden brown in 425 degree oven, about 9 minutes.

**Filling:**

2½ squares semi-sweet chocolate
2 tablespoons sugar
3 tablespoons milk

1 teaspoon vanilla flavoring
3 eggs
½ cup whipping cream
1 teaspoon sugar

Melt chocolate in the top of a double boiler. Add sugar and milk and stir very well with a spoon. Add the vanilla and stir well. Remove from the top of the double boiler. Separate the eggs putting the yolks, one at a time, in with the chocolate mixture and beating well each time with a spoon. Place the whites of the eggs in a mixing bowl. Beat with mixer until stiff. Fold into chocolate mixture. Pour into cooled pie shell. Place in refrigerator for 4 hours. Top with whipping cream whipped with 1 teaspoon sugar. Serves 8.

Mrs. Chambliss Mizelle
Lafayette, Louisiana

## ELLEN'S CHOCOLATE PIE

**Crust:**

3 egg whites
Pinch of salt
1 teaspoon vanilla

1 cup sugar
1 teaspoon baking powder
¾ cup chopped pecans
½ cup saltine cracker crumbs

Beat egg whites, salt and vanilla gradually adding sugar. Beat until stiff. Mix together baking powder, nuts and crumbs. Fold into egg white mixture. Grease a deep 10-inch pie pan or two 8-inch pans and spread the mixture to make crust. Bake at 300 degrees for 40 minutes.

**Filling:**

1 cup sugar
⅓ cup cocoa, minus 1 teaspoon
⅓ cup flour
3 egg yolks

1¾ cups milk
1 teaspoon vanilla
2 tablespoons butter, softened
1 cup whipping cream, whipped

Mix in double boiler, sugar, cocoa, flour, egg yolks and milk. Cook on medium heat until very thick. Remove from heat and add vanilla and butter. Pour into baked shell. Cool. Top with whipped cream. Serves 10 to 12.

Mrs. Billy J. Smith

## RASPBERRY PIE

**Crumb Crust:**

| | |
|---|---|
| 1⅓ cups crushed graham crackers | ¼ cup butter or margarine, melted |
| | 3 tablespoons powdered sugar |

Combine cracker crumbs, melted butter or margarine, and sugar and pat in 8- or 9-inch pie pan.

**Filling:**

| | |
|---|---|
| One 8-ounce package cream cheese | 1 teaspoon vanilla |
| 2 eggs | ½ cup sugar |

Beat cream cheese, eggs, vanilla and sugar together and pour over crumb crust. Bake in 350 degree oven until set, 15 or 18 minutes. Let cool.

**Topping:**

| | |
|---|---|
| 1 package frozen raspberries | 2 tablespoons cornstarch |
| 3 tablespoons sugar | whipped cream, sweetened |

Heat raspberries and add 3 tablespoons sugar. Thicken with cornstarch. Cool. Put raspberry mixture over filling and frost with sweetened whipped cream. Refrigerate for several hours before serving. Serves 6 to 8.

Mrs. Torrence H. Sneed
Balboa, Canal Zone

## BLUEBERRY COOL WHIP PIE

| | |
|---|---|
| One 8-inch baked pie shell | 2 cups powdered sugar |
| ⅓ cup chopped pecans | 1 small carton Cool Whip |
| One 9-ounce package cream cheese | ½ cup milk |
| | ½ can blueberry pie filling |

Sprinkle chopped pecans on crust. In one bowl mix cream cheese and sugar. Cream together. In another bowl mix Cool Whip and milk. Beat until thoroughly mixed. Add cream cheese mixture and whipped topping and beat until well mixed. Pour into crust and add ½ can pie filling to middle of pie. Do not cover all of pie. It's prettier if an inch or an inch and a half of the pie filling around the edge is showing. Serves 6 to 8.

Mrs. William J. Carona
Mrs. W. A. Whitley

## APPLE PIE

| | |
|---|---|
| 4 cups thinly sliced apples | 2 tablespoons flour |
| ½- to ¾-cup sugar, depending on | Double pie crust for 9-inch pan |
| tartness of apples | 1 tablespoon butter |

Mix apples, sugar and flour together and place in unbaked 9-inch pie shell. Dot with small pieces of butter, then cover with unbaked pie crust which has slits in it to allow steam to escape. Bake at 425 degrees until crust is set, about 12 minutes; then lower oven temperature to 350 degrees and bake until fruit is tender; about 35 minutes. Crust should be lightly browned. Serves 6.

Mrs. Charles C. Garvey

# CANDY

### PECAN PRALINES

1½ cups sugar
½ cup buttermilk
1 tablespoon white corn syrup

½ teaspoon baking soda
¼ cup butter
½ teaspoon vanilla
1 cup chopped pecans

Combine sugar, buttermilk, syrup and soda. Cook slowly in a heavy pot until the mixture forms a soft ball, about 20 minutes. Be sure to use candy thermometer (235 degrees). Remove from heat. Add butter, vanilla and pecans. Beat mixture until smooth and creamy using a wooden spoon. Drop by tablespoonsful onto waxed paper. If candy does not harden within 10 minutes of dropping, it can be cooked a few minutes more. Yield: 2 dozen small pieces.

Mrs. Earl Geroy

### MAPLE PRALINES

2 cups white granulated sugar
1 cup dark brown sugar
3 tablespoons white corn syrup

1 cup whipping cream
Pinch of salt
3 teaspoons maple flavoring
3 or more cups pecans

Cook sugars, syrup, cream and salt over high heat until the mixture forms a soft ball (235 degrees) when dropped in water. Remove from heat. Add maple flavoring and pecans. Beat or stir until creamy. Drop from spoon onto waxed paper in bite size pieces. Yield: 4 to 5 dozen.

Mrs. Julius H. Mullins

### ORANGE-PECAN PRALINES

2 cups sugar
1 tablespoon grated orange peel
1 cup milk

¼ cup orange juice
1½ cups pecan halves or
large pieces

Combine sugar, orange peel and milk. Bring to a boil. Boil until the mixture forms a soft ball (235 degrees), about 20 minutes. Stir in orange juice. Let cool. Add pecans, stirring until almost dry. Drop quickly by teaspoonsful onto waxed paper. Yield: 3 dozen.

Mrs. J. Dawson Gasquet

## QUICK PRALINE CANDY

One 3-ounce package regular (not         ½ cup dark brown sugar
   instant) vanilla pudding mix          ½ cup evaporated milk
1 cup granulated sugar                   1 tablespoon butter
                                         1½ cups pecans

Combine ingredients in a 2-quart saucepan. Cook until sugar dissolves and mixture boils, stirring constantly. Continue cooking until mixture forms a soft ball in water. Remove from heat; beat until thick, but *no longer*. Drop on waxed paper by spoonsful. Yield: 20 to 25 pralines.

Mrs. Jack V. Holmes

## DIVINITY

4 cups sugar                             3 egg whites
1 cup light corn syrup                   1 teaspoon vanilla
¾ cup water                              1 cup slightly chopped nuts

Place sugar, syrup and water in a heavy 4-quart saucepan over low heat. Stir until sugar is dissolved, then cook without stirring to 255 degrees (hard ball stage). Remove from heat and pour in a fine stream, beating constantly into the stiffly beaten egg whites. Continue beating until mixture holds its shape and loses its gloss. Add vanilla and nuts. Drop quickly from tip of spoon onto waxed paper in individual peaks or spread in a buttered 9-inch square cake pan. Cut into squares when firm.

Mrs. Robert Witcher
Manhasset, New York

## MOTHER'S FUDGE

Two 1-ounce unsweetened chocolate        ¾ cup milk
   squares                               5 tablespoons white corn syrup
2 cups sugar                             4 teaspoons butter or margarine
⅛ teaspoon salt                          1 cup chopped pecans
                                         2 teaspoons vanilla

Cook the first 5 ingredients to a soft ball (235 degrees). Remove from heat and add butter. Cool slightly; then beat until almost stiff. Add nuts and vanilla. Drop by teaspoonsful quickly onto waxed paper or pour onto slightly greased plate. Cool and cut.

Mrs. Dave Cowden
Shreveport, Louisiana

## PEANUT BUTTER FUDGE

| | |
|---|---|
| 1 cup dark brown sugar | 2 tablespoons butter |
| 1 cup white sugar | 1 cup marshmallow pieces |
| ½ cup evaporated milk | ¾ cup peanut butter |
| | 1 teaspoon vanilla |

Combine sugars, milk and butter in a heavy 4-quart saucepan. Cook until soft ball stage (235 degrees). Just before removing pan from heat, add remaining ingredients. Stir until marshmallows are almost melted. Now remove from heat and beat until mixture begins to thicken, about 1 minute. Pour immediately into a buttered 8-inch square pan. When cool, cut into serving size squares. Yield: 1½ pounds.

Mrs. Robert Witcher
Manhasset, New York

## ORANGE NUTS

| | |
|---|---|
| 1 cup sugar | 1 teaspoon lemon extract |
| ⅓ cup concentrated orange juice | 2 tablespoons butter or margarine |
| | 2½ cups walnut or pecan halves |

Combine sugar and orange juice concentrate and cook until mixture forms a soft ball (235 degrees). Add extract and butter. Beat well until mixture has a very creamy look and begins to thicken. Add nut meats and stir until well coated. Pour out on waxed paper and pull apart to form small clusters. Yield: 1 pound.

Mrs. G. Ross Murrell, Jr.

## CHOCOLATE COATED ORANGE PEEL

| | |
|---|---|
| 4 large oranges | 1 cup water |
| ½ teaspoon salt | ¼ cup white corn syrup |
| 2 cups sugar | One 6-ounce package semi-sweet chocolate pieces |

Peel oranges in quarters. Remove pulp and membrane. Place peel in saucepan with salt and enough water to cover. Bring quickly to a boil and simmer 30 minutes. Drain. Add fresh water and continue simmering until peel is tender, about 15 minutes. Drain and cool. Scrape off white part, then cut in ¼-inch strips. Combine sugar, water and corn syrup. Cook and stir until sugar is dissolved. Add peel and cook until a small amount of mixture forms a very soft ball (230 degrees). Drain peel and roll in sugar. Spread on tray and dry overnight. Heat chocolate slowly until partly melted. Remove from heat and stir rapidly until entirely melted. Cool slightly. Hold strips by ends and dip quickly in chocolate. Harden on waxed paper. Will keep at least a week in a candy tin.

Mrs. G. Ross Murrell, Jr.

## DOT'S MINTS

¼ cup margarine
1 pound powdered sugar
½ egg white

½ teaspoon oil of peppermint
2 drops food coloring (for a
    pastel color)
Very little bit of cream

Mix all ingredients well. Amount of cream to use depends on consistency of mixture (should be about as thick as softened butter). Form into small patties or force through star shape of a cookie press. Place on wax paper and let sit for 12 hours. (Drying time will be longer on highly humid days. The drier the day, the better the mint.) Store in cookie tin. Will keep indefinitely. Yield: 100 mints.

Mrs. Julius H. Mullins

## HEAVENLY HASH

2 cups marshmallows
3 cups sugar
1½ cups evaporated milk
½ cup cocoa

¼ cup butter or margarine
2 cups chopped pecans
1¾ cups marshmallow crème
1 teaspoon vanilla

Cut marshmallows into pieces and place in a greased 9x12-inch pan. Mix sugar, milk, cocoa and butter. Cook mixture until a soft ball is formed when dropped into water (235 degrees). Add pecans, marshmallow crème and vanilla. Beat until mixture begins to thicken. Pour over the broken pieces of marshmallows. Let cool and harden. Cut into squares.

Mrs. Earle R. Weaver

## MARTHA WASHINGTON FUDGE

**Candy:**

2 boxes powdered sugar
1 can condensed milk

¼ cup soft butter
2 teaspoons vanilla
3 cups chopped nuts

Mix powdered sugar, condensed milk, butter, vanilla, and nuts together. Chill. Roll into balls.

**Dipping Chocolate:**

1½ to 2 packages semi-sweet
    brick chocolate

¾ block paraffin wax

Melt chocolate and paraffin in top of double boiler. Drop one ball at a time into chocolate mixture. Retrieve with a fork and shake off excess chocolate. Dry on waxed paper Yield: 5 pounds.

Mrs. William D. Wilkinson

## CHOCOLATE WHISKEY BALLS

**Candy:**

½ cup margarine, at room
  temperature
Two 1-pound boxes confectioners
  sugar

One 15-ounce can sweetened
  condensed milk
2 tablespoons whiskey
4 cups chopped pecans

Mix all ingredients together. Shape into 1-inch balls. Place in single layer on waxed paper. Let dry several hours or overnight. Reshape and dip in chocolate mixture.

**Dipping Chocolate:**

12 ounces chocolate chips                ¾ block paraffin wax

Melt chocolate chips and paraffin in top of double boiler. Drop one ball at a time into chocolate mixture. Retrieve with a fork and shake off excess chocolate. Place on waxed paper. Let cool and harden. Store in tin in cool place. Yield: 12 dozen.

Mrs. Billy Ezell
Lake Charles, Louisiana

Candy

# EQUIVALENTS

## LIQUID MEASURE VOLUME EQUIVALENTS

60 drops = 1 teaspoon
3 teaspoons = 1 tablespoon
2 tablespoons = 1 fluid ounce
4 tablespoons = ¼ cup
5 ⅓ tablespoons = ⅓ cup
8 tablespoons = ½ cup or 4 ounces or 1
   gill or 1 tea cup

16 tablespoons = 1 cup or 8 ounces
⅜ cup = ¼ cup plus 2 tablespoons
⅝ cup = ½ cup plus 2 tablespoons
⅞ cup = ¾ cup plus 2 tablespoons
1 cup = ½ pint or 8 ounces
2 cups = 1 pint or 16 ounces
1 quart = 2 pints or 64 tablespoons
1 gallon = 4 quarts

## DRY MEASURE VOLUME EQUIVALENTS

2 cups = 1 pint
2 pints = 1 quart

4 quarts = 1 gallon
2 gallons or 8 quarts = 1 peck
4 pecks = 1 bushel

## MISCELLANEOUS MEASURE EQUIVALENTS

A few grains = Less than ⅛ teaspoon
Pinch = As much as can be taken between
   tip of finger and thumb
Speck = Less than ⅛ teaspoon

1 jigger = 2 ounces
1 minim = 1 drop
10 drops = dash
6 dashes = 1 teaspoon
8 teaspoons = 1 ounce

## WEIGHT OR AVOIRDUPOIS EQUIVALENTS

1 ounce = 16 drams

1 pound = 16 ounces
1 kilo = 2.20 pounds

## METRIC ABBREVIATIONS

cc = cubic centimeter
l = liter
ml = milliliter
cm = centimeter
m = meter
mm = millimeter

mµ = millimicron
°C = degrees Centigrade
g = gram
kg = kilogram
mcg = microgram
µg = microgram
mg = milligram

## METRIC LIQUID MEASURE VOLUME EQUIVALENTS

1 teaspoon = 5 milliliters
1 tablespoon = 14.8 milliliters
66⅔ tablespoons = 1 liter
1 cup = ¼ liter, approximately, or 236.6
   milliliters

1 gill = .118 liters
1 pint = .4732 liters
1 quart = .9464 liters
1 gallon = 3.785 liters
1 liter = 1000 milliliters or 1.06 quarts

## METRIC DRY MEASURE VOLUME EQUIVALENTS

1 pint = .551 liters                    1 peck = 8.81 liters
1 quart = 1.101 liters                  1 bushel = 35.24 liters

## WEIGHT EQUIVALENTS IN GRAMS

1 ounce = 28.35 grams                   1 kilogram = 2.21 pounds
1 pound = 453.59 grams                  1 microgram = 0.001 milligram
1 gram = 0.035 ounces                   1 milligram = 1000 micrograms
                                        1 gram = 1000 milligrams

## METRIC LINEAR EQUIVALENTS

1 centimeter = 0.394 inches             1 inch = 2.54 centimeters
                                        1 meter = 39.37 inches

## TEMPERATURE CONVERSIONS

To convert Fahrenheit to Centigrade:
    Subtract 32, miltiply by 5, divide by 9
To convert Centigrade to Fahrenheit:
    Multiply by 9, divide by 5, add 32

## CAN SIZES

| Can size | Weight | Approximate Cups |
|---|---|---|
| 8 ounces | 8 ounces | 1 |
| Picnic | 10½ to 12 ounces | 1¼ |
| 12 ounces | 12 ounces | 1½ |
| No. 300 | 14 to 16 ounces | 1¾ |
| No. 303 | 16 to 17 ounces | 2 |
| No. 2 | 1 lb. 4 ounces or | |
| | 1 pint 2 fluid ounces | 2½ |
| No. 2½ | 1 lb. 13 ounces | 3½ |
| No. 3 Cyl. | 3 lb. 3 ounces or | |
| | 1 quart 14 fluid ounces | 5¾ |
| Baby Foods | 3½ to 8 ounces | |
| No. 10 | 6½ lbs. to | |
| | 7 lbs. 5 ounces | 12 to 13 |
| Condensed Milk | 15 ounces | 1½ |
| Evaporated Milk | 6 ounces | ⅔ |
| Evaporated Milk | 14½ ounces | 1⅔ |

## BUTTER OR MARGARINE MEASUREMENTS

1 pound = 4 sticks or 2 cups            ½ cup = 1 stick
1 cup = 2 sticks                        ¼ cup = ½ stick

## CHEESE MEASUREMENTS

1 pound American cheese = 4 cups grated
1 pound Cheddar cheese = 4 cups grated
4 ounces Cheddar cheese = 1 cup grated, sieved or chopped
1 pound Cottage cheese = 2 cups
½ pound Cottage cheese = 1 cup or 8 ounces
½ pound Cream cheese = 1 cup or 8 ounces
6 ounces Cream cheese = 12 tablespoons or ¾ cup
5 ounces Cheese spread = 8 tablespoons or ½ cup


## APPROXIMATE INGREDIENT SUBSTITUTIONS AND EQUIVALENTS

1 teaspoon baking powder = ¼ teaspoon baking soda plus ½ cup buttermilk
     = ¼ teaspoon baking soda plus ½ teaspoon cream of tartar

Leavening
    (per cup flour) = Use 1¼ teaspoon baking powder, or ¼ teaspoon soda with 2 tablespoons vinegar

1 pound sifted flour = 4 cups
1 cup sifted all purpose flour = 1 cup plus 2 tablespoons sifted cake flour
1 cup sifted cake flour = ⅞ cup sifted all purpose flour
1 pound granulated sugar = 2 to 2¼ cups
1 teaspoon sugar = ¼ grain saccharin
    = ⅛ teaspoon non-caloric sweetner
1 pound confectioners sugar = 4 to 4½ cups
1¾ cups packed confectioners sugar = 1 cup granulated
1 pound brown sugar = 2¼ to 2½ cups
1 cup packed brown sugar = 1 cup granulated
1 cup honey = 1 to 1¼ cups sugar plus ¼ cup liquid
1 cup corn syrup = 1 cup sugar plus ¼ cup liquid
1 cup butter = 1 cup margarine
    = 14 tablespoons hydrogenated fat and ½ teaspoon salt
    = 14 tablespoons lard and ½ teaspoon salt
1 cup fresh milk = ½ cup evaporated milk plus ½ cup water
    = ½ cup condensed milk plus ½ cup water (reduce sugar in recipe)
    = 4 teaspoons powdered whole milk plus 1 cup water
    = 4 tablespoons powdered skim milk plus 2 teaspoons butter plus 1 cup water
1 cup buttermilk or sour milk = 1 tablespoon vinegar or lemon juice plus enough sweet milk to make one cup (let stand 5 minutes) or 1¾ teaspoon cream of tartar plus 1 cup sweet milk
1 cup yogurt = 1 cup buttermilk
1 cup coffee or light cream = 3 tablespoons butter and about ¾ cup milk
1 cup heavy cream = ½ cup butter and about ¾ cup milk

1 cup whipping cream = 2 cups or more after whipping
2 large eggs = 3 small eggs
1 ounce chocolate = 1 square or 3 tablespoons cocoa plus 1 teaspoon to
                    1 tablespoon fat (less for Dutch-type cocoa)
1 tablespoon flour = ½ tablespoon cornstarch or arrowroot, or 2 teaspoons
                    quick-cooking tapioca (as thickener)
1 tablespoon cornstarch = 2 tablespoons flour (as thickener)
1 tablespoon potato flour = 2 tablespoons flour (as thickener)
1 teaspoon lemon juice = ½ teaspoon vinegar
Herbs, ½ to 1½ teaspoon dried = 1 tablespoon fresh
⅛ teaspoon garlic powder = 1 small clove
1 tablespoon candied ginger, washed of sugar or 1 tablespoon raw ginger = ⅛
                    teaspoon powdered ginger
1 tablespoon fresh horseradish = 2 tablespoons bottled
1 cup raw rice = approximately 3 cups cooked
1 cup uncooked macaroni = 2 to 2¼ cups cooked
1 cup uncooked noodles = 1¾ cups cooked
1 pound fresh mushrooms = 3 ounces dried or 6 ounces canned
15 pounds whole crawfish = 1 pound peeled tails

# METRIC CONVERSION TABLE

## COMPARISON OF AVOIRDUPOIS AND METRIC UNITS OF WEIGHT

| Ounces to Pounds to Grams | | | Pounds to Kilograms | | Grams to Ounces | | Kilograms to Ounces | |
|---|---|---|---|---|---|---|---|---|
| 1 | 0.06 | 28.35 | 1 | 0.454 | 1 | 0.035 | 1 | 2.205 |
| 2 | 0.12 | 56.70 | 2 | 0.91 | 2 | 0.07 | 2 | 4.41 |
| 3 | 0.19 | 85.05 | 3 | 1.36 | 3 | 0.11 | 3 | 6.61 |
| 4 | 0.25 | 113.40 | 4 | 1.81 | 4 | 0.14 | 4 | 8.82 |
| 5 | 0.31 | 141.75 | 5 | 2.27 | 5 | 0.18 | 5 | 11.02 |
| 6 | 0.38 | 170.10 | 6 | 2.72 | 6 | 0.21 | 6 | 13.23 |
| 7 | 0.44 | 198.45 | 7 | 3.18 | 7 | 0.25 | 7 | 15.43 |
| 8 | 0.50 | 226.80 | 8 | 3.63 | 8 | 0.28 | 8 | 17.64 |
| 9 | 0.56 | 255.15 | 9 | 4.08 | 9 | 0.32 | 9 | 19.84 |
| 10 | 0.62 | 283.50 | 10 | 4.54 | 10 | 0.35 | 10 | 22.05 |
| 11 | 0.69 | 311.85 | 11 | 4.99 | 11 | 0.39 | 11 | 24.26 |
| 12 | 0.75 | 340.20 | 12 | 5.44 | 12 | 0.42 | 12 | 26.46 |
| 13 | 0.81 | 368.55 | 13 | 5.90 | 13 | 0.46 | 13 | 28.67 |
| 14 | 0.88 | 396.90 | 14 | 6.35 | 14 | 0.49 | 14 | 30.87 |
| 15 | 0.94 | 425.25 | 15 | 6.81 | 15 | 0.53 | 15 | 33.08 |
| 16 | 1.00 | 453.59 | 16 | 7.26 | 16 | 0.56 | 16 | 35.28 |

## COMPARISON OF U. S. AND METRIC UNITS OF LIQUID MEASURE

| Ounces (fluid) to Milliliters | | Quarts to Liters | | Gallons to Liters | |
|---|---|---|---|---|---|
| 1 | 29.573 | 1 | 0.946 | 1 | 3.785 |
| 2 | 59.15 | 2 | 1.89 | 2 | 7.57 |
| 3 | 88.72 | 3 | 2.84 | 3 | 11.36 |
| 4 | 118.30 | 4 | 3.79 | 4 | 15.14 |
| 5 | 147.87 | 5 | 4.73 | 5 | 18.93 |
| 6 | 177.44 | 6 | 5.68 | 6 | 22.71 |
| 7 | 207.02 | 7 | 6.62 | 7 | 26.50 |
| 8 | 236.59 | 8 | 7.57 | 8 | 30.28 |
| 9 | 266.16 | 9 | 8.52 | 9 | 34.07 |
| 10 | 295.73 | 10 | 9.46 | 10 | 37.85 |

| Milliliters to Ounces (fluid) | | Liters to Quarts | | Liters to Gallons | |
|---|---|---|---|---|---|
| 1 | 0.034 | 1 | 1.057 | 1 | 0.264 |
| 2 | 0.07 | 2 | 2.11 | 2 | 0.53 |
| 3 | 0.10 | 3 | 3.17 | 3 | 0.79 |
| 4 | 0.14 | 4 | 4.23 | 4 | 1.06 |
| 5 | 0.17 | 5 | 5.28 | 5 | 1.32 |
| 6 | 0.20 | 6 | 6.34 | 6 | 1.59 |
| 7 | 0.24 | 7 | 7.40 | 7 | 1.85 |
| 8 | 0.27 | 8 | 8.45 | 8 | 2.11 |
| 9 | 0.30 | 9 | 9.51 | 9 | 2.38 |
| 10 | 0.34 | 10 | 10.57 | 10 | 2.64 |

# FOOD TO SERVE FIFTY

## AMOUNTS OF FOOD TO SERVE 50 PEOPLE
### Approximate amounts of foods as purchased to serve 50

| FOOD | SERVING UNIT | PURCHASE |
|---|---|---|
| Beverages | | |
| Coffee | 5 ounces | 1 pound coffee plus |
| | 100 Demitasse | 2¼ gallons water |
| | 5 ounces | ½ pound coffee plus |
| | 50 Demitasse | 1 gallon water |
| Fruit Juice, frozen | ½ cup | 4 to 12 ounce cans |
| Canned Fruit and | ½ cup | Four 46 ounce cans |
| Vegetable Juice | ⅓ cup | 5 quarts |
| Cereals and Cereal Products | | |
| Noodles | 5 ounces | 4 pounds |
| Rice | 5 ounces | 3 to 4 pounds |
| Spaghetti | 5 ounces | 4 to 5 pounds |
| Dairy Product and Eggs | | |
| Butter for table | 1 to 1½ pats | 1 to 1½ pounds |
| Cream, coffee | 1 teaspoon | 3 quarts |
| Cheese, cottage | ⅓ cup | 10 pounds |
| Cheese for sandwiches | 1¼ ounces | 4 pounds |
| Eggs | 1 to 2 | 4 to 8 dozen |
| Ice Cream | ⅓ cup | 2 gallons |
| Milk | 6 ounce glass | 2½ gallons |
| Fruits | | |
| Canned Fruits | ½ cup | 6 to 7 pounds |
| MEATS | | |
| Beef | | |
| Creamed Beef, ground meat | 3 ounces | 10 pounds |
| Ground Meat Patties | 3½ ounces | 14 pounds |
| Pot Roast, chuck | 3 ounces | 20 to 22 pounds |
| Stew with vegetables | 5½ ounces | 15 pounds |
| Swiss steak, round ¾ inch | 3½ ounces | 16 pounds |
| Veal | | |
| Breaded veal round | 3 ounces | 12½ pounds |
| Chops, 3 to 1 pound | 1 each | 17 pounds |
| Cutlets, 4 to 1 pound | 3 ounces | 12½ pounds |
| Fish | | |
| Fish, fillets | 4 ounces | 12½ to 15 pounds |
| Oysters, large | | 1½ to 2 gallons |

| FOOD | SERVING UNIT | PURCHASE |
|---|---|---|
| Shrimp | 2½ ounces, ¼ cup | 10 to 12 pounds |
| Lamb | | |
| Roast Leg, 6 pounds each | 2½ ounces | 4 legs |
| Pork | | |
| Cold cuts | 2 ounces | 6 to 8 pounds |
| Frankfurters | 2 each | 8 to 10 pounds |
| Ham | | |
| Baked, sliced | 2 ounces | 16 to 20 pounds |
| Pork chops | 1 each | 12½ to 16 pounds |
| Sausage | 1 cake each | 12½ pounds |
| Sausage link | 2 each | 6¼ pounds |
| Poultry | | |
| Chicken, ready to cook | | |
| Baked | 4 ounces | 30 pounds, 8 hens 5 to 6 pounds each |
| Creamed | 5 ounces | 18 to 20 pounds, 4 hens 4½ to 5 pounds each |
| Fried | ¼ or ½ chicken | 13 to 25 fryers 2½ to 3½ pounds each |
| Stewed | 5 ounces | 35 to 40 pounds, 8 hens 4½ to 5 pounds each |
| Turkey, roast | 2½ ounces | 35 to 40 pounds |
| Turkey, roll | 3 ounces | 12 to 15 pounds |
| Vegetables | | |
| Canned Vegetables | ½ cup | Ten no. 2 cans |
| Dried Peas and Beans | ½ cup | 5 pounds |
| Asparagus, fresh | 3 ounces, ¼ cup | 18 to 20 pounds |
| Beans, green, fresh | 3 ounces | 10 to 12 pounds |
| Beans, lima, fresh | 3 ounces | 22 to 25 pounds |
| Broccoli, fresh | 3 ounces | 16 to 20 pounds |
| Cabbage, raw | 1 to 2 ounces ⅛ to ¼ cup | 8 pounds |
| Carrots, topped | 3 ounces | 12½ pounds |
| Cauliflower, fresh | 3 ounces | 28 to 32 pounds |
| Celery | 1 to 2 pieces | 2 pounds |
| Cucumber, 9 inch | 2 slices | 4 |
| Eggplant, 1¼ pounds each | 2 to 2½ ounces ¼ cup | 8 |
| Lettuce, head | 1½ to 2 ounces | 8 to 10 heads |
| Potatoes, to mash | ½ cup | 12 pounds |

| FOOD | SERVING UNIT | PURCHASE |
|---|---|---|
| Potatoes, to scallop | ½ cup | 15 pounds |
| Potatoes, sweet | ½ cup | 18 to 20 pounds |
| Spinach, to cook | ¼ cup | 12 to 15 pounds |
| Spinach, for salad | ⅛ cup | 5 to 6 pounds |
| Squash, to bake or mash | 3 ounces | 12 to 15 pounds |
| Miscellaneous | | |
| Jelly | 2 tablespoons | 3 pounds |
| Syrup | ¼ cup | 3¼ quarts |
| Sugar, granulated | 1½ teaspoon | ¾ pound |

## APPROXIMATE AMOUNTS OF PREPARED
## FOOD TO SERVE 50

| FOOD | SERVING UNIT | PURCHASE |
|---|---|---|
| Beverages | | |
| Tea, Iced | 8 ounces, 1 glass | 3 gallons |
| Punch | 3 ounces, 1 punch cup | 1¼ gallons |
| | 6 ounces | 2½ gallons |
| Breads | | |
| Bread, thin for | 2 slices | 7 pounds |
| sandwiches | | 4½ to 5 loaves |
| Bread, quick loaf | 2 to 3 loaves | 5 loaves, 4x9-inch |
| brown, nut, orange | | |
| Desserts | | |
| Ice Cream, plain, bulk | ⅓ cup | 8 quarts |

Emily Wray Lamont

# INDEX